D1257719

Grasses of the Texas
Gulf Prairies and Marshes

NUMBER TWENTY-FOUR:
W. L. Moody, Jr., Natural History Series

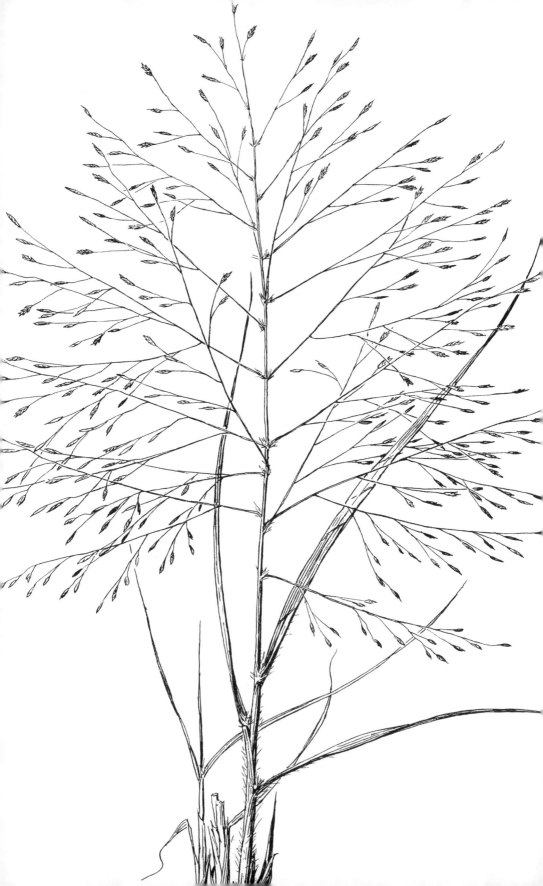

Grasses of the Texas Gulf Prairies and Marshes

Stephan L. Hatch, Joseph L. Schuster,
& D. Lynn Drawe

Texas A&M University Press
College Station

Copyright © 1999 by Stephan L. Hatch,
Joseph L. Schuster, and D. Lynn Drawe
Manufactured in the United States of America
All rights reserved
First edition

The paper used in this book meets the minimum requirements
of the American National Standard for Permanence
of Paper for Printed Library Materials, Z39.48-1984.
Binding materials have been chosen for durability.

Library of Congress Cataloging-in-Publication Data

Hatch, Stephan L., 1945–
       Grasses of the Texas Gulf prairies and marshes / Stephan L. Hatch,
   Joseph L. Schuster, and D. Lynn Drawe. — 1st ed.
           p.   cm. — (W.L. Moody, Jr., natural history series ; no. 24)
       Includes bibliographical references (p.   ) and index.
       ISBN 0-89096-875-6 (cloth);   ISBN 0-89096-889-6 (pbk.)
       1. Grasses—Texas—Identification.   I. Schuster, Joseph L., 1932–
   . II. Drawe, Dale Lynn, 1942–   .   III. Title.   IV. Series.
   QK495.G74H3436   1999
   584'.9'09764—dc21   98-47488
                                                               CIP

Contents

— Acknowledgments

We thank and acknowledge Lucile Gould Bridges and Texas A&M University Press for granting permission to use grass illustrations from the following publications: *Grasses of the Texas Coastal Bend* (Gould and Box 1965), *The Grasses of Texas* (Gould 1975), *Common Texas Grasses* (Gould 1978), and *Grass Systematics* (Gould and Shaw 1983). We thank Texas A&M University Press and the Texas Agricultural Experiment Station respectively for the use of illustrations from *Texas Range Plants* (Hatch and Pluhar 1993) and *Grasses (Poaceae) of the Texas Cross Timbers and Prairies* (Hignight et al. 1988). Original line drawings were prepared by Keith Westover (*Poa arachnifera*), John E. Dawson III (*Luziola peruviana* in part, and *Sporobolus compositus* var. *clandesinus* in part), and Lucretia Hamilton (*Eragrostis curvula*). Most of the remaining artwork is from Hitchcock-Chase Collection of Grass Drawings, Hunt Institute for Botanical Documentation, Carnegie Mellon University, Pittsburgh, Pennsylvania, and on indefinite loan from Smithsonian Institution and is used with their permission.

We are indebted to the Rob and Bessie Welder Wildlife Foundation for financial support and for making office space available for initiation of this project. Special appreciation is extended to Jim Teer and Elizabeth Burke of the Welder Wildlife Foundation. Jim provided support and encouragement and Elizabeth typed the original descriptions.

Thanks to the many range students from Texas A&M University who used the keys, or portions thereof, in agrostology classes. Special thanks is due to Kimberly D'Angelo for typing, editing, and proofing the manuscript several times. Thanks to Andrew Lee for preparing the electronic images for this publication.

Acknowledgment is also due Stan Reinke, James Alderson, and Mike Stellbauer of the Natural Resources Conservation Service for providing input on the value or ecology of many of the species. We appreciated and used their expert opinions on species of the Texas Gulf Coast. We assume responsibility, however, for the correctness of the ratings. This is Welder Wildlife Foundation Contribution B-15.

Grasses of the Texas
Gulf Prairies and Marshes

— Introduction

Grasses of the Texas Gulf Prairies and Marshes is written for grass taxonomists, conservationists, environmentalists, students, and laypeople. The manual should be useful for the identification and study of grasses in the prairies and marshes adjacent to the Gulf of Mexico, from northern Mexico to western Louisiana. It is intended as a systematic and descriptive treatment of the grasses in the Coastal Zone of Texas and adjacent areas.

Keys to both genera and species are provided. For convenience in locating specific taxa, the grasses are listed alphabetically, first by genus and then by species within the genus. The common name for each species is provided when known. Species descriptions include longevity, vegetative and floral dimensions, and descriptions. The measurements of morphological characters may include parentheses before or after the range of variation. This usually means that the measurements are "rarely" less than or more than the regular range of variation. Common names and synonyms generally follow those of *A Checklist of the Vascular Plants of Texas* (Hatch et al. 1990).

Notes on abundance, habitat, and distribution provide information on the ecological niche of each species. When known, grass species growth requirements such as moisture, soils, and other environmental conditions are given. For distribution indices, we divided the Texas Gulf Coast geographically into lower, mid, and upper. Our mid and upper coastal delineations correspond to those described by Smeins et al. (1982). Our lower coast designation extends from Baffin Bay to the mouth of the Rio Grande. The mid extends from the 100th meridian to Baffin Bay south of Corpus Christi, and the upper extends from where the coast intersects the 100th meridian to Sabine Bay.

Notes on the utilization of grass species by livestock and wildlife include designations of poor, fair, and good. These values are based on the literature or expert opinion, and vary in usage even within species.

The forage value given to a grass for livestock is based on its potential forage value. A good rating reflects relatively high values for forage factors such as volume, palatability, and nutritive value. A low rating reflects low values of one or more attributes, while a fair rating indicates intermediate production, palatability, or nutritive value.

Good, fair, and poor values assigned to grasses for wildlife reflect food value, such as with a livestock forage, or some other habitat value, or both. When known, specific information about food or habitat value is given for the kind of wildlife involved.

If the rating is for livestock only and there is no rating for wildlife, then the terms good, fair, or poor forage are used without designating the kind of animal. If forage values for both livestock and wildlife are given, the terms good, fair, or poor forage are assigned to livestock and wildlife. If the ratings differ for livestock and wildlife, then the rating for each is given separately. If known, other values of plants for wildlife habitat, such as for nesting cover or roosting, are described.

Original plant measurements were made from specimens housed in the S. M. Tracy Herbarium, Texas A&M University. These measurements were compared with data from Allred (1973), Gould (1975), Gould and Box (1965), Lonard (1993), and Correll and Johnston (1970).

Grasses of the Texas Gulf Prairies and Marshes is an outgrowth of Gould and Box's *Grasses of the Texas Coastal Bend* (1965) containing 72 genera and 218 species. Our new treatment adds 27 genera and 86 species, for a combined total of 304 species in 99 genera, and is applicable to the entire Texas Gulf Coast.

The checklist in *Grasses of the Texas Gulf Prairies and Marshes* summarizes data and includes the following information:

1. **Correct names are in boldface.** Appropriate synonyms, in italics, are provided. Synonyms within the same genus are listed first. Although most of the synonyms are mentioned in parentheses or square brackets, several also are listed alphabetically within the genus to indicate their present taxonomic status.

2. **Authorities are given for genera, species, subspecies, and varieties** (typical subspecies and varieties, called autonyms, do not have authorities).

3. **Scientific names are followed by common names** (if available). The first or only common name of a species is shown in all capital letters, and additional common names appear in lowercase letters. The initial letters of common names for genera, if any, are capitalized. If the common name of a genus is used, the name is abbreviated to its first letter for the species.

4. **The codes for origin, longevity, phenology, and distribution are given at the bottom of the first page of the checklist.**

5. **Wetland designations for each grass species are identified in our checklist**

and follow Reed (1988). The grasses not listed in Reed (1988) are given as upland species and included in the checklist.

The Texas Gulf Prairies and Marshes

The Texas Gulf Prairies and Marshes extend inland along the coast from the mouth of the Rio Grande northward to Sabine Bay (Figure 1). The Gulf Prairies, about 3.6 million hectares (9 million acres), include the nearly flat plain extending 50 to 135 kilometers (30–80 miles) inland from the Gulf of Mexico. The Gulf Marshes, approximately 200,000 hectares (495,000 acres), occupy a narrow strip of lowlands adjacent to the coast and the barrier islands (e.g., Padre Island) extending from Mexico to Louisiana.

The climate of the Texas Gulf Coastal Region varies considerably. The marine-type climate along the coast is modified by surges of continental air. The persistent flow of warm air from the Gulf of Mexico produces a humid subtropical climate with hot summers. Mean annual rainfall increases gradually from 658 mm (26 inches) in Cameron County at the Texas-Mexican border to 1417 mm (56 inches) in Jefferson County at the mouth of the Sabine River. Mean annual temperatures vary from 74°F (23°C) in the south to 68°F (20°C) in the north. The average frost-free period decreases gradually from 320 days in the southern portion to 245 days in the northern portion.

The Gulf Prairies are nearly level and virtually undissected plains having slow surface drainage, with elevations from sea level to 80 meters (250 feet). The Gulf Marshes are low, wet, marshy coastal areas, commonly covered with saline or brackish water, and range from sea level to a few meters in elevation.

Gulf coastal prairie soils are dark, neutral to slightly acid, clay loams and loams, with clays in the northeastern parts. Farther south in the subhumid Coastal Bend, the soils are slightly alkaline to slightly acid. A narrow band of light, acid sands and darker, loamy to clayey soils stretches along the coast. Inland from the dark clayey soils is a narrow belt of lighter, acid, fine sandy loam soils with gray to brown and red-mottled subsoils. Soils of the river bottomlands and broad deltaic plains are reddish-brown to dark gray, slightly acid to calcareous, and loamy to clayey alluvial. A characteristic feature of nearly all these soils is poor surface and internal drainage. Soils of the Gulf Marshes are dark, poorly drained, sandy loams and clays, and light, neutral sands, typically showing little textural change with depth. The loamy and clayey soils of the marshes are commonly saline and sodic.

The original vegetation types of the Gulf Prairie were tallgrass prairie and oak

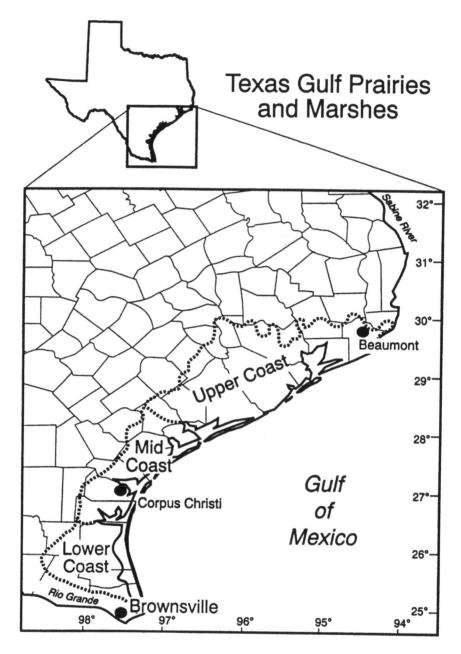

Figure 1. Texas map with a detailed inset of county boundaries and the location of lower, mid, and upper coast divisions of the Texas Gulf Prairies and Marshes.

savannah. Trees and shrubs, such as honey mesquite (*Prosopis glandulosa* Torr.), oak (*Quercus*), and acacia (*Acacia*), however, have increased and formed thickets in many places (Figure 2). Characteristic oak species are live oak (*Quercus virginiana* Mill.) and post oak (*Q. stellata* Wang). Typical acacias are huisache (*Acacia smallii* Isely) and blackbrush (*A. rigidula* Benth.). Bushy sea-ox-eye [*Borrichia frutescens* (L.) DC.], a dwarf shrub, is also typical.

Primary climax grasses of the Gulf Prairie are gulf cordgrass [*Spartina spartinae* (Trin.) Merr. *ex* A. S. Hitchc.], big bluestem (*Andropogon gerardii* Vitman var. *gerardii*), little bluestem [*Schizachyrium scoparium* (Michx.) Nash], yellow indiangrass [*Sorghastrum nutans* (L.) Nash], eastern gamagrass [*Tripsacum dactyloides* (L.) L.], hairy awn muhly [*Muhlenbergia capillaris* (Lam.) Trin.], tanglehead [*Heteropogon contortus* (L.) Beauv. *ex* Roem. & Schult.], Texas wintergrass [*Nassella leucotricha* (Trin. & Rupr.) Pohl], and many species of *Panicum* and *Paspalum*. Common increasers and invaders accompanying overgrazing are yankeeweed (*Eupatorium compositifolium* Walt.), broomsedge bluestem (*Andropogon virginicus* L.), smutgrass [*Sporobolus indicus* (L.) R. Br.], western ragweed (*Ambrosia cumanensis* Kunth in H.B.K.), tumblegrass [*Schedonnardus paniculatus* (Nutt.) Trel.], threeawns (*Aristida*), and many annual forbs and grasses (Figure 3). Pricklypear (*Opuntia*) species are common throughout the area. Characteristic forbs include asters (*Aster*), Indian paintbrush (*Castilleja indivisa* Engelm.), poppy mallows (*Callirhoe*), phlox (*Phlox*), bluebonnets (*Lupinus*), and evening primroses (*Oenothera*) (Jones 1982).

Gulf Marshes, variously salty and fresh, support species of sedges (*Carex* and *Cyperus*), rushes (*Juncus*), bulrushes (*Scirpus*), several cordgrasses (*Spartina*), coastal saltgrass [*Distichlis spicata* (L.) Greene var. *spicata*], common reed [*Phragmites australis* (Cav.) Trin. *ex* Steud.], marshmillet [*Zizaniopsis miliacea* (Michx.) Doell & Aschers.], longtom (*Paspalum lividum* Trin.), seashore dropseed [*Sporobolus virginicus* (L.) Kunth], and knotroot bristlegrass [*Setaria parviflora* (Sw.) Kerguelen] (Figure 4). Marshmillet and maidencane (*Panicum hemitomon* Schult.) are two of the most important grasses in the freshwater marshes of the upper coast. Common aquatic forbs are pepperweeds (*Lepidium*), smartweeds (*Polygonum*), docks (*Rumex*), bushy seedbox (*Ludwigia alternifolia* L.), green parrotfeather [*Myriophyllum pinnatum* (Walt.) B.S.P.], pennyworts (*Hydrocotyle*), water lilies (*Nymphaea*), narrowleaf cattail (*Typha domingensis* Pers.), spiderworts (*Tradescantia*), and duckweeds (*Lemna*). Common halophytic herbs and shrubs on salty sands are spikesedges (*Eleocharis*), fimbries (*Fimbristylis*), glassworts (*Salicornia*), sea-rockets (*Cakile*), maritime saltwort (*Batis maritima* P. Br.), morning glories (*Ipomoea*), and bushy sea-ox-eye (*Borrichia*) (Jones 1982).

Figure 2. Upland prairie and savannah vegetation.

Figure 3. Vegetation dominated by *Spartina spartinae* (gulf cordgrass).

Introduction

The Gulf Prairies are used for crops, livestock grazing, wildlife production, and increasingly, for urban and industrial centers. About one-third of the area is cultivated, mostly for rice (*Oryza sativa* L.), grain sorghum [*Sorghum bicolor* (L.) Moench], corn (*Zea mays* L.), cotton (*Gossypium hirsutum* L.), and tame pastures. Bermudagrass [*Cynodon dactylon* (L.) Pers.] and several introduced bluestems (*Dichanthium* and *Bothriochloa*) are common tame pasture grasses.

Texas Gulf Marshes and barrier islands (Figure 5) contain most of our national seashore parks. The low, marshy areas provide an excellent natural habitat for wildlife such as upland game and waterfowl, and the higher elevations are important for livestock and wildlife production. Urban, industrial, and recreational developments, however, have increased in recent years. Most land is not well suited for cultivation because of periodic flooding and saline soils. Ranch units are mostly in large land holdings.

In the Gulf Prairies and Marshes, ranches are primarily cow-calf operations using forage produced from rangeland and tame pasture. Zebu (*Bos indicus*), or crossbreeds having Zebu blood, are the most widely adapted and used cattle. Recreation, hunting, and fishing provide excellent multiuse opportunities in these areas of the Texas Gulf Coast.

Figure 4. Fresh and saltwater vegetation represented by *Spartina alterniflora* and *S. patens* (smooth and marshhay cordgrass).

Figure 5. Barrier island vegetation: *Uniola paniculata* (sea-oats).

In Texas, the Gulf Prairies and Marshes have seen the greatest industrial development since World War II. The major industrial concentration has been from Orange and Beaumont to Houston. Corpus Christi, the surrounding Coastal Bend region, Brownsville, and the adjacent Lower Rio Grande Valley area are developing naval, agricultural, and industrial sections at a rapid pace.

The Grass Plant

The grass family (Poaceae) is composed of highly evolved monocotyledonous plants distantly related to the sedge (Cyperaceae), rush (Juncaceae), and lily (Liliaceae) families. Our native grasses are typically herbaceous (except for *Arundinaria gigantea,* a native bamboo species) and are of perennial or annual longevity. Perennial culms die back to the ground each year and produce new culms the following year from axillary buds at the basal culm nodes. Annuals complete their life cycle in a year or less, and die at the completion of that one cycle. The grass plant consists of roots, culms, leaves, and inflorescences of small flowers borne in spikelets (Figure 6A). Characteristics and variation found within each of these structures are discussed separately.

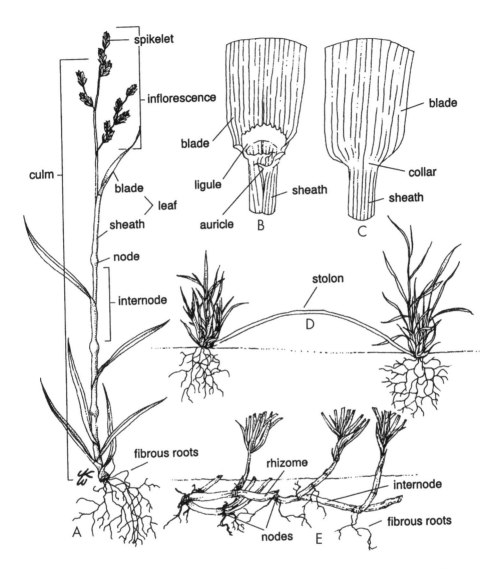

Figure 6. The grass plant: (A) general habit of *Poa annua* (annual bluegrass); (B-C) junction of the blade and sheath of *Hordeum leporinum* (hair barley); (B) adaxial surface; (C) abaxial surface; (D) stolon of *Hilaria belangeri* (common curlymesquite); and (E) rhizomes of *Cynodon dactylon* (bermudagrass).

The root system in grasses, as in most monocotyledons, is fibrous. The primary or seminal root system, developed from the embryo, is short-lived and persists until the plant is established. An adventitious or secondary root system begins to develop one to two weeks after seed germination, and then supports plant growth. These roots develop from the lower culm nodes. In many grasses, when the culm is decumbent or prostrate, roots will arise from culm nodes in contact with the soil. Branching of roots occurs at irregular intervals, but not at nodes, as in branching of the culm.

Grass culms are generally smooth and cylindrical with solid internodes, axillary buds, leaves, and in most plants, enlarged ("swollen") nodes. Leaves, branches, axillary buds, and adventitious roots are borne at the nodes. Culm internodes are solid, semisolid, or hollow. The terminal (apical) meristem and intercalary meristems at the base of the internodes account for the growth of the culm, resulting from cell division, elongation, and differentiation.

Asexual reproduction can occur in the grass plant, attributable to modifications of the culm. Tillers (suckers) are subterranean or ground-level lateral shoots, erect and usually associated with a caespitose (bunchgrass) habit. Rhizomes (Figure 6E) are underground stems with leaves reduced to scales and roots, arising from the culm nodes at regular intervals. Generally, the internode of a rhizome is greatly shortened compared to the internode of the aboveground culm. Stolons (runners) (Figure 6D) spread horizontally along the ground surface and can initiate a "new plant" at a node by developing roots and an erect culm. Leaves at the nodes may resemble erect culm leaves or could be reduced to scales. Typically, plants that reproduce vegetatively will be stoloniferous or rhizomatous (except *Cynodon dactylon*, which is both). Depending on environmental conditions, however, a rhizomatous stem axis may become stoloniferous at the ground surface, or a stolon may become subterranean and rhizomatous (Figure 6E).

Grass leaves occur in two ranks, or rows, and are arranged alternately on the culm. Nearly all leaves are differentiated into three parts: sheath, ligule, and blade (Figure 6B). The sheath is attached just below the culm node and ascends, typically, clasping the internode. Margins of the sheath are generally free or open to the base. In some genera (most species of *Bromus, Glyceria,* and *Melica*) the margins are connate, forming a tubular structure, or are fused along the lower portion. Leaf blades are typically flat and elongated. Many species having evolved under arid conditions, however, have folded or involute leaves, an adaptation that reduces the loss of transpired water. Dermal appendages on the sheath and blade vary from smooth, without visible hairs, to densely pilose or hispid. The ligule (Figure 6B), typically present (except in most *Echinochloa* species), is a membrane, a ciliate membrane, or a ring of hairs on the adaxial surface at the junction of the sheath and blade. Auricles (Figure 6B) are membranous projections of tissue present on some plants on either side of the leaf, at the apex of the sheath, or at the base of the blade. The collar (Figure 6C) is the abaxial area at the junction of the blade and sheath. The collar may be strongly differentiated in color.

The prophyll, the first leaf of a lateral branch, provides some protection to the developing branch in early growth stages. Typically short and membranous, the prophyll consists only of a sheath. The prophyll develops with its dorsal surface fitted tightly against the culm axis and its margins folded over the axillary meristem or base of the branch. The prophyll has two prominent veins and often has been compared to the palea of the spikelet and the coleoptile of the embryo.

Inflorescence Types

Grass inflorescences (Figures 7–9) are delimited by the uppermost culm leaf or portion thereof. By our definition, multiple inflorescences can occur on a single culm. We have used the grass inflorescence terminology of spike, spicate raceme, raceme, and panicle in the traditional sense. Other terms are used for specialized panicle inflorescences. The spike, spicate raceme, and raceme inflorescences do not have branches arising from the central axis (rachis). The spikelets either are attached directly or individually pedicelled (or stalked) upon the central axis. The panicle inflorescence has branches arising from the central axis nodes. The spikelets are seldom borne on the central axis, but on the branches. Spike inflorescences (Figure 7A) are those in which the spikelets are sessile on the central axis (rachis). A spicate raceme (Figures 7B and 9A) has an unbranched central axis (rachis) with sessile spikelets and short pedicellate spikelets at inflorescence nodes. Raceme inflorescences (Figure 7C) have pedicels supporting single spikelets, with the pedicel attached to the central axis (rachis). Panicle inflorescences (Figures 7D, 8, and 9B–D) can have only primary branches or primary branches that branch and rebranch, or have several spikelets supported by each branch or branchlet. By definition, the central axis of a panicle is not a rachis. The rachis is only the axis of a spike, spicate raceme, or raceme.

A panicle of spicate primary unilateral branches (Figure 8) is a common modification of the typical grass inflorescence. Branches developing from the nodes at the central axis of the inflorescence are called primary branches. Spikelets on this inflorescence type are racemose (subsessile) or spicate (sessile) on the primary

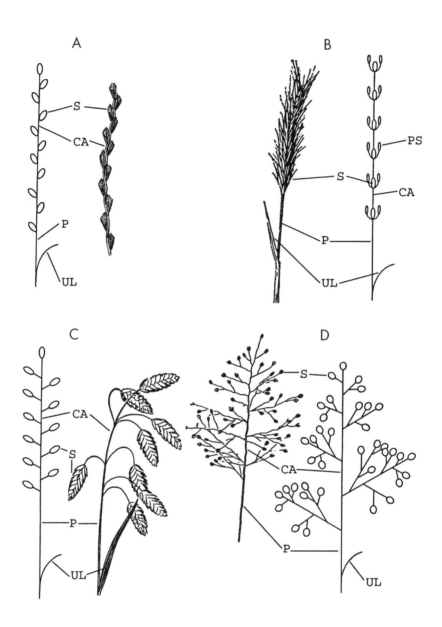

Figure 7. Diagrammatic representation and examples of grass inflorescence types: (A) spike (*Lolium*); (B) spicate raceme (*Hordeum*); (C) raceme (*Bromus*); and (D) open panicle (*Dichanthelium*). S = spikelet, CA = central axis, P = peduncle, SS = sessile spikelet, PS = pedicellate spikelet, and UL = uppermost leaf.

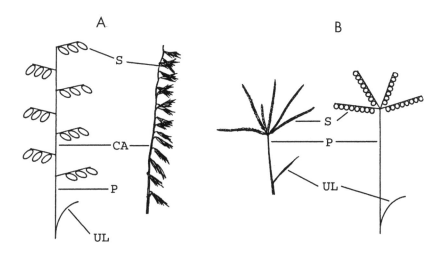

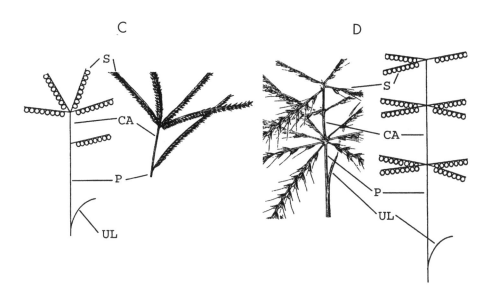

Figure 8. Diagrammatic representation and examples of grass inflorescence types: (A) panicle of alternate spicate primary unilateral branches (*Bouteloua*); (B) panicle of digitate spicate primary unilateral branches (*Cynodon*); (C) panicle of subdigitate spicate primary unilateral branches (*Eleusine*); and (D) panicle of verticillate spicate primary unilateral branches (*Chloris*). S = spikelet, CA = central axis, P = peduncle, and UL = uppermost leaf.

branch and make the branch appear spikelike, hence the term "spicate." The spikelets are attached along one side of the branch and give the branch a unilateral or one-sided appearance. Panicles with spicate primary unilateral branches may be described by the arrangement of the branches using modifiers such as alternate (Figure 8A), digitate (Figure 8B), subdigitate (Figure 8C), or verticillate (Figure 8D).

A panicle of racemose branches (Figure 9B-D) is a specialized inflorescence composed of branches and branchlets bearing both sessile and pedicellate spikelets at each node; this condition, found in the Andropogoneae tribe, is repeated at all nodes of the inflorescence except the terminal node, where one sessile and two pedicellate spikelets are normal. The inflorescence types in the Andropogoneae tribe are spicate raceme (Figure 9A), panicle of subdigitate racemose branches (Figure 9B), panicle of alternate racemose branches (Figure 9C), and an open panicle (Figure 9D).

Spikelet Parts

The grass spikelet (Figure 10) is the basic unit of the grass inflorescence. Understanding the variation in spikelet structure is essential to using this diagnostic key. Spikelets typically consist of a pair of glumes with one or more florets and the associated rachilla. Florets consist of a lemma, palea, floral axis, and "grass flower" (lodicules, stamens, and pistils) or some portion thereof (Figure 10). Determining where the spikelet disarticulates (breaks apart) at maturity is often important. Spikelets disarticulate from the pedicel below the glumes (or at the spikelet base), or above the glumes and between the florets. Spikelets from four of the common tribes found in the area are illustrated in Figure 11.

Glumes are empty bracts occurring at the base of the spikelet, and their presence delimits or defines the spikelet. Most spikelets have two glumes that may vary in relative size, texture, presence or absence of awns, and several other characters. Some taxa may lack one (e.g., many species in the Paniceae tribe) or both (e.g., species in the Oryzeae tribe) glumes. When lacking, the first (lowermost) glume is more likely to be absent than the second glume. Glumes are typically odd-veined (1, 3, 5, etc., to as many as 13 veins), and the veins may extend into awns.

The floret consists of two protective bracts, the lemma and the palea, and the included grass flower (if present). The lemma is attached to the rachilla, and in many species, partly conceals or completely encloses the palea. The lemma typically has an odd number of veins that could extend from the tissue to form an awn or a mucro. Commonly, only the midvein extends into an awn, although all the veins could extend, as in *Pappophorum*. The palea and grass flower are

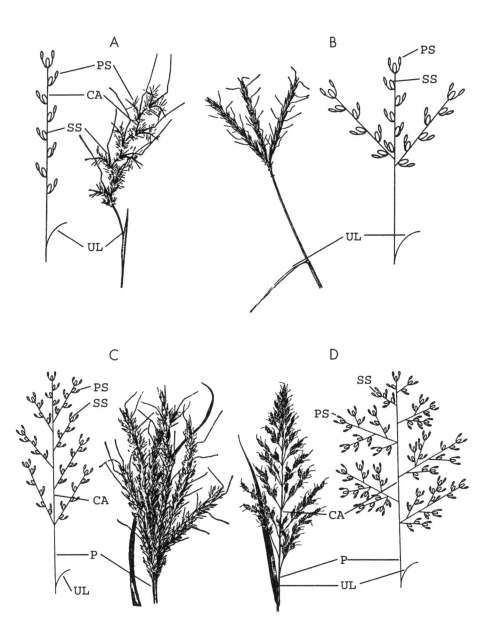

Figure 9. Diagrammatic representation and examples of Andropogoneae tribe inflorescence types: (A) spicate raceme (*Schizachyrium*); (B) panicle of subdigitate racemose branches (*Andropogon*); (C) panicle of alternate racemose branches (*Bothriochloa*); and (D) open panicle (*Sorghum*). PS = pedicellate spikelet, CA = central axis, SS = sessile spikelet, and UL = uppermost leaf.

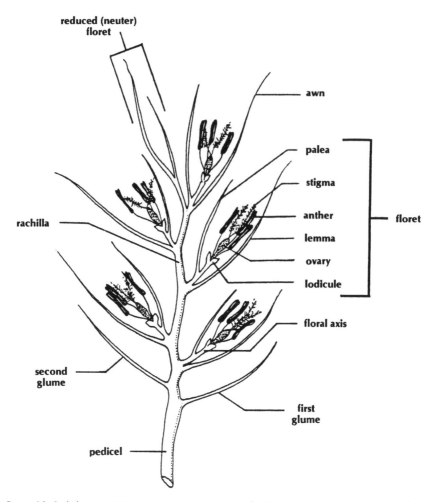

reduced (neuter) floret

awn

palea

stigma

anther — floret

lemma

ovary

lodicule

floral axis

rachilla

second glume

first glume

pedicel

Figure 10. Spikelet parts. Diagrammatic representation of a *Bromus* (brome) spikelet with six florets (Gould and Shaw 1983).

attached to the floral axis. This very short axis arises from the rachilla and is adaxial to the lemma. The palea is an even-veined (2) bract, typically shorter than the lemma, lighter in texture, and usually awnless. The palea is adaxial to the grass flower relative to the rachilla, and protects the developing flower parts from moisture loss or extreme temperatures. In the Paniceae and Andropogoneae tribes, the palea of the lower floret is typically reduced or absent.

Florets may be perfect, imperfect, fertile, sterile, staminate, pistillate, or reduced (Figures 10 and 11). A reduced floret can consist of a lemma and palea, or become reduced to one or several awnlike structures. The position of the fertile floret(s) in relation to the sterile, or reduced, floret(s) is an important taxonomic character in distinguishing among tribes. In the Paniceae and Andropogoneae tribes, the sterile floret is below the fertile floret, whereas in all other tribes, the sterile floret(s) is above the fertile floret or absent (except in the Centotheceae tribe where the sterile florets located below and above the fertile florets, and in the genus *Phalaris* of the tribe Aveneae, in which the reduced florets are below the fertile florets).

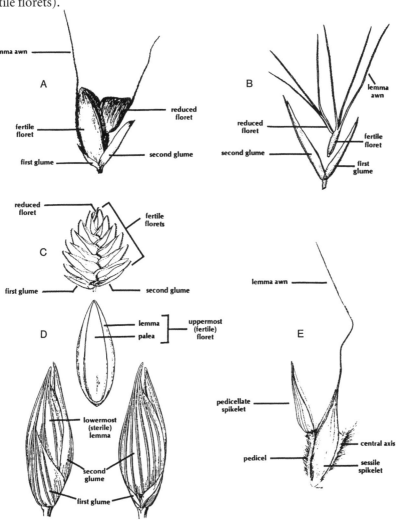

Figure 11. Spikelets representing major genera and tribes found in the area. Species shown may not be found in the area: (A) spikelet of *Chloris* x *subdolichostachya* (Chlorideae) (Gould and Box 1965); (B) spikelet of *Bouteloua trifida* (Chlorideae) (Gould 1951); (C) spikelet of *Eragrostis superba* (Eragrosteae) (Hatch et al. 1984); (D) spikelet of *Panicum harvardii* (Paniceae) (Hitchcock 1951); and (E) spikelet of *Cymbopogon caesius* (Andropogoneae) (Hatch et al. 1984).

The fruit of most grasses is a caryopsis, a hard, single-seeded, dry indehiscent fruit with the pericarp fused to the seed coat. Exceptions occur in a few genera, such as *Sporobolus* in which the fruit is an achene, and the pericarp is not fused to the seed coat. The embryo of grasses is lateral to the endosperm.

Poaceae Classification of Subfamilies, Tribes, and Genera Represented in the Texas Gulf Prairies and Marshes
(Number in parentheses is the number of species in the genus.)

ARUNDINOIDEAE

Aristideae	1	*Aristida* (6)
Arundineae	2	*Arundo* (1)
	3	*Cortaderia* (1)
	4	*Phragmites* (1)
Centotheceae	5	*Chasmanthium* (2)

BAMBUSOIDEAE

Bambuseae	6	*Arundinaria* (1)
Oryzeae	7	*Leersia* (5)
	8	*Luziola* (1)
	9	*Oryza* (1)
	10	*Zizaniopsis* (1)

CHLORIDOIDEAE

Aeluropodeae	11	*Distichlis* (1)
	12	*Monanthochloë* (1)
Chlorideae	13	*Bouteloua* (5)
	14	*Buchloë* (1)
	15	*Chloris* (12)
	16	*Cynodon* (1)
	17	*Enteropogon* (1)
	18	*Eustachys* (2)
	19	*Gymnopogon* (1)
	20	*Hilaria* (1)
	21	*Schedonnardus* (1)
	22	*Spartina* (5)

	23	*Tragus* (1)
	24	*Trichloris* (1)
	25	*Willkommia* (1)
Eragrosteae	26	*Dactyloctenium* (1)
	27	*Eleusine* (1)
	28	*Eragrostis* (19)
	29	*Erioneuron* (1)
	30	*Leptochloa* (8)
	31	*Muhlenbergia* (5)
	32	*Sporobolus* (10)
	33	*Trichoneura* (1)
	34	*Tridens* (8)
	35	*Triplasis* (1)
	36	*Vaseyochloa* (1)
Pappophoreae	37	*Pappophorum* (2)
Unioleae	38	*Uniola* (1)

PANICOIDEAE

Andropogoneae	39	*Andropogon* (5)
	40	*Bothriochloa* (7)
	41	*Chrysopogon* (1)
	42	*Coelorachis* (2)
	43	*Dichanthium* (3)
	44	*Elionurus* (1)
	45	*Hemarthria* (1)
	46	*Heteropogon* (2)
	47	*Rottboellia* (1)
	48	*Saccharum* (4)
	49	*Schizachyrium* (1)
	50	*Sorghastrum* (2)
	51	*Sorghum* (2)
	52	*Trachypogon* (1)
	53	*Tripsacum* (1)
	54	*Zea* (1)
Paniceae	55	*Anthaenantia* (1)
	56	*Axonopus* (2)
	57	*Cenchrus* (3)

58	*Dichanthelium* (9)
59	*Digitaria* (10)
60	*Echinochloa* (6)
61	*Eriochloa* (4)
62	*Melinis* (1)
63	*Oplismenus* (1)
64	*Panicum* (24)
65	*Paspalidium* (1)
66	*Paspalum* (23)
67	*Pennisetum* (6)
68	*Sacciolepis* (1)
69	*Setaria* (13)
70	*Stenotaphrum* (1)
71	*Urochloa* (8)

POOIDEAE

Aveneae	72	*Agrostis* (3)
	73	*Aira* (1)
	74	*Alopecurus* (3)
	75	*Avena* (1)
	76	*Holcus* (1)
	77	*Limnodea* (1)
	78	*Phalaris* (4)
	79	*Polypogon* (1)
	80	*Rostraria* (1)
	81	*Sphenopholis* (1)
	82	*Trisetum* (1)
Hainardieae	83	*Hainardia* (1)
	84	*Parapholis* (1)
Meliceae	85	*Glyceria* (1)
	86	*Melica* (1)
Poeae	87	*Briza* (2)
	88	*Bromus* (4)
	89	*Dactylis* (1)
	90	*Dezmazeria* (1)
	91	*Lolium* (2)
	92	*Poa* (3)

	93	*Vulpia* (1)
Stipeae	94	*Nassella* (1)
	95	*Piptochaetium* (1)
Triticeae	96	*Elymus* (2)
	97	*Hordeum* (3)
	98	*Secale* (1)
	99	*Triticum* (1)

Checklist

AGROSTIS L. Bentgrass

    A. elliottiana Schult. ELLIOTT B., annual ticklegrass   NAC¤U

    A. hyemalis (Walt.) B.S.P. WINTER B., fly-away grass, ticklegrass   NPC FW

    A. stolonifera L.

        var. **palustris** (Huds.) Farw. CREEPING B.   IPC FW

AIRA L. Hairgrass

    A. caryophyllea L. ANNUAL H.   IAC F

    A. elegans (= **A. caryophyllea**)

ALOPECURUS L. Foxtail

    A. carolinianus Walt. CAROLINA F.   NAC FW

    A. myosuroides Huds. MOUSE F., slimspike f.   IAC FW

ANDROPOGON L. Bluestem

    A. gerardii Vitman

        var. **gerardii** BIG B.   NPW FU

    A. glomeratus (Walt.) B.S.P. [*A. virginicus* var. *abbreviatus* (Hack.)

        Fern. & Griscom] BUSHY B., bushy beardgrass   NPW FW

    A. gyrans Ashe (*A. elliottii* of Texas auth., not Chapm.)

        ELLIOTT B., Elliott beardgrass   NPW U

    A. ternarius Michx. (*A. elliottii* Chapm., not of Texas auth.)

¤ The following codes denote plant origin, longevity, season of growth, and wetland classification.

Origin: N=Native, I=Introduced

Longevity: A=Annual, B=Biennial, P=Perennial

Season of growth: W=Warm season growth, C=Cool season growth

Wetland classification (indicator categories): U=Upland, FU=Facultative upland, F=Facultative, FW= Facultative wetland, O=Obligative wetland

SPLITBEARD B., splitbeard beardgrass, silvery beardgrass,
feather b.   NPW FU

A. virginicus L. BROOMSEDGE B., yellowsedge b., Virginia b.,
broomsedge   NPW FU

ANTHAENANTIA Beauv. Silkyscale
  A. rufa (= **A. villosa**)
  A. villosa (Michx.) Beauv. GREEN S., purple s.   NPW FU

ARISTIDA L. Threeawn
  A. desmantha Trin. & Rupr. CURLY T., western tripleawn grass,
  western t.   NAW U
  A. lanosa Muhl. *ex* Ell. WOOLLYSHEATH T., woolly tripleawn
  grass, woolly t.   NPW U
  A. longespica Poir.
    var. **geniculata** (Raf.) Fern. (*A. intermedia* Scribn. and Ball)
    KEARNEY T., plains t.   NAW FU
    var. **longespica** SLIMSPIKE T., slender t.   NAW FU
  A. oligantha Michx. OLDFIELD T., prairie t., few-flowered aristida NAW U
  A. purpurea Nutt.
    var. **longiseta** (Steud.) Vasey (*A. longiseta* Steud. and var. *rariflora*
    A. S. Hitchc. and var. *robusta* Merr.) RED T., dogtown-grass,
    longawned aristida, longawned t.   NPW U
    var. **purpurea** (Incl. var. *laxiflora* Merr., *A. roemeriana* Scheele)
    PURPLE T., purple needlegrass   NPW U
  A. purpurescens Poir. ARROWFEATHER T., broomsedge,
  arrowgrass   NPW F
  A. virgata (= **A. purpurescens**)

ARUNDINARIA Michx.
  A. gigantea (Walt.) Muhl. GIANTCANE, southern cane   NPC FW

ARUNDO L.
  A. donax L. GIANTREED   IPW F

AVENA L. Oat
  A. fatua L.

var. **fatua** WILD O. IAC U

var. **sativa** (L.) Hausskn. (*A. sativa* L.) COMMON O.,
cultivated o. IAC U

AXONOPUS Beauv. Carpetgrass
A. affinis (= **A. fissifolius**)
A. fissifolius (Raddi) Kuhlman COMMON C. NPW F
A. furcatus (Flugge) A. S. Hitchc. BIG C., flat crabgrass NPW O

BOTHRIOCHLOA O. Ktze. Bluestem
B. barbinodis (Lag.) Herter
var. **barbinodis** (*Andropogon barbinodis* Lag.)
CANE B., cane beardgrass, bristlejoint b. NPW U
var. **perforata** (Fourn.) Gould (*Andropogon perforatus* Trin.
ex Fourn.) PINHOLE B., pinhole beardgrass, perforated b. NPW U
B. bladhii (Retz.) S. T. Blake [*B. intermedia* (R. Br.) A. Camus]
AUSTRALIAN B. IPW U
B. exaristata (Nash) Henr. [*Andropogon exaristatus* (Nash) A. S.
Hitchc.] AWNLESS B. NPW U
B. hybrida (Gould) Gould (*Andropogon hybridus* Gould)
HYBRID B. NPW U
B. ischaemum (L.) Keng
var. **songarica** (Fisch. & Mey.) Celarier & Harlan KING
RANCH B. IPW U
B. laguroides (DC.) Herter
subsp. **torreyana** (Steud.) Allred & Gould
[*B. saccharoides* (Sw.) Rydb. var. *torreyana* (Steud.) Gould]
SILVER B., silver beardgrass NPW U
B. longipaniculata (Gould) Allred & Gould
[*B. saccharoides* (Sw.) Rydb. var. *longipaniculata* (Gould) Gould,
Andropogon longipaniculatus Gould] LONGSPIKE SILVER B. NPW U

BOUTELOUA Lag. mut. Lag. Grama
B. barbata Lag. SIXWEEKS G. NAW U
B. curtipendula (Michx.) Torr.
var. **curtipendula** SIDEOATS G. NPW U
B. hirsuta Lag. HAIRY G. NPW U
B. rigidiseta (Steud.) A. S. Hitchc.

var. **rigidiseta** TEXAS G., mesquitegrass NPW U
B. trifida Thurb. RED G., threeawn g. NPW U

BRACHIARIA in part (= **UROCHLOA**)
   B. ciliatissima (= **U. ciliatissima**)
   B. fasciculata (= **U. fasciculata**)
   B. mutica (= **U. mutica**)
   B. platyphylla (= **U. platyphylla**)
   B. reptans (= **U. reptans**)
   B. texana (= **U. texana**)

BRIZA L. Quakinggrass
   B. maxima L. BIG Q. IAC F
   B. minor L. LITTLE Q. IAC U

BROMUS L. Brome
   B. catharticus M. A. Vahl
      RESCUEGRASS, rescue b., Schraders-grass IAC U
   B. japonicus Thunb. *ex* Murray JAPANESE B., Japanese chess,
      spreading b. IAC FU
   B. secalinus L. RYE B. IAC U
   B. texensis (Shear) A. S. Hitchc. TEXAS B. NPC U
   B. unioloides (= **B. catharticus**)

BUCHLOË Engelm.
   B. dactyloides (Nutt.) Engelm. BUFFALOGRASS NPW FU

CATAPODIUM (= **DEZMAZERIA**)
   C. rigidum (= **Dezmazeria rigida**)

CENCHRUS L. Sandbur, Cenchrus
   C. ciliaris (= **Pennisetum ciliare**)
   C. echinatus L. SOUTHERN S., hedge-hog grass NAW U
   C. incertus (= **C. spinifex**)
   C. myosuroides Kunth in H.B.K. BIG C., big sandbur, cadillo NPW FU
   C. pauciflorus (= **C. spinifex**)
   C. spinifex A. Cavanilles COMMON S.

CHASMANTHIUM Link Woodoats

    C. latifolium (Michx.) Yates (*Uniola latifolia* Michx.)

        BROADLEAF W.   NPW   F

    C. laxum (L.) Yates [*Uniola laxa* (L.) B.S.P.] NARROWLEAF W.   NPW   F

    C. sessiliflorum (= **C. laxum**)

CHLORIS Sw. Windmillgrass, Chloris

    C. andropogonoides Fourn. SLIMSPIKE W.   NPW   U

    C. canterai Arech.   IPW   U

    C. chloridea (= **Enteropogon chlorideus**)

    C. ciliata Swartz FRINGED C.   NPW   U

    C. cucullata Bisch. HOODED W., hooded fingergrass   NPW   U

    C. divaricata R. Br.   IPW   U

    C. gayana Kunth RHODESGRASS   IPW   U

    C. pluriflora (= **Trichloris pluriflora**)

    C. x subdolichostachya. C. Muell. SHORTSPIKE W.   NPW   U

    C. texensis Nash TEXAS W.   NPW   U

    C. verticillata Nutt. TUMBLE W.   NPW   U

    C. virgata Sw. SHOWY C., feather fingergrass   NAW   U

CHRYSOPOGON Trin.

    C. pauciflorus (Chapm.) Benth. *ex* Vasey   NAW   U

COELORACHIS Brongn. Jointtail

    C. cylindrica (Michx.) Nash (*Manisuris cylindrica* Michx.)

        CAROLINA J.   NPW   F

    C. rugosa (Nutt.) Nash [*Manisuris rugosa* (Nutt.) O. Ktze.]

        WRINKLED J.   NPW   FW

CORTADERIA Stapf

    C. selloana (Schult. & Schult.) Aschers. & Graebn.

        PAMPASGRASS   IPW   U

CYNODON L. Rich.

    C. dactylon (L.) Pers. BERMUDAGRASS, pata del gallo   IPW   FU

DACTYLIS L.

    D. glomerata L. ORCHARDGRASS   IPC   FU

DACTYLOCTENIUM Willd.

    D. aegyptium (L.) Beauv. DURBAN CROWFOOTGRASS, Egyptian
        crowfootgrass   IAW   U

DESMAZERIA Dumort

    D. rigida (L.) T. Tutin STIFFGRASS   IAC   U

DICHANTHELIUM (A. S. Hitchc. & Chase) Gould Rosettegrass

    D. aciculare (Poir.) Gould & Clark [*D. angustifolium* (Ell.) Gould,
        Panicum angustifolium Ell.] NARROW-LEAF R.   NPC   FU

    D. acuminatum (Sw.) Gould & Clark

        var. **acuminatum** [*D. lanuginosum* (Ell.) Gould, *Panicum*
            acuminatum Sw., *P. lanuginosum* Ell., *P. huachucae* Ashe,
            P. tennesseense Ashe] WOOLLY R.   NPC   F

        var. **densiflorum** (Rand & Redf.) Gould & Clark
            [*Panicum acuminatum* var. *densiflorum* (Rand & Redf.) Lelong] NPC   U

        var. **lindheimeri** (Nash) Gould & Clark [*D. lindheimeri* (Nash)
            Gould, *Panicum acuminatum* var. *lindheimeri* (Nash) Lelong,
            P. lindheimeri Nash] LINDHEIMER R.   NPC   U

    D. commutatum (Schult.) Gould (*Panicum commutatum* Schult.)
        VARIABLE R.   NPC   F

    D. dichotomum (L.) Gould (*Panicum dichotomum* L.)
        var. **dichotomum**   NPC   F

        var. **ensifolium** (Baldwin) Gould & Clark [*D. ensifolium*
            (Ell.) Gould, *Panicum ensifolium* Ell.] FORKED R.   NPC   U

    D. linearifolium (Scribn.) Gould (*Panicum linearifolium* Scribn.,
        P. perlongum Nash, *P. werneri* Scribn.) SLIMLEAF R.   NPC   U

    D. nodatum (A. S. Hitchc. & Chase) Gould
        (*Panicum nodatum* A. S. Hitchc. & Chase) SARITA R.   NPC   U

    D. oligosanthes (Schult.) Gould
        var. **oligosanthes** (*Panicum oligosanthes* Schult.)   NPC   FU

        var. **scribnerianum** (Nash) Gould (*Panicum scribnerianum* Nash,
            P. helleri Nash) SCRIBNER'S R.   NPC   FU

    D. ravenelii (Scribn.) Gould (*Panicum ravenelii* Scribn.)   NPC   U

    D. sphaerocarpon (Ell.) Gould & Clark
        var. **sphaerocarpon** (*Panicum sphaerocarpon* Ell.)
        ROUNDSEED R.   NPC   FU

DICHANTHIUM Willem. Bluestem

D. annulatum (Forssk.) Stapf (*Andropogon annulatus* Forssk.)
    KLEBERG B.   IPW   U

D. aristatum (Poir.) C. E. Hubb. [*Andropogon nodosus*
    (Willem.) Nash] ANGLETON B.   IPW   U

D. sericeum (R. Br.) A. Camus (*Andropogon sericeus* R. Br.)
    SILKY B.   IPW   U

DIGITARIA Fabr. Crabgrass, Cottontop

D. arenicola (Swallen) Beetle [*Leptoloma arenicola* Swallen,
    L. cognatum (Schult.) Chase var. *arenicola* (Swallen) Gould]
    SAND WITCHGRASS   NPW   U

D. bicornis (Lam.) Roem. & Schult. (*D. diversiflora* Swallen)
    CRABGRASS   IAW   U

D. californica (Benth.) Henr. [*Trichachne californica* (Benth.)
    Chase] ARIZONA COTTONTOP, California cottontop   NPW   U

D. ciliaris (= **D. sanguinalis**)

D. cognata (Schult.) Pilger [*Leptoloma cognatum* (Schult.) Chase]
    FALL WITCHGRASS, diffuse crabgrass   NPW   U
    ssp. **cognata**   NPW   U
    ssp. **pubiflora** (Vasey *ex* L. H. Dewey) Wipff   NPW   U

D. filiformis (L.) Koel. SLENDER CRABGRASS, slender
    fingergrass   NPW   U

D. insularis (L.) Mez *ex* Ekman [*Trichachne insularis* (L.) Nees]
    SOURGRASS   NPW   F

D. patens (Swallen) Henr. (*Trichachne patens* Swallen) TEXAS
    COTTONTOP   NPW   U

D. runyoni (= **D. texana**)

D. sanguinalis (L.) Scop. [*D. adscendens* (Kunth in H.B.K.) Henr.]
    HAIRY CRABGRASS, southern c.   IAW   FU

D. texana A. S. Hitchc. TEXAS CRABGRASS, Texas fingergrass,
    dune c.   NPW   U

D. villosa (Walt.) Pers. [*D. filiformis* var. *villosa* (Walt.) Fern.]
    SHAGGY CRABGRASS   NPW   U

DISTICHLIS Raf. Saltgrass

D. spicata (L.) Greene
    var. **spicata** COASTAL S., spicate s.   NPW   FW

ECHINOCHLOA Beauv. Cockspur, Barnyardgrass

E. colonum (L.) Link JUNGLERICE	IAW	FW
E. crusgalli (L.) Beauv. BARNYARDGRASS		
var. **crusgalli** BARNYARDGRASS	IAW	FW
var. **frumentacea** (Link) W. F. Wight JAPANESE MILLET	IAW	FW
E. crus-pavonis (Kunth) Schult. GULF COCKSPUR		
var. **crus-pavonis**	NAW	O
var. **macera** (Wieg.) Gould	NAW	O
E. muricata (Beauv.) Fern.		
var. **microstachya** Wieg.	NAW	FW
var. **muricata**	NAW	FW
E. polystachya (Kunth in H.B.K.) A. S. Hitchc.	NPW	FW
E. walteri (Pursh) Heller COAST COCKSPUR	NAW	O

ELEUSINE Gaertn.

E. indica (L.) Gaertn. GOOSEGRASS, yardgrass, zacate guacima	IAW	FU

ELIONURUS Willd. Balsamscale

E. tripsacoides Humb. & Bonpl. *ex* Willd. PAN AMERICAN B., b.	NPW	U

ELYMUS L. Wildrye

E. canadensis L.var. **canadensis** CANADA W., nodding w.	NPC	F
E. virginicus L. VIRGINIA W.	NPC	F

ENTEROPOGON Nees Windmillgrass

E. chlorideus (J. Presl) W. Clayton [*C. chloridea* (J. Presl) A. S. Hitchc.] BURYSEED W.	NPW	U

ERAGROSTIS Wolf Lovegrass

E. barrelieri Daveau MEDITERRANEAN L.	IAW	U
E. capillaris (L.) Nees LACEGRASS, tiny l.	NAW	U
E. cilianensis (All.) Janchen [*E. megastachya* (Koel.) Link] STINKGRASS	IAW	FU
E. ciliaris (L.) R. Br. GOPHERTAIL L.	NAW	FU
E. curtipedicellata Buckl. GUMMY L., shortstalked l.	NPW	U
E. curvula (Schrad.) Nees WEEPING L.	IPW	U
E. elliottii S. Wats. ELLIOTT L.	NPW	FW

E. **hirsuta** (Michx.) Nees BIGTOP L.   NPW   FU

E. **hypnoides** (Lam.) B.S.P. TEAL L., smooth creeping grass   NAW   O

E. **intermedia** A. S. Hitchc. PLAINS L.   NPW   U

E. **lugens** Nees MOURNING L.   NPW   FU

E. **pectinacea** (Michx.) Nees *ex* Steud.

    var. **miserrima** (Fourn.) J. Reeder (*E. tephrosanthes* Schult.)   IAW   F

    var. **pectinacea** (*E. diffusa* Buckl.) SPREADING L.   IAW   F

E. **refracta** (Ell.) Scribn. COASTAL L., meadow l.   NPW   FW

E. **reptans** (Michx.) Nees [*Neeragrostis reptans* (Michx.) Nicora]

    CREEPING L.   NAW   O

E. **secundiflora** Presl

    ssp. **oxylepis** (Torr.) S. D. Koch [*E. oxylepis* (Torr.) Torr.] RED L. NPW   FU

E. **sessilispica** Buckl. TUMBLE L.   NPW   U

E. **silveana** Swallen SILVEUS L.   NPW   U

E. **spectabilis** (Pursh) Steud. PURPLE L.   NPW   FU

E. **swallenii** A. S. Hitchc. SWALLEN L.   NPW   U

ERIANTHUS (= **SACCHARUM**)

    E. alopecuroides (= **S. alopecuroideum**)

    E. contortus (= **S. brevibarbe** var. **contortum**)

    E. giganteus (= **S. giganteum**)

    E. strictus (= **S. baldwinii**)

ERIOCHLOA Kunth in H.B.K. Cupgrass

E. **contracta** A. S. Hitchc. PRAIRIE C.   NAW   F

E. **pseudoacrotricha** (Stapf *ex* Thell.) C. E. Hubb. *ex* Blake   IPW   U

E. **punctata** (L.) Desv. *ex* Hamilton LOUISIANA C., everlasting-

    grass   NPW   FW

E. **sericea** (Scheele) Munro *ex* Vasey TEXAS C., silky c.   NPW   U

ERIONEURON Nash Erioneuron, Woollygrass

E. **pilosum** (Buckl.) Nash [*Tridens pilosus* (Buckl.) A. S. Hitchc.]

    HAIRY E., hairy tridens   NPW   U

EUSTACHYS Desv. Eustachys

E. **caribea** (Spreng.) Herter   IPW   U

E. **petraea** (Sw.) Desv. (*Chloris petraea* Sw.) STIFFLEAF E.   NPW   F

GLYCERIA R. Br. Mannagrass
  G. septentrionalis A. S. Hitchc. EASTERN M., floating m.   NPC   U

GYMNOPOGON Beauv. Skeletongrass
  G. ambiguus (Michx.) B.S.P. BEARDED SKELETONGRASS,
    broad-leaved beardgrass   NPW   FU

HAINARDIA Greuter
  H. cylindrica (Willd.) Tutin THINTAIL   IAC   F

HEMARTHRIA R. Br.
  H. altissima (Poir.) Stapf & Hubb. [*Manisuris altissima* (Poir.)
    A. S. Hitchc.] AFRICAN JOINTTAIL   IPW   FW

HETEROPOGON Pers.
  H. contortus (L.) Beauv. *ex* Roem. & Schult. TANGLEHEAD,
    retorcido moreno, barba negra   NPW   U

HILARIA Kunth
  H. belangeri (Steud.) Nash COMMON CURLYMESQUITE,
    creeping mesquite   NPW   U

HOLCUS L.
  H. lanatus L. COMMON VELVETGRASS   IPC   F

HORDEUM L. Barley
  H. leporinum Link HARE B.   IAC   FU
  H. murinum (= **H. leporinum**)
  H. pusillum Nutt. LITTLE B., mouse b.   NAC   FU
  H. vulgare L. BARLEY   IAC   U

KOELERIA in part (= **ROSTRARIA**)
  K. gerardii (= **Rostraria cristata**)
LEERSIA Sw. Cutgrass
  L. hexandra Sw. CLUBHEAD C.   NPW   O
  L. lenticularis Michx. CATCHFLYGRASS   NPW   O
  L. monandra Sw. BUNCH C.   NPW   FW

L. oryzoides (L.) Sw. RICE C.   NPW O
L. virginica Willd. WHITEGRASS, Virginia c.   NPW FW

LEPTOCHLOA Beauv. Sprangletop
  L. chloridiformis (Hack.) Parodi ARGENTINE S.   NPW U
  L. dubia (Kunth in H.B.K.) Nees GREEN S., Texas crowfoot   NPW U
  L. fascicularis (Lam.) Gray BEARDED S., salt meadowgrass, salt s.   NAW FW
  L. filiformis (= **L. mucronata**)
  L. mucronata (Michx.) Kunth RED S., slendergrass   NAW FW
  L. nealleyi Vasey NEALLEY S.   NAW FW
  L. panicoides (Presl) A. S. Hitchc. AMAZON S.   NAW FW
  L. uninervia (Presl) A. S. Hitchc. & Chase MEXICAN S.   NAW FW
  L. virgata (L.) Beauv. TROPIC S.   NPW FW

LEPTOLOMA (= **DIGITARIA**)
  L. arenicola (= **Digitaria arenicola**)
  L. cognatum (= **Digitaria cognata**)

LIMNODEA Dewey
  L. arkansana (Nutt.) L. H. Dewey OZARKGRASS   NAC U

LOLIUM L. Ryegrass
  L. perenne L. [*L. multiflorum* Lam., *L. perenne* var. *italicum*
    (R. Br.) Parnell] PERENNIAL R., English r., ryegrass   IPC FU
  L. temulentum L.
    var. **temulentum** DARNEL R., poison darnel   IAC U

LUZIOLA Juss.
  L. peruviana Gmel.   IPW O

MANISURIS (= **HEMARTHRIA**)
  M. altissima (= **Hemarthria altissima**)
  M. cylindrica (=**Coelorachis cylindrica**)
  M. rugosa (=**Coelorachis rugosa**)

MELICA L. Melic
  M. mutica Walt. TWO-FLOWERED M., narrow m.   NPC U

MELINIS P. Beauv.

    M. repens (Willd.) Zizka [*Rhynchelytrum repens* (Willd.)
      C. E. Hubb.] NATALGRASS   IPW   U

MONANTHOCHLOË Engelm.

    M. littoralis Engelm. SHOREGRASS, dwarfstand saltgrass   NPW O

MONERMA (= **HAINARDIA**)

    M. cylindrica (= **Hainardia cylindrica**)

MUHLENBERGIA Schreb. Muhly

    M. capillaris (Lam.) Trin. HAIRYAWN M., long-awned hairgrass,
      slender m.   NPW FU
    M. expansa (Poir.) Trin. CUTOVER M.   NPW FW
    M. filipes M. A. Curtis GULF M.   NPW U
    M. fragilis Swallen DELICATE M.   NAW U
    M. schreberi Gmel. NIMBLEWILL, satingrass, Schreber's m. NPW F

NASSELLA Desv. Needlegrass

    N. leucotricha (Trin. & Rupr.) Pohl TEXAS WINTERGRASS,
      Texas n., speargrass   NPC U

NEERAGROSTIS (= **ERAGROSTIS**)

    N. reptans (= **Eragrostis reptans**)

OPLISMENUS Beauv. Basketgrass

    O. hirtellus (L.) Beauv. BASKETGRASS   IPW FU

ORYZA L. Rice

    O. sativa L. RICE   IAW O

PANICUM L. Panicum

    P. amarum Ell. (*P. amarulum* A. S. Hitchc. & Chase) BITTER P. NPW FU
    P. anceps Michx. BEAKED P.   NPW F
    P. antidotale Retz. BLUE P.   IPW U
    P. brachyanthum Steud. PIMPLE P.   NPW FU
    P. capillare L. COMMON WITCHGRASS   NAW F
    P. capillarioides Vasey SOUTHERN WITCHGRASS, slender

panicgrass	NPW	U
P. dichotomiflorum Michx. FALL P., spreading witchgrass	NAW	FW
P. diffusum Sw. SPREADING P.	NPW	F
P. fasciculatum (= **Brachiaria fasciculata**)		
P. ghiesbreghtii Fourn. GHIESBREGHT P.	NPW	U
P. gymnocarpon Ell. SAVANNAH P.	NPW	O
P. hallii Vasey		
var. **filipes** (Scribn.) Waller (*P. filipes* Scribn.) FILLY P.	NPW	U
var. **hallii** HALLS P.	NPW	FU
P. hemitomon Schult. MAIDENCANE, Simpson's grass	NPW	O
P. hians Ell. GAPING P.	NPW	FW
P. hirsutum Sw. HAIRY P.	NPW	U
P. maximum Jacq. GUINEAGRASS	IPW	F
P. miliaceum L. BROOMCORN MILLET, proso	IAW	U
P. obtusum Kunth in H.B.K. VINE MESQUITE, grapevine-mesquite, wiregrass	NPW	F
P. pilcomayense Hack.	IPW	FW
P. purpurascens (= **Brachiaria mutica**)		
P. repens L. TORPEDOGRASS	IPW	F
P. rigidulum Nees (*P. agrostoides* Spreng., *P. condensum* Nash) REDTOP P.	NPW	FW
P. tenerum Beyr. *ex* Trin.	NPW	FW
P. trichoides Sw.	NAW	F
P. verrucosum Muhl. WARTY P.	NAW	FW
P. virgatum L. SWITCHGRASS	NPW	U
PAPPOPHORUM Schreb. Pappusgrass		
P. bicolor Fourn. PINK P., two-colored p.	NPW	U
P. vaginatum Buckl. WHIPLASH P., mucronulate p.	NPW	U
PARAPHOLIS Hubb.		
P. incurva (L.) C. E. Hubb. [*Lepturus incurvus* Druce, *Pholiurus incurvus* (L.) Schinz & Thell.] SICKLEGRASS	IAC	F
PASPALIDIUM Stapf		
P. geminatum (Forssk.) Stapf		
var. **geminatum** (*Panicum geminatum* Forssk.) EGYPTIAN PASPALIDIUM	IPW	O

var. **paludivagum** (A. S. Hitchc. & Chase) Gould
(*Panicum paludivagum* A. S. Hitchc. & Chase) WATER
PASPALIDIUM   IPW   O

PASPALUM L.   Paspalum

P. almum Chase COMBS P.   NPW   U
P. bifidum (Bertol.) Nash PITCHFORK P.   NPW   U
P. boscianum Flugge BULL P.   NPW   FW
P. conjugatum Bergius SOUR P.   NPW   FW
P. dilatatum Poir. DALLISGRASS, paspalum grass   IPW   F
P. dissectum (L.) L. MUDBANK P.   NPW   O
P. floridanum Michx.
  var. **floridanum** FLORIDA P.   NPW   F
  var. **glabratum** Engelm. *ex* Vasey FLORIDA P., big Florida p.,
      big p.   NPW   FW
P. fluitans (Ell.) Kunth WATER P.   NAW   O
P. hartwegianum Fourn. HARTWEG P.   NPW   FW
P. laeve Michx.
  var. **circulare** (Nash) Fern. (*P. circulare* Nash) ROUNDSEED P. NPW   U
  var. **laeve** FIELD P., smooth p.   NPW   FW
P. langei (Fourn.) Nash RUSTYSEED P., Lange's p.   NPW   U
P. lividum Trin. LONGTOM, pull-and-be-damned   NPW   O
P. minus Fourn. MAT P.   NPW   U
P. monostachyum Vasey GULFDUNE P, single-spike p.   NPW   FW
P. notatum Flugge BAHIAGRASS   IPW   F
P. plicatulum Michx. (*P. texanum* Swallen) BROWNSEED P.,
    plaited p.   NPW   F
P. praecox Walt. (*P. lentiferum* Lam.) EARLY P.   NPW   FW
P. pubiflorum Rupr. *ex* Fourn.
  var. **pubiflorum** HAIRYSEED P., hairyflowered p.   NPW   FW
P. setaceum Michx. THIN P.
  var. **ciliatifolium** (Michx.) Vasey FRINGELEAF P.   NPW   F
  var. **muhlenbergii** (Nash) D. Banks   NPW   F
  var. **stramineum** (Nash) D. Banks (*P. stramineum* Nash) NPW   F
P. unispicatum (Scribn. & Merr.) Nash ONESPIKE P.   NPW   U
P. urvillei Steud. VASEYGRASS, Urville's p.   IPW   F
P. vaginatum Sw. SEASHORE P., sand knotgrass   NPW   FW
P. virgatum L. TALQUEZAL   NPW   FW

PENNISETUM L. A. Rich. Pennisetum

   P. ciliare (L.) Link (*Cenchrus ciliaris* L.) BUFFELGRASS   IPW   U

   P. nervosum (Nees) Trin. BENTSPIKE P.   IPW   U

   P. orientale L. C. Rich. LAURISAGRASS   IPW   U

   P. purpureum Schumach. NAPIERGRASS, elephantgrass   IPW   U

   P. setaceum (Forssk.) Chiov. FOUNTAINGRASS   IPW   U

   P. villosum R. Br. *ex* Fresen. FEATHERTOP P.   IPW   U

PHALARIS L. Canarygrass

   P. angusta Nees *ex* Trin. TIMOTHY C.   NAC   FW

   P. canariensis L. C.   IAC   FW

   P. caroliniana Walt. CAROLINA C., southern c.   NAC   FW

   P. minor Retz. LITTLESEED C.   IAC   U

PHRAGMITES Adans.

   P. australis (Cav.) Trin. *ex* Steud. (*P. communis* Trin.)

      COMMON REED   NPW   FW

PIPTOCHAETIUM Presl

   P. avenaceum (L.) Parodi (*Stipa avenacea* L.)

      BLACKSEEDNEEDLEGRASS, black oatgrass, oats needlegrass NPC   U

POA L. Bluegrass

   P. annua L. ANNUAL B., low speargrass, dwarf meadowgrass   IAC   F

   P. arachnifera Torr. TEXAS B.   NPC   U

   P. autumnalis Muhl. *ex* Ell. AUTUMN B., flexuous speargrass   NPC   F

POLYPOGON Desf. Polypogon

   P. monspeliensis (L.) Desf. RABBITFOOT P., annual beardgrass,

      rabbitfoot-grass   IAC   FW

RHYNCHELYTRUM (= **MELINUS**)

   R. repens (= **Melinus repens**)

ROSTRARIA Trin.

   R. cristata (L.) Tzvelev ANNUAL JUNEGRASS, annual koeleria   IAC   U

ROTTBOELLIA L.f.

    R. cochinchinensis (Lour.) W. D. Clayton ITCHGRASS   IAW   U

SACCHARUM L. Plumegrass

    S. alopecuroideum (L.) Nutt. [*Erianthus alopecuroides* (L.)
        Ell.] SILVER PLUMEGRASS   NPW FW

    S. baldwinii Spreng. (*Erianthus strictus* Baldw.) NARROW
        PLUMEGRASS   NPW FW

    S. brevibarbe (Michx.) Pers.

        var. **contortum** (Ell.) R. Webster (*Erianthus contortus* Baldw.
        ex Ell.) BENTAWN PLUMEGRASS   NPW F

    S. giganteum (Walt.) Pers. [*Erianthus giganteus* (Walt.) F. T. Hubb.]
        SUGARCANE PLUMEGRASS   NPW FW

SACCIOLEPIS Nash

    S. striata (L.) Nash AMERICAN CUPSCALE   NPW O

SCHEDONNARDUS Steud.

    S. paniculatus (Nutt.) Trel. TUMBLEGRASS   NPW U

SCHIZACHYRIUM Nees Bluestem

    S. scoparium (Michx.) Nash (*Andropogon scoparius* Michx.)
        LITTLE B.

        var. **divergens** (Hack.) Gould [*Andropogon divergens* (Hack.)
        Andress. ex A. S. Hitchc.] EASTERN LITTLE B.   NPW U

        var. **littorale** (Nash) Gould [*Andropogon littoralis* (Nash)
        A. S. Hitchc.] SEACOAST B., seacoast beardgrass   NPW FU

        var. **scoparium** (C. E. Hubb.) Gould (*Andropogon frequens*
        C. E. Hubb.) LITTLE B.   NPW FU

SECALE L. Rye

    S. cereale L. RYE   IAC   U

SETARIA Beauv. Bristlegrass, Millet

    S. adhaerans (Forssk.) Chiov.   IAW   U

    S. corrugata (Ell.) Schult.   NPW U

    S. firmula (A. S. Hitchc. & Chase) Pilger
        (*Panicum firmulum* A. S. Hitchc. & Chase) KNOTGRASS   NPW U

S. geniculata (= **S. parviflora**)

S. glauca (= **S. pumila**)

S. italica (L.) Beauv. FOXTAIL MILLET	IAW	FU
S. leucopila (Scribn. & Merr.) K. Schum. PLAINS B.	NPW	U
S. macrostachya Kunth in H.B.K. PLAINS B.	NPW	U
S. magna Griseb. GIANT B., giant foxtail grass	NAW	FW
S. parviflora (Sw.) Kerguelen KNOTROOT B.	NPW	F
S. pumila (Poir) Roem. & Schult. [*S. lutescens* (Weigel.) F. T. Hubb.]		
YELLOW B.	IAW	F
S. ramiseta (Scribn.) Pilger (*Panicum ramisetum* Scribn.)	NPW	U
S. reverchonii (Vasey) Pilger (*Panicum reverchonii* Vasey)		
REVERCHON B.	NPW	U
S. scheelei (Steud.) A. S. Hitchc. SOUTHWESTERN B., Scheele's b.	NPW	U
S. texana W.H.P. Emery TEXAS B.	NPW	U

SORGHASTRUM Nash Indiangrass

S. elliottii (Mohr) Nash SLENDER I., long-bristled i.	NPW	U
S. nutans (L.) Nash YELLOW I., indianreed	NPW	FU

SORGHUM Moench Sorghum

S. bicolor (L.) Moench (*S. vulgare* Pers.) GRAIN S.	IAW	FU
S. halepense (L.) Pers. JOHNSONGRASS	IPW	FU

SPARTINA Schreb. Cordgrass

S. alterniflora Loisel.

var. **glabra** (Bigel.) Fern. SMOOTH C., salt-marshgrass	NPW	O
S. bakeri Merr.	NPW	U
S. cynosuroides (L.) Roth BIG C., salt-reedgrass	NPW	O
S. patens (Ait.) Muhl. MARSHHAY C., rush saltgrass	NPW	FW
S. spartinae (Trin.) Merr. *ex* A. S. Hitchc.		
GULF C., coastal sacahuista, sacahuista grass	NPW	FW

SPHENOPHOLIS Scribn. Wedgescale

S. obtusata (Michx.) Scribn.

var. **major** (Torr.) Erdman [*S. intermedia* (Rydb.) Rydb.,		
S. longiflora (Vasey) A. S. Hitchc.]	NPC	FW
var. **obtusata** PRAIRIE W.	NPC	FW

SPOROBOLUS R. Br. Dropseed

    S. airoides (Torr.) Torr. ALKALI SACATON   NPW F

    S. asper (= **S. compositus**)

        var. *asper* (= **S. compositus** var. **compositus**)

        var. *clandestinus* (= **S. compositus** var. **clandestinus**)

        var. *drummondii* (= **S. compositus** var. **drummondii**)

    S. buckleyi Vasey BUCKLEY D.   NPW U

    S. compositus (Poir.) Merr.

        var. **clandestinus** (Biehl.) Wipff & S. D. Jones   NPW U

        var. **compositus** TALL D., longleaved rushgrass, rough

            rushgrass   NPW U

        var. **drummondii** (Trin.) Kartesz & Gandhi MEADOW D.   NPW U

    S. coromandelianus (Retz.) Kunth WHORLED D.   NPW F

    S. cryptandrus (Torr.) Gray SAND D., covered-spike d.   NPW FU

    S. indicus (L.) R. Br. [*S. poiretii* (Roem. & Schult.) A. S. Hitchc.]

        SMUTGRASS   NPW F

    S. junceus (Beauv.) Kunth PINEYWOODS D., purple d.   NPW U

    S. purpurascens (Sw.) Hamilt. PURPLE D.   NPW U

    S. pyramidatus (= **S. coromandelianus**)

    S. silveanus Swallen SILVEUS D.   NPW U

    S. tharpii (= **S. airoides**)

    S. virginicus (L.) Kunth SEASHORE D., seashore rushgrass   NPW FW

STENOTAPHRUM Trin.

    S. secundatum (Walt.) O. Ktze. ST. AUGUSTINEGRASS   IPW F

STIPA in part (= **NASSELLA**)

    S. leucotricha (= **Nassella leucotricha**)

TRACHYPOGON Nees

    T. secundus (Presl) Scribn. (*T. montufari* of Hitchcock's *Manual*

        of U.S. Grasses, ed. I.) CRINKLEAWN   NPW U

TRAGUS Haller Burgrass

    T. racemosus (L.) All. STALKED B.   IAW U

TRICHLORIS Fourn. *ex* Benth.

    T. pluriflora Fourn. [*Chloris pluriflora* (Fourn.) Clayton]

MULTIFLOWERED FALSE RHODESGRASS NPW U

TRICHONEURA Anderss.
T. **elegans** Swallen SILVEUSGRASS, hairy-nerve grass NAW U

TRIDENS Schult. & Schult. Tridens
T. **albescens** (Vasey) Woot. & Standl. WHITE T. NPW F
T. **ambiguus** (Ell.) Schult. PINEBARREN T. NPW F
T. **congestus** (L. H. Dewey) Nash PINK T. NPW U
T. **eragrostoides** (Vasey & Scribn.) Nash LOVEGRASS T. NPW U
T. **flavus** (L.) A. S. Hitchc.
   var. **flavus** PURPLETOP, redtop NPW U
T. **muticus** (Torr.) Nash
   var. **muticus** SLIM T. NPW U
T. *pilosus* (= **Erioneuron pilosum**)
T. **strictus** (Nutt.) Nash LONGSPIKE T. NPW F
T. **texanus** (S. Wats.) Nash TEXAS T. NPW U

TRIODIA of Hitchcock's *Manual of U.S. Grasses,* ed. I. (= **TRIDENS**)

TRIPLASIS Beauv.
T. **purpurea** (Walt.) Chapm. PURPLE SANDGRASS NAW U

TRIPSACUM L.
T. **dactyloides** (L.) L. EASTERN GAMAGRASS NPW F

TRISETUM Pers. Trisetum
T. **interruptum** Buckl. PRAIRIE T. NAC U

TRITICUM L.
T. **aestivum** L. WHEAT IAC U

UNIOLA L.
U. **paniculata** L. SEA-OATS, beachgrass NPW FU

UROCHLOA Beauv. Signalgrass
U. **ciliatissima** (S. Buckl.) R. D. Webster [*Brachiaria ciliatissima*
(Buckl.) Chase] FRINGED S. NPW U

U. fasciculata (O. Swartz) R. D. Webster

    (*Panicum fasciculatum* Sw., *Brachiaria fasciculata* Sw. Parodi)

    BROWNTOP S., fieldgrass, browntop   NAW   F

U. mosambicensis (Hack.) Dandy   IPW   U

U. mutica (P. Forssk.) T. Q. Nguyen [*Panicum purpurascens* Raddi,

    Brachiaria mutica (Forssk.) Stapf] PARAGRASS   IPW   FW

U. panicoides Beauv. LIVERSEED GRASS   IAW   U

U. platyphylla (Munro *ex* Wright) R. D. Webster [*Brachiaria*

    platyphylla (Griseb.) Nash, *B. plantaginea* (Link) A. S. Hitchc.]

    BROADLEAF S.   NAW   F

U. reptans (L.) Stapf [*Brachiaria reptans* (L.) C. E. Hubb.]

    SPRAWLING S.   IAW   U

U. texana (S. Buckl.) R. D. Webster

    [*Panicum texanum* Buckl., *Brachiaria texana* (Buckl.) S. T. Blake]

    TEXAS S., Texas millet, Colorado grass   NAW   U

VASEYOCHLOA A. S. Hitchc.

    V. multinervosa (Vasey) A. S. Hitchc. TEXASGRASS   NPW   U

VULPIA Gmel. Sixweeksgrass

    V. octoflora (Walt.) Rydb.

        var. **hirtella** (Piper) Henr. HAIR S.   NAC   U

        var. **octoflora** (*Festuca octoflora* Walt.) COMMON S.   NAC   U

WILLKOMMIA Hack.

    W. texana A. S. Hitchc.

        var. **texana** TEXAS WILLKOMMIA   NPC   U

ZEA L.

    Z. mays L. CORN   IAW   U

ZIZANIOPSIS Doell

    Z. miliacea (Michx.) Doell & Aschers.

        MARSHMILLET, water millet, giant cutgrass, southern wildrice   NPW   O

— Generic Key to Groups or Selected Genera

1. Leaf blades less than 1 cm long; leaves in fascicles; spikelets unisexual, inconspicuous in axils of fascicled leaves .... *Monanthochloë*
1. Leaf blades more than 1 cm long; leaves not in fascicles; spikelets perfect or unisexual, usually conspicuous 2
2(1). Second glumes with three rows of hooked spines on abaxial surface .... *Tragus*
2. Second glumes without hooked spines on abaxial surface 3
3(2). Spikelets with unisexual florets only; staminate and pistillate spikelets conspicuously different .... Group A
3. Spikelets, at least some, with one or more perfect florets; if unisexual, then staminate and pistillate spikelets not conspicuously different 4
4(3). Florets one per spikelet 5
4. Florets two or more per spikelet, on at least some spikelets 7
5(4). Inflorescence a spike or spicate raceme .... Group B
5. Inflorescence a panicle (depauperate specimens may be reduced to a raceme) 6
6(5). Panicle open, contracted, or with racemose branches, but without spicate primary unilateral branches .... Group C
6. Panicle with spicate primary unilateral branches .... Group D
7(4). Reduced florets below perfect florets (both above and below in some *Chasmanthium* and *Uniola*) 8
7. Reduced florets above perfect floret, or all florets perfect 13
8(7). Reduced florets both above and below fertile florets 9
8. Reduced florets below fertile floret, or both florets reduced/staminate 10
9(8). Disarticulation above glumes; plants of inland or woodland sites .... *Chasmanthium*

9. Disarticulation below glumes; plants of coastal dunes .... *Uniola*

10(8). Glumes absent; spikelets appear to have one floret **11**

10. Glumes present; spikelets have two or three florets **12**

11(10). Plants perennial, native; upper florets less than 6 mm long .... *Leersia*

11. Plants annual, cultivated; upper florets 7–12 mm long .... *Oryza*

12(10). Spikelets paired (except at branch or inflorescence apex where spikelets are in threes), one sessile or subsessile and perfect, one pedicellate and sterile; upper floret usually membranous or leaflike; first glume nearly the length of spikelet (Andropogoneae tribe) .... **Group E**

12. Spikelets paired or not paired; when paired, both spikelets perfect; upper floret dissimilar from lower floret or florets; first glume usually reduced or absent (except in *Phalaris* and some *Panicum* species) (Paniceae tribe and *Phalaris*) .... **Group F**

13(7). Inflorescence a spike or spicate raceme .... **Group G**

13. Inflorescence a panicle (depauperate specimens may be reduced to a raceme) **14**

14(13). Panicle of spicate primary unilateral branches .... **Group H**

14. Panicle of open, contracted, or racemose branches but without spicate primary unilateral branches .... **Group I**

Group A
(unisexual spikelets only, staminate and pistillate spikelets conspicuously different)

1. Plants dioecious **2**

1. Plants monoecious **5**

2(1). Plants erect **3**

2. Plants mat-forming, not erect **4**

3(2). Plant height 1–3 m tall; rhizomes absent .... *Cortaderia*

3. Plant height 35–60 cm tall; rhizomes present .... *Poa*

4(2). Pistillate and staminate inflorescences similar in appearance; lemmas 3-veined .... *Eragrostis*

4. Pistillate inflorescences in burlike clusters and staminate spikelets in clusters on spicate primary unilateral branches; lemmas 3-veined .. *Buchloë*

5(1). Staminate and pistillate spikelets borne on separate inflorescences **6**

5. Staminate and pistillate spikelets borne on the same inflorescence **7**

6(5). Leaf blades 3 cm or wider; plants of terrestrial habitats .... *Zea*

6. Leaf blades less than 0.5 cm wide; plants of wet habitats .... *Luziola*

7(5). Pistillate spikelets below staminate spikelets on inflorescence branch; glume texture indurate .... *Tripsacum*

7. Pistillate spikelets above staminate spikelets on inflorescence branch; glume texture leaflike .... *Zizaniopsis*

Group B
(one floret/spikelet; spike or spicate raceme)

1. Spikelets solitary, one per inflorescence node 2

1. Spikelets, three per inflorescence node 3

2(1). First glumes present .... *Parapholis*

2. First glumes absent .... *Hainardia*

3(1). Glumes reduced to awns; inflorescence a spicate raceme (except in *H. vulgare* a spike) .... *Hordeum*

3. Glumes not reduced to awns, but rather obvious bracts; inflorescence a spike .... *Hilaria*

Group C
(one floret/spikelet;
panicles without spicate primary unilateral branches)

1. Lemmas 3-veined 2

1. Lemmas not conspicuously 3-veined; either 1-, 5-, or more veined 3

2(1). Lemma awn branched to three awns; sometimes the lateral awns greatly reduced .... *Aristida*

2. Lemma awn unbranched or lemma awnless .... *Muhlenbergia*

3(1). Lemmas indurate and completely enclose palea for most of its length.. 4

3. Lemmas membranous or leaflike, but not obviously indurate; usually not enclosing the palea for entire length 5

4(3). Ligule, a firm membrane 1.4–4.8 mm long .... *Piptochaetium*

4. Ligule, a thin membrane to 1 mm long .... *Nassella*

5(3). Glumes absent .... *Leersia*

5. Glumes present 6

6(5). Glumes, at least the first, shorter than floret 7

6. Glumes both longer than floret 8

7(6). Lemmas 5-veined; plants of wet habitats .... *Oryza*

7. Lemmas 1-veined; plants of mesic or xeric habitats .... *Sporobolus*

8(6). Glumes and lemmas awnless .... *Agrostis*

8. Glumes or lemmas awned **9**

9(8). Glumes awned .... *Polypogon*

9. Glumes awnless **10**

10(9). Disarticulation of spikelet above glumes .... *Agrostis*

10. Disarticulation of spikelet below glumes **11**

11(10). Lemmas awned from below middle; inflorescence a tightly contracted, cylindrical panicle .... *Alopecurus*

11. Lemmas awned from near apex; inflorescence contracted but not tightly cylindrical .... *Limnodea*

Group D
(one floret/spikelet; panicle with spicate primary unilateral branches)

1. Panicle branches digitate .... *Cynodon*

1. Panicle branches generally alternate but definitely not digitate **2**

2(1). Spikelets borne on central axis of inflorescence as well as the branches .... *Schedonnardus*

2. Spikelets not borne on central axis of inflorescence, occurring only on the branches **3**

3(2). Lemmas conspicuously 3-veined; paleas 2-veined **4**

3. Lemmas 5-veined; paleas 3-veined .... *Leersia*

4(3). Plants 50 cm or taller; spikelets 6–25 mm long .... *Spartina*

4. Plants 49 cm or shorter; spikelets 4–5 mm long .... *Willkommia*

Group E
ANDROPOGONEAE TRIBE
(two florets/spikelet; spikelets paired; reduced floret below perfect floret)

1. Inflorescence a spicate raceme, several to many per culm **2**

1. Inflorescence a panicle of racemose branches (rarely a panicle with a single branch) **8**

2(1). Upper lemmas awned **3**

2. Upper lemmas awnless **5**

3(2). Lemma awn less than 3 cm long .... *Schizachyrium*

3. Lemma awn more than 3.5 cm long **4**

4(3). Inflorescences less than 8 cm long (excluding awns) .... *Heteropogon*

4. Inflorescences more than 9 cm long (excluding awns) ..... *Trachypogon*

5(2). Inflorescences pubescent .... *Elionurus*

5. Inflorescences glabrous **6**

6(5). Basal leaf sheaths with stiff, sharp, papilla-based hairs to 3 mm long that irritate the skin; plants annual .... *Rottboellia*

6. Basal leaf sheaths glabrous; plants perennial **7**

7(6). First glumes of sessile spikelets smooth on back; inflorescences flattened. .... *Hemarthria*

7. First glumes of sessile spikelets with pits or ridges; inflorescences cylindrical .... *Coelorachis*

8(1). Branches of inflorescence reduces to a triad; lemma awn 10 cm or longer .... *Chrysopogon*

8. Branches of inflorescence rebranched, or at least not a triad of spikelets; lemma awn less than 5 cm long **9**

9(8). Panicles of two to seven paired, digitate, or subdigitate racemose branches; a spathe subtending inflorescence bases can be present or absent; pedicels of upper spikelets without central groove or membranous area **10**

9. Panicles of more than seven racemose branches (occasionally reduced to three branches in *Bothriochloa ischaemum*); spathe not subtending inflorescences; pedicels of upper spikelet with or without a central or membranous area **11**

10(9). Pedicellate spikelets about as large as sessile spikelets, apex broadly rounded; species introduced .... *Dichanthium*

10. Pedicellate spikelets shorter and narrower than sessile spikelets, or apex narrow and tapering; species native .... *Andropogon*

11(9). Pedicels, and usually upper branch internodes, on upper part of the inflorescence with a central groove or membranous area .... *Bothriochloa*

11. Pedicels and upper branch internodes on upper part of the inflorescence without a central groove or membranous area **12**

12(11). Spikelets, both sessile and pedicellate, fertile .... *Saccharum*

12. Spikelets, sessile one fertile and pedicellate one usually reduced and staminate or sterile or neuter **13**

13(12). Pedicellate spikelets absent, only hairy pedicel remaining . *Sorghastrum*

13. Pedicellate spikelets present .... *Sorghum*

Group F
PHALARIS and PANICEAE TRIBE
(two or three florets/spikelet; reduced floret below perfect floret; panicle inflorescences)

1. Glumes equal, 1 mm or more longer than fertile floret; two (occasionally one) scalelike rudimentary florets below fertile floret; disarticulation below glumes; upper floret coriaceous .... *Phalaris*
1. Glumes unequal (rarely equal) or only second glume present (in some species of *Axonopus, Digitaria,* and *Paspalum*); if equal, then reduced floret as long as spikelet; disarticulation below the glumes; upper floret usually firm to indurate (except in *Pennisetum* and *Cenchrus*) **2**
2(1). Inflorescence a spike or spicate raceme; spikelets embedded into cavities of rachis .... *Stenotaphrum*
2. Inflorescence a panicle; spikelets not embedded into cavities of inflorescence branches **3**
3(2). Panicles of spicate (or racemose) primary unilateral branches **4**
3. Panicles open or contracted, but not having spicate primary unilateral branches **16**
4(3). First glumes absent or reduced to a cuplike structure on all or some spikelets **5**
4. First glumes present on all spikelets **9**
5(4). Spikelets subtended by a cuplike or disklike ring; upper lemma mucronate .... *Eriochloa*
5. Spikelets not subtended by a cuplike or disklike ring; upper lemma awnless **6**
6(5). Lemma of the fertile florets with rounded back away from inflorescence branch axis .... *Axonopus*
6. Lemma of fertile florets with rounded back toward inflorescence branch axis **7**
7(6). Upper lemma margins folded over palea, not clasping, appearing thin. .... *Digitaria*
7. Upper lemma margins clasping the palea, appearing thick **8**
8(7). Lemma of lower florets awned; upper florets mucronate .. *Echinochloa*
8. Lemma of lower florets awnless; upper florets rounded to obtuse to acute, not mucronate .... *Paspalum*
9(4). Ligules absent; plants annual .... *Echinochloa*
9. Ligules present; plants annual or perennial **10**

22. Ligules present **23**

23(22). Inflorescences of spicate unbranched primary branches .... ***Urochloa***

23. Inflorescences with branches that rebranch **24**

24(23). Plants forming a basal rosette of leaves different from cauline leaves; culm simple in cool season with a primary panicle inflorescence per culm, later becoming much- branched with small axillary inflorescences in summer and fall .... ***Dichanthelium***

24. Plants not forming a basal rosette of leaves; leaves at base similar to cauline leaves; culms with a primary panicle inflorescence in summer and fall (see also *Dichanthelium pedicellatum*) **25**

25(24). Plants annual; lemma of perfect florets transversely rugose .... ***Urochloa***

25. Plants annual or perennial; when annual, lemma of perfect florets not transversely rugose .... ***Panicum***

Group G
(two or more florets/spikelet; spike or spicate raceme)

1. Inflorescence with one spikelet per node **2**

1. Inflorescence with two or more spikelets per node **3**

2(1). First glume absent on all except the terminal spikelet .... ***Lolium***

2. First glume present on all spikelets .... ***Triticum***

3(1). Plants annual; florets two per spikelet.. ***Secale***

3. Plants perennial; florets not consistently two per spikelet **4**

4(3). Spikelets disarticulate in clusters as a complete unit; lemmas 3-veined, distinct; stolons present ....***Hilaria***

4. Spikelets disarticulate above the glumes; lemmas 5- to 7-veined, indistinct; stolons not present... ***Elymus***

Group H
(two or more florets/spikelet; inflorescence
a panicle of spicate primary unilateral branches)

1. Inflorescence branches digitate, subdigitate, or verticillate................... **2**

1. Inflorescence branches alternate or occasionally paired (*Eleusine* occasionally reduced to one or two branches per inflorescence) **8**

2(1). Fertile florets three or more per spikelet **3**

2. Fertile florets one or two per spikelet **4**

3(2). Inflorescence primary branches terminating in a bare point .... ***Dactyloctenium***

3. Inflorescence primary branches terminating in a spikelet .... ***Eleusine***

4(3). Leaf blades without a midvein, conspicuously distichous; second glumes equal to or longer than spikelet .... ***Gymnopogon***

4. Leaf blades with midvein, not conspicuously distichous; second glumes shorter than spikelet **5**

5(4). Lemmas laterally compressed; caryopses triangular or subterete in cross section **6**

5. Lemmas dorsally compressed; caryopses dorsally compressed............. **7**

6(5). Second glumes acute to bidentate, awnless or rarely short-awned, lowermost lemmas usually awned, usually pale .... ***Chloris***

6. Second glumes obtuse to bilobed, distinctly awned; lowermost lemmas awnless to mucronate, dark brown or pale .... ***Eustachys***

7(5). Lowermost lemmas 1-awned .... ***Enteropogon***

7. Lowermost lemmas 3-awned .... ***Trichloris***

8(1). Lemmas obscurely 5-veined; plants annual .... ***Desmazeria***

8. Lemmas conspicuously 3-veined; plants perennial or annual **9**

9(8). Fertile florets one per spikelet .... ***Bouteloua***

9. Fertile florets two or more per spikelet **10**

10(9). Glumes 8 mm or longer; lemma veins ciliate .... ***Trichoneura***

10. Glumes less than 7.8 mm long; lemma veins glabrous or puberulent but not with spreading ciliate hairs **11**

11(10). Lemmas glabrous, acute, awnless; spikelets not overlapping on inflorescence branches .... ***Eragrostis***

11. Lemmas glabrous or pubescent on veins or near the base, apex acute to obtuse or notched, awned or awnless; when lemmas awnless, spikelets overlapping on branches .... ***Leptochloa***

Group I
(two or more florets/spikelet; reduced floret at spikelet apex; panicle inflorescence)

1. Plants 2–6 m tall **2**

1. Plants less than 2 m tall **5**

2(1). Spikelets 3.5–7.0 cm long; inflorescences not plumose ...... ***Arundinaria***

2. Spikelets less than 3.5 cm long; inflorescences a plumelike panicle **3**

3(2). Plants without rhizomes (caespitose); glumes 1-veined ...... *Cortaderia*

  3. Plants rhizomatous; glumes 3- to many-veined **4**

4(3). Lemmas densely pubescent; rachilla glabrous .... *Arundo*

  4. Lemmas glabrous; rachilla villous .... *Phragmites*

5(1). Lemmas conspicuously 3-veined **6**

  5. Lemmas 5- to many-veined, or veins obscure (midvein may be conspicuous) **11**

6(5). Veins of lemma glabrous or minutely scabrous **7**

  6. Veins of lemma pubescent (occasionally puberulent) to long hairy **8**

7(6). Lemma apex without a notch, midvein not extending into an awn; panicles open or narrow .... *Eragrostis*

  7. Lemma apex with a slight notch, midvein extending into a mucro; panicles contracted .... *Tridens*

8(6). Paleas densely long-ciliate on upper half; plants annual .... *Triplasis*

  8. Paleas not densely long-ciliate on upper half; plants annual or perennial **9**

9(8). Leaf blades with thick white margins; inflorescences usually less than 4 cm long .... *Erioneuron*

  9. Leaf blades without thick white margins; inflorescences more than 5 cm long **10**

10(9). Inflorescence a panicle of spicate primary branches .... *Leptochloa*

  10. Inflorescence a panicle without spicate primary branches .... *Tridens*

11(5). Lemmas 11- or more veined, each extending into 11 awns .... *Pappophorum*

  11. Lemmas with fewer than 11 veins and 11 awns, or lemmas awnless .. **12**

12(11). Ligules a ring of hairs or a ciliate membrane **13**

  12. Ligules membranous for most or all its length **14**

13(12). Lemmas strongly 7- to 9-veined, apex slightly bifid; caryopsis apex with two persistent hornlike bases .... *Vaseyochloa*

  13. Lemmas 1-veined, apex entire; caryopsis apex without persistent style bases .... *Eragrostis*

14(12). Glumes or lemmas awned **15**

  14. Glumes and lemmas awnless **21**

15(14). Lemmas awned from back with a dorsally attached awn **16**

  15. Lemmas awned from apex or from between the lobes of bifid apex .. **18**

16(15). Glumes 1.5 cm or longer .... *Avena*

  16. Glumes 0.5 cm or shorter **17**

17(16). Spikelets to 2.5 mm long (excluding awn); upper lemmas with geniculate awn; sheaths glabrous to scabrous .... *Aira*

17. Spikelets 4–6 mm long; upper lemmas with a hooked awn; sheaths velvety pubescent .... *Holcus*

18(15). Lemmas bifid, awned from between teeth **19**

18. Lemmas acute, not bifid, awned from apex **20**

19(18). Paleas not adnate to caryopsis; spikelets less than 8 mm long; plants annual .... *Trisetum*

19. Paleas adnate to caryopsis; spikelets more than 8 mm long; plants annual or perennial .... *Bromus*

20(18). Plants annual; stamen one (rarely three); leaves less than 2 mm wide; lemmas inconspicuously 5-veined .... *Vulpia*

20. Plants perennial; stamens three; leaves more than 4 mm wide; lemmas conspicuously 5-veined .... *Dactylis*

21(14). Glumes longer than 1.7 cm .... *Avena*

21. Glumes shorter than 1.7 cm **22**

22(21). Glumes and lemmas spreading at right angles to rachilla, appearing inflated; pedicels slender .... *Briza*

22. Glumes and lemmas ascending, not close to a right angle to rachilla, not appearing obviously inflated; pedicels various **23**

23(22). Sheath margins connate at least one-fourth the length **24**

23. Sheath margins free for more than three-fourths the length **26**

24(23). Lemma veins strongly and uniformly developed and equally spaced .... *Glyceria*

24. Lemma veins not strongly and not uniformly developed and not equally spaced **25**

25(24). Paleas adnate to caryopsis; lemma usually awned from between the lobes of a bifid apex, some species awnless .... *Bromus*

25. Paleas free from caryopsis; lemma awnless (Texas species), apex entire .... *Melica*

26(23). Paleas colorless **27**

26. Paleas yellow, green, or brown, at least on veins **28**

27(26). Second glumes obovate, widest above the middle, apex obtuse .... *Sphenopholis*

27. Second glumes lanceolate, widest below the middle, apex acute .... *Rostraria*

28(26). Lemma apex bifid **29**

28. Lemma apex acute, not bifid **30**

29(28). Rachilla extended beyond upper floret; panicles narrow, congested ......
.... ***Trisetum***

29. Rachilla not extended beyond upper floret; panicles open, diffuse ....
.... ***Aira***

30(28). Lemma apex obtuse to broadly acute; lemma 5-veined, distinct........ **31**

30. Lemma apex attenuate to narrowly acute; lemma 5-veined or more, often indistinct **32**

31(30). Panicles of stiff spicate primary branches; plants annual ... ***Desmazeria***

31. Panicles of rebranched primary branches, branches not appearing stiff
.... ***Poa***

32(30). Plants annual; stamen one (rarely three); rhizomes absent; spikelets with at least one perfect floret .... ***Vulpia***

32. Plants perennial; stamens three; rhizomes present; spikelets unisexual
.... ***Distichlis***

Generic Descriptions, Key to Species, and Species Descriptions

Figure 12. *Agrostis hyemalis*
plant and spikelet (Gould and Box 1965).

1. **AGROSTIS** L. • Bentgrass

Culms hollow. Leaves basal and cauline; sheaths rounded; ligules membranous; blades flat, folded or involute. Panicles open or contracted with 1-floreted spikelets. Spikelets small, disarticulation above the glumes; glumes thin, 1-veined; lemmas 3- to 5-veined, awnless or dorsally awned; paleas absent or vestigial to equaling lemma, 2-veined or veinless.

1. Lemmas awned; plants annuals; paleas present .... *A. elliottiana*
1. Lemmas awnless; plants perennials; paleas absent or present **2**
2(1). Palea present, 1 mm or longer; plants stoloniferous; panicle branches bearing spikelets on upper two-thirds .... *A. stolonifera* var. *palustris*
2. Palea absent or shorter than 0.5 mm; plants not stoloniferous; panicle branches bearing spikelets on upper one-third .... *A. hyemalis*

Agrostis elliottiana Schult. **ELLIOTT BENTGRASS** Tufted annuals. Culms to 30 cm tall, slender, weak. Leaves glabrous; ligules 1.5–5.0 mm long; blades 2–7 cm long, to 1.6 mm wide. Panicles 5–18 cm long, delicate, open. Spikelets 1.2–2.2 mm long; lemmas dorsally awned; paleas absent or a veinless scale.

Common along ditches, roadsides, and wooded borders of upper Gulf Coast. Poor livestock and wildlife values.

Agrostis hyemalis (Walt.) B.S.P. **WINTER BENTGRASS** (Figure 12) Annuals or weak perennials. Culms to 70 cm tall, glabrous. Leaves with ligules 1–4 mm long; blades thin. Spikelets 1.5–2.1 mm long, closely spaced; glumes subequal, awnless; lemmas hyaline, slightly shorter than glumes, awnless; paleas absent.

Abundant in late winter and early spring as an invader on disturbed sites. Poor livestock and wildlife values.

Agrostis stolonifera L. var. *palustris* (Huds.) Farw. **CREEPING BENTGRASS** Sod-forming perennials, often rhizomatous but spreading primarily by leafy stolons. Culms to 45 cm tall, decumbent. Leaf blades less than 10 cm long, 1–5 mm wide, flat. Panicles densely spikeleted. Spikelets 2–5 mm long, awnless; glumes 1-veined; lemmas shorter than glumes, awnless; paleas present.

Found in lowlands of upper Gulf Coast. Poor livestock and wildlife values.

2. AIRA L. • Hairgrass
Culms hollow. Leaves mostly basal; sheaths open, rounded; ligules membranous; blades narrow, subfiliform, lax. Panicles open or contracted with 2-floreted spikelets. Spikelets laterally compressed, disarticulation above the glumes; glumes about equal, membranous, longer than lemmas, 1- (obscurely 3-) veined; lemmas 5-veined, bifid, firmer than glumes, dorsally awned from below the middle of lemma; awn geniculate, twisted, and usually exserted; paleas present, awnless.

Aira caryophyllea L. **ANNUAL HAIRGRASS** (Figure 13) Annuals. Culms to 40 cm tall, tufted, geniculate to erect, glabrous to scabrous, delicate. Leaf ligules to 4 mm long, whitish; blades flat to involute, about 0.5 mm wide. Panicles 5–15 cm long, usually open, spikelets borne on pedicels near or at apex of capillary branches.

Figure 13. *Aira caryophyllea*
plant, (A) spikelet, and (B) floret (Hitchcock 1951).

Spikelets to 2.3 mm long, excluding awn; glumes lanceolate; lemmas awnless or dorsally awned; upper lemmas dorsally awned to 2 mm long.

Occasional along sterile, sandy prairie sites or open woods of upper Gulf Coast.

Figure 14. *Alopecurus carolinianus* plant, (A) glumes, and (B) lemma (Hitchcock 1951).

3. ALOPECURUS L. • Foxtail

Culms hollow. Leaves basal and cauline; sheaths rounded; ligules membranous; blades flat. Panicles compact and cylindrical with 1-floreted spikelets. Spikelets laterally compressed, disarticulation below the glumes; glumes long, nearly equal, awnless; lemmas length equals glumes length, 3- to 5-veined, dorsally awned from below the middle, awns straight to geniculate; paleas absent.

1. Glume midveins glabrous to scabrous to puberulent at base; spikelets 4.5–7.0 mm long .... *A. myosuroides*
1. Glume midveins hispid-ciliate; spikelets shorter than 3 mm .... *A. carolinianus*

Alopecurus carolinianus Walt. **CAROLINA FOXTAIL** (Figure 14) Tufted annuals. Culms to 50 cm tall. Leaf sheaths much shorter than internodes; ligules 3–7 mm long; blades 1–4 mm wide. Panicles 2–6 cm long, contracted, cylindrical. Spikelets 1.8–3.0 mm long; lemmas shorter than glumes, dorsally awned, awn 3–5 mm long.

Usually occurs as a weed on moist, open, disturbed sites such as ditch banks and roadsides along the mid and upper Gulf Coast. Available only for a short period from late winter to early spring. Produces little seed or forage.

Alopecurus myosuroides Huds. **MOUSE FOXTAIL** Tufted annuals. Culms to 70 cm tall. Leaf sheaths glabrous, shorter than culm internodes; ligules 2–5 mm long; blades 3–20 cm long, 2–8 mm wide. Panicles 3–14 cm long, compact. Spikelets about 6 mm long; glumes

4.5–7.0 mm long, equals the length of spikelets, slightly keeled; lemmas awned from base, awn 5–8 mm long, twisted.

Infrequent in moist soil of upper Gulf Coast. Available only for a short period from late winter to early spring.

4. **ANDROPOGON** L. • Bluestem

Culms solid and branched. Leaves basal and cauline; sheaths keeled; ligules membranous or a ciliate membrane; blades flat or folded. Panicles of two to six racemose branches in a more or less digitate arrangement with spikelet disarticulation at the base of sessile spikelets, spikelet pair usually falling together with rachis joint (node and internode) and pedicel. Spikelets in pairs, one sessile and perfect, one pedicelled and staminate or rudimentary (represented by pedicel only in a few species). Sessile spikelets with perfect floret above reduced floret; glumes subequal, flat; upper lemma awned; paleas small or absent.

1. Flowering culms without leaflike spathes subtending inflorescence; spikelets 6.5–11.0 mm long; pedicellate spikelet usually as large as sessile spikelet .... *A. gerardii* var. *gerardii*
1. Flowering culms containing leaflike spathes subtending inflorescence; spikelets less than 7 mm long; pedicellate spikelets reduced and rudimentary or completely absent with only pedicel remaining 2
2(1). Sessile spikelets 5–7 mm long .... *A. ternarius*
   2. Sessile spikelets shorter than 4 mm **3**
3(2). Flowering culms greatly branched and rebranched, giving broomlike appearance; spathes usually 2.5 mm or less wide .... *A. glomeratus*
   3. Flowering culms rebranched but not broomlike in appearance; spathes 3–5 mm wide **4**
4(3). Spathe or sheath subtending inflorescence 6–10 mm wide, conspicuously inflated .... *A. gyrans*
   4. Spathe or sheath subtending inflorescence 2–5 mm wide, not conspicuously inflated .... *A. virginicus*

Andropogon gerardii Vitman var. *gerardii* BIG BLUESTEM (Figure 15) Tall perennial bunchgrasses, sometimes with rhizomes. Culms to 2 m tall, often glaucous, sparingly branched. Leaves usually villous; blades 5–10 mm wide, elongate, margins scabrous. Panicles with two to five racemose branches, branches digitate or subdigitate. Sessile spikelets 8–11 mm long with awn 1–2 cm long, twisted;

Figure 15. *Andropogon gerardii* var. *gerardii*
plant and paired spikelets (Hitchcock 1951).

Figure 16. *Andropogon glomeratus* inflorescence (Gould and Box 1965).

glumes the length of spikelets, purplish. Pedicellate spikelets as large as sessile one, staminate, awnless.

Once a climax dominant in upland prairies throughout Gulf Coast; decreases with livestock grazing. Good forage for livestock; fair for wildlife.

Andropogon glomeratus (Walt.) B.S.P. **BUSHY BLUESTEM** (Figure 16) Tufted perennial bunchgrasses. Culms to 130 cm tall, flattened. Leaf sheaths usually over-

Figure 17. *Andropogon gyrans* inflorescence (Hitchcock 1951).

lapping, keel strongly compressed; ligules to 3 mm long, ciliate membranes; blades mostly 2.5–6.0 mm wide, usually much narrower than sheaths, elongate, frequently folded. Flowering culms profusely branched and rebranched; ultimate branches with reduced, villous, broomlike inflorescences; uppermost branchlets silky-villous, at least just below nodes; bracteate sheaths of terminal branchlets reddish-brown or bronze colored. Panicles with two to four racemose branches, each 1.5–3.0 cm long, partially enclosed by sheath; branch axis delicate, not or only slightly flattened, villous. Sessile spikelets 3.0–4.5 mm long; glumes glabrous; upper lemma awns 1–2 cm long, straight or undulant. Pedicels slender, terete or slightly flattened, villous with long hairs. Pedicellate spikelets completely absent or vestigial.

Present along ditches, swales, and other poorly drained sites throughout Gulf Coast. Poor forage. Provides nesting cover for mottled ducks (*Anas fulvigula*), as it occurs in lowlands and freshwater marshes of coastal prairie, and fawning cover for white-tailed deer (*Odocoileus virginianus*).

Andropogon gyrans Ashe **ELLIOTT BLUESTEM** (Figure 17) Tufted perennials. Culms to 80 cm tall, erect, much-branched toward summit. Leaf sheaths bearded at base. Panicles of two to four racemose branches, subtended by wide spathes; branches 3–5 cm long. Sessile spikelets less than 4 mm long. Pedicellate spikelets absent or vestigial.

Figure 18. *Andropogon ternarius*
inflorescence with sessile and pedicellate spikelets (Gould and Box 1965).

Figure 19. *Andropogon virginicus*
plant and paired spikelet (Hitchcock 1951).

Occurs in open grounds, old fields, and open woods of mid and upper Gulf Coast.

Andropogon ternarius Michx. **SPLITBEARD BLUESTEM** (Figure 18) Perennial bunchgrasses. Culms to 120 cm tall, mostly glabrous except for silvery hairs below uppermost leaf- or bract-bearing node. Leaf blades 2–4 mm wide. Panicles of two racemose branches; branch axis and pedicels densely villous with silvery hairs 6–9 mm long. Sessile spikelets 5–7 mm long; glumes glabrous; lemma of upper florets membranous, awns 1.5–2.5 cm long, geniculate. Pedicellate spikelets less than 2 mm long.

Infrequent on upper Gulf Coast. Fair to poor forage.

Andropogon virginicus L. **BROOMSEDGE BLUESTEM** (Figure 19) Tufted perennials. Culms 0.5–1.0 m tall, erect, basal nodes glabrous, much-branched above. Leaf sheaths compressed-keeled basally, margins hairy; ligules 1 mm long, membranous; blades 2–5 mm wide, flat or folded, orangish or straw colored at maturity. Panicles per culm numerous; each of two to four racemose branches enclosed in subtending spathe; branches 2–3 cm long; spikelets paired. Sessile spikelets 3–4 mm long, perfect; glumes indurate; upper lemmas hyaline with delicate, straight awn. Pedicellate spikelets absent or vestigial; pedicels villous.

Common in old fields and sterile or shallow soils throughout Gulf Coast. Frequently grows with *A. glomeratus* but tends to occupy higher, better-drained sites. Poor forage; increases under grazing. Provides nesting habitat for ground- nesting birds.

5. **ANTHAENANTIA** Beauv. • Silkyscale
Culms solid. Leaves basal and cauline; ligules a ciliate membrane; blades flat, narrow. Panicles loosely contracted. Spikelets laterally compressed, disarticulation below the glumes; florets two, lower sterile, upper fertile; first glumes absent; second glumes and lower lemmas similar in size and texture; upper lemmas cartilaginous, smooth, muticous.

Anthaenantia villosa (Michx.) Beauv. **GREEN SILKYSCALE** (Figure 20) Rhizomatous perennials. Culms to 110 cm tall, erect. Leaf blades relatively long, 3–10 mm wide. Panicles 6–20 cm long, to 4 cm wide; branches stiffly erect to spreading. Spikelets 3–4 mm long, greenish to purplish, conspicuously hirsute usually with spreading hairs; hairs 0.6–1.0 mm long, awnless. Some Texas material referred to as *A. rufa*.

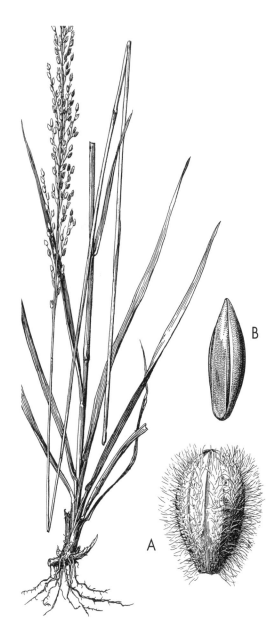

Figure 20. *Anthaenantia villosa*
plant, (A) spikelet, and (B) floret (palea view) (Hitchcock 1951).

Infrequent in savannahs and sandy woodlands of upper Gulf Coast; decreases under livestock grazing. Poor forage for wildlife.

6. ARISTIDA L. • Threeawn

Culms branched or unbranched, hollow. Leaves usually basal and cauline; sheath margins open; ligules a ciliate membrane or ring of hairs; blades without midvein. Panicles open or contracted. Spikelets laterally compressed, disarticulation above the glumes; floret one, callus sharp; glumes thin, longer or shorter than floret; lemmas 3-veined, extending into three awns, indurate, sometimes the lateral awns short to vestigial; paleas indistinctly veined.

1.	Plants annual	2
1.	Plants perennial	5
2(1).	Central awn of lemma with semicircular bend	*A. desmantha*
2.	Central awn of lemma without semicircular bend	3
3(2).	Lemma awns (excluding awn column) 4–7 cm long, nearly equal length	*A. oligantha*
3.	Lemma awns (excluding awn column) shorter than 3 cm, unequal length	4
4(3).	Lateral awns one-third to one-half length of central awn; central awn 4–15 mm long, reflexed on some spikelets	*A. longespica* var. *longespica*
4.	Lateral awns two-thirds to three-fourths length of central awn; central awn 15–36 mm long, spreading	*A. longespica* var. *geniculata*
5(1).	Lower sheaths lanate-pubescent	*A. lanosa*
5.	Lower sheaths not lanate-pubescent	6
6(5).	Panicles open; spikelets ascending but not appressed	7
6.	Panicles contracted; spikelets typically appressed	8
7(6).	Lemma awns 3–6 cm long; second glume shorter than 15 mm	*A.purpurea* var. *purpurea*
7.	Lemma awns 5–10 cm or longer; second glume 15 mm or longer	*A.purpurea* var. *longiseta*
8(7).	First glume nearly equal in length to second glume, either slightly longer or shorter	*A purpurescens*
8.	First glume one-half to two-thirds length of second glume	*A. purpurea* var. *longiseta*

Aristida desmantha Trin. & Rupr. **CURLY THREEAWN** (Figure 21) Tall annuals. Culms unbranched with stiffly erect branches. Panicles 10–20 cm long;

Figure 21. *Aristida desmantha*
inflorescence and spikelet (Gould and Box 1965).

branches erect to spreading. Spikelets 10–13 mm long, large; glumes yellowish-brown with 3–5 mm awn; lemmas 3-awned, each 1–2 cm long, awn bases with spiral coils when dry.

Found on coastal prairies of upper Gulf Coast. Poor livestock forage and wild-life values.

Aristida lanosa Muhl. *ex* Ell. **WOOLLYSHEATH THREEAWN** Tufted perenni-als from firm, often knotty bases. Culms to 150 cm tall, usually branching only near base. Leaf sheaths densely lanate with soft, kinky hairs, glabrate with age; blades (lower culm) 50 cm or longer, 1–3 mm wide, scabrous. Panicles 15–40 cm long, narrow. Spikelets with glumes awnless or short-awned; lemmas 3-awned, flexuous, somewhat twisted below; lateral awns mostly 10–15 mm long; central awn 15–25 mm long, strongly deflexed at maturity.

Frequent in open forest, mostly in sandy soil of upper Gulf Coast. Poor forage.

Aristida longespica Poir. var. *longespica* **SLIMSPIKE THREEAWN** Tufted an-nuals. Culms branching above base, slender, often geniculate. Leaves mostly cauline. Inflorescence a panicle or reduced to a raceme, contracted with spikelets appressed on central axis or on short pedicels. Spikelets with glumes 3–7 mm long, about equal; lemmas 4–7 mm long, 3-awned; central awns 6–15 mm long; lateral awns shorter, reflexed or erect.

var. *geniculata* (Raf.) Fern. **KEARNEY THREEAWN** (Figure 22) Similar to var. *longespica*. Panicles mostly 15–35 cm long; glumes mostly 8–9 mm long; lem-mas 7–9 mm long, awns geniculate; central awns 15–36 mm long; lateral awns slightly shorter.

Occurs in sandy soils of woodland clearings and along wooded borders of mid and upper Gulf Coast. Poor forage.

Aristida oligantha Michx. **OLDFIELD THREEAWN** (Figure 23) Tufted annu-als. Culms to 45 cm tall, wiry, usually much-branched. Panicles of large purplish spikelets. Glumes 18–25 mm long, subequal; first glumes awnless; second glumes with awn to 10 mm long; lemmas 6–28 mm long, 3-awned; awns about equal.

Abundant in heavily grazed pastures on all upland sites along mid and upper Gulf Coast. Poor forage.

Aristida purpurea Nutt. var. *longiseta* (Steud.) Vasey **RED THREEAWN** Tufted perennials. Culms to 50 cm tall, erect or geniculate, unbranched. Leaves mainly

Figure 22. *Aristida longespica* var. *geniculata*
inflorescence and spikelet (Gould and Box 1965).

Grasses of the Texas Gulf Prairies and Marshes

Figure 23. *Aristida oligantha* plant (Gould and Box 1965), (A) glumes, and (B) floret (Hitchcock 1951).

basal; sheaths about one-half the length of internodes, glabrous; blades 4–10 cm long, 0.4–1.5 mm wide, margins scabrous. Panicles to 22 cm long, branches ascending or spreading. Spikelets to 18 mm long, scabrous; glumes unequal, brownish, linear; first glumes 6.5–7.5 mm long; second glumes 16.5–18.0 mm long; lemmas purple-tinged, 3-awned; awns 4–10 cm long, straight.

Frequent in overgrazed pastures and roadsides, but only occasionally when range condition is good. Poor forage.

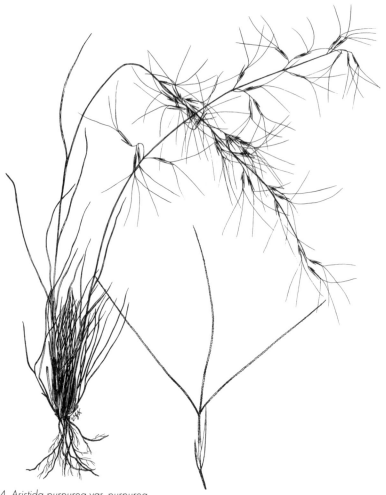

Figure 24. *Aristida purpurea* var. *purpurea* plant and spikelet (Gould and Box 1965).

var. ***purpurea*** **PURPLE THREEAWN** (Figure 24) Similar to red threeawn but with second glumes 11–15 mm long and lemma awns 3–6 cm long.

Dominant on many heavily grazed pastures and disturbed sites throughout lower and mid Gulf Coast. Poor forage. These perennials can provide good nesting cover for bobwhite quail (*Colinus virginianus*), but have no forage or seed value for wildlife.

Aristida purpurescens Poir. **ARROWFEATHER THREEAWN** Tufted perennials. Culms to 80 cm tall, erect, little-branched from knotty, somewhat rhizomatous base. Leaf blades 15–30 cm long, 1.0–2.5 mm wide. Panicles 12–35 cm long, narrow, contracted. Spikelets with first glumes scabrous, acuminate; second glumes similar but shorter; lemmas mostly 5–7 mm long, purple or mottled with purple at maturity; lemma awns not twisted; central awns 15–28 cm long, usually spreading more than laterals; lateral awns shorter.

Found in sandy, wooded openings or wooded borders along mid and upper Gulf Coast. Poor forage.

7. ARUNDINARIA Michx.

Culms hollow (bamboolike). Leaves cauline; sheaths auriculate; ligules membranous; blades flat, tessellate, base petiolate. Inflorescences of one to several spikelets. Spikelets large, laterally compressed, reduced florets at apex, disarticulation above the glumes; glumes variable in development, shorter than lemmas; lemmas attenuate to awn-tipped.

Arundinaria gigantea (Walt.) Muhl. **GIANTCANE** (Figure 25) Rhizomatous perennials. Culms to 8 m tall much-branched, somewhat woody. Leaves extremely variable; lower sheaths about one-half the length of internodes; blades of main culm and primary branches 15–27 cm long, 2.5–4.0 cm wide, rounded at base. Inflorescence a simple panicle or raceme with few to several spikelets. Spikelets 4–7 cm long, about 8 mm wide; florets mostly 8–12; glumes sometimes absent; lemmas 1.5–2.0 cm long, awnless or tapering into awn 4 mm long. Rachilla segments densely hairy.

Forms dense colonies in low moist woodlands and along streams and swales of mid and upper Gulf Coast. Useful for shoreline and stream bank stabilization. Good forage; usually grazed out if livestock have continuous access. Provides cover for wildlife but no forage; seldom produces seed.

8. ARUNDO L. • Giantreed

Culms more than 3 m tall, hollow. Leaves cauline; ligules a ciliate membrane; blades flat, midvein obvious. Panicles large, erect, branches ascending, peduncle glabrous. Spikelets laterally compressed, plumose, florets two to five, disarticulation above glumes; glumes nearly equal; lemmas 5-veined with apical awn to 1.5 mm; paleas about one-half lemma length.

Arundo donax L. **GIANTREED** (Figure 26) Stout rhizomatous perennials. Culms to 6 m tall. Leaves uniformly spaced, distichous; blades 4–7 cm wide, thick, margins scabrous. Panicles to 60 cm long, large plumose, many-spikeleted. Spikelets 10–15 mm long; florets two to four; glumes wide, nearly equal; lemmas 5–10 mm

Figure 25. *Arundinaria gigantea*
plant, (A) lemma, (B) floret (palea view), and (C) leaf (sheath and blade showing ligule and auricles) (Hitchcock 1951).

Grasses of the Texas Gulf Prairies and Marshes

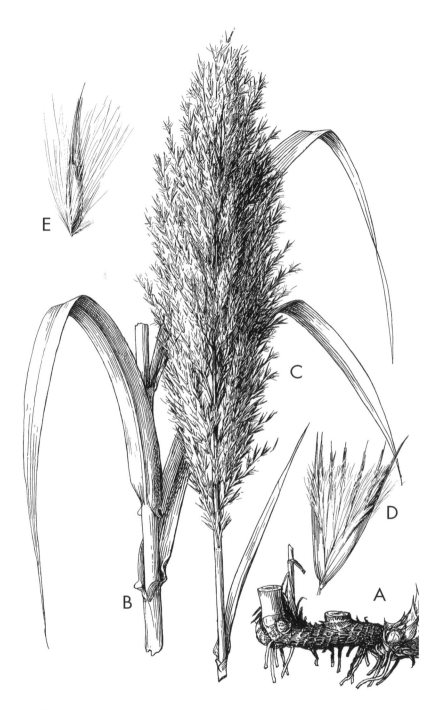

Figure 26. *Arundo donax*
(A) rhizome, (B) section of culm, (C) inflorescence, (D) spikelet, and (E) floret (Hitchcock 1951).

long, thin, densely pilose with soft hairs 6–9 mm long, acuminate, often short-awned at apex; paleas wide, shorter than lemmas.

Common along ditches and waterways throughout Gulf Coast; planted to prevent soil erosion. Reproduces only by vegetative means in our area. Palatable to both cattle and wildlife, usually grazed out in pastures; provides nesting habitat for mottled ducks and cover for other shorebirds such as rails (*Rallidae*).

9. AVENA L. • Oat

Culms hollow. Leaves cauline; sheaths open; ligules membranous; blades flat. Panicles open, drooping with pedicellate spikelets. Spikelets not conspicuously compressed, florets two to four, disarticulation above the glumes, reduced florets above, rachilla extended above upper lemma; glumes about equal, longer than lemmas, awn-tipped; lemmas awned or awnless, awn attached about middle of lemmas; paleas glabrous.

1. Lemma awn geniculate, well developed; florets three or four per spikelet .... *A. fatua* var. *fatua*
1. Lemma awnless or awn not geniculate, or poorly developed; florets usually two per spikelet .... *A. fatua* var. *sativa*

Avena fatua L. var. *fatua* **WILD OAT** (Figure 27A–C) Tufted annuals. Culms to 1 m tall, erect, glabrous. Leaf blades 6–12 mm wide, flat, loose. Panicles with 10–30 large spikelets. Spikelets with three or four florets; glumes thin, several-veined, longer than florets; lemmas firmer than glumes and usually bearing a stout, geniculate dorsal awn with reddish-brown hairs on dorsal surface.

var. *sativa* (L.) Hausskn. **COMMON OAT** (Figure 27D) The common cereal grain and winter pasture species. Differs from var. *fatua* in that spikelets usually have only two florets and lemma awns are straight, absent, or sometimes irregularly developed.

Found as occasional escapee along roadsides and fields throughout Gulf Coast. Good livestock and wildlife forage and seed.

10. AXONOPUS Beauv. • Carpetgrass

Culms solid, angular. Leaves basal and cauline; sheaths keeled, ligules a ciliate membrane; blades flat or folded. Panicles of spicate primary unilateral branches, with branches terminating in a spikelet; spikelets in two rows. Spikelets with second glumes and upper florets oriented away from the branch, disarticulation below the glumes; first glumes absent; second glumes awnless, rounded; upper lemma muticous.

Figure 27. *Avena fatua*
(A) var. *fatua* plant, (B) var. *fatua* spikelet, (C) var. *fatua* floret (Hitchcock 1951), and (D) var. *sativa* spikelet (Gould and Box 1965).

1. Spikelets 1.7–2.7 mm long; second glumes sparsely pubescent .... *A.fissifolius*

1. Spikelets longer than 4 mm; second glumes glabrous .... **A. furcatus**

Axonopus fissifolius (Raddi) Kuhlman **COMMON CARPETGRASS** (Figure 28) Low, mat-forming, stoloniferous perennials. Culms to 70 cm tall, somewhat laterally flattened. Leaves glabrous except near ligules; blades to 7 mm wide, apex obtuse. Panicles of two to four spicate primary unilateral branches 2–10 cm long. Spikelets about 2 mm long, subacute; second glumes and lower lemmas covering indurate upper florets; upper florets finely rugose.

Frequent along upper Gulf Coast on moist sandy meadows, in open woods, and waste places. Fair forage but not highly productive; increases under grazing on bottomland sites. Poor wildlife value.

Axonopus furcatus (Flugge) A. S. Hitchc. **BIG CARPETGRASS** Stoloniferous perennials with same general characteristics as *A. fissifolius.* Culms to 100 cm tall. Leaf blades to 10 mm wide. Spikelets 4.0–5.5 mm long; second glumes elongated; lemma of lower florets with strong midvein, mucro extending 1.5–2.0 mm beyond tip.

Same habitat adaptation as *A. fissifolius* but less frequent.

Figure 28. *Axonopus fissifolius* plant, (A) spikelet (first lemma view), (B) spikelet (second glume view), and (C) upper floret (palea view) (Hitchcock 1951).

11. **BOTHRIOCHLOA** O. Ktze.
• Bluestem

Culms solid. Leaves basal and cauline; ligules membranous; blades flat, midvein present. Panicles usually of numerous racemose branches (few in *B. ischaemum*), branches ascending, aromatic when crushed. Spikelets dorsally compressed; paired, sessile spikelets fertile and pedicellate spikelets sterile, reduced; pedicels with thin membranous area for most of their length, disarticulation below glumes; glumes equal, length of glumes equals lemmas length; lemmas narrow, hyaline; upper lemma awned.

1. Inflorescence a panicle of two to eight subdigitate racemose branches .... *B. ischaemum* var. *songarica*
1. Inflorescence a panicle of nine to many racemose branches 2
2(1). Pedicellate spikelets about as long and wide as sessile ones, staminate or neuter .... *B. bladhii*
2. Pedicellate spikelets shorter and narrower than sessile ones, neuter 3
3(2). Spikelets 4.5–7.5 mm long; lemma awn 20–28 mm long 4
3. Spikelets shorter than 4.5 mm; lemma awnless or awn less than 20 mm long 6
4(3). Panicle central axis shorter than 5 cm; panicle branches two to eight .... *B.hybrida*
4. Panicle central axis longer than 5 cm; panicle branches 9–40 5
5(4). First glume of sessile spikelets with glandular pit (pinhole) or depression on back .... *B. barbinodis* var. *perforata*
5. First glume of sessile spikelets without glandular pit or depression on back .... *B. barbinodis* var. *barbinodis*
6(3). Upper lemma awnless, or awn to 6 mm long .... *B. exaristata*
6. Upper lemma awn 8–18 mm long 7
7(6) Panicles 4–12 cm long; glumes dull green to glaucous, ovate, relatively broad and blunt; one mainly basal .... *B. laguroides* subsp. *torreyana*
7. Panicles 10 cm or longer; glumes shiny green, narrowly ovate to lanceolate; leaves evenly distributed on culm .... *B. longipaniculata*

Bothriochloa barbinodis (Lag.) Herter var. ***barbinodis*** **CANE BLUESTEM** (Figure 29) Tall, coarse perennial bunchgrasses. Culms to 120 cm tall, erect, nodes bearded. Leaves with ligules 1–2 mm long; blades firm. Panicles of numerous racemose branches; branches and pedicels with villous hairs. Sessile spikelets 4.3–7.3 mm long; upper lemma awns 20–30 mm or longer, geniculate and twisted.

Adapted to loose, calciferous soils. Good forage but infrequent; relatively unimportant along Gulf Coast.

var. *perforata* (Fourn.) Gould **PINHOLE BLUESTEM** Similar to var. *barbinodis* but with glandular-pitted glumes on the sessile spikelets.

Bothriochloa bladhii (Retz.) S. T. Blake **AUSTRALIAN BLUESTEM** (Figure 30) Perennial bunchgrasses. Culms to 110 cm tall, nodes bearded, branching above base. Generally similar to *B. ischaemum* but with larger and longer panicle axis;

Figure 29. *Bothriochloa barbinodis* var. *barbinodis* plant and spikelet (Hitchcock 1951).

Figure 30. *Bothriochloa bladhii* inflorescence (Gould and Box 1965).

central axis longer than basal branches; panicle branches numerous. Sessile spikelets 3–4 mm long; first glumes glabrous, apex obtuse to widely acute with or without a glandular pit; upper floret awns 1.0–1.5 cm long, geniculate.

Infrequent outside cultivated areas along lower and mid Gulf Coast. Good forage.

Bothriochloa exaristata (Nash) Henr. **AWNLESS BLUESTEM** Tufted perennials. Culms to 130 cm tall, erect. Leaf blades long, 3–8 mm wide. Panicles 9–15 cm long, silvery pubescent, contracted and densely spikeleted; branches racemose, erect to spreading, numerous, much shorter than central axis. Sessile spikelets about 3 mm long; upper lemmas hyaline, awnless or with awns to 4 mm long. Pediceled spikelets 2–4 mm long, neuter, much narrower than sessile ones, awnless.

Found only along upper Gulf Coast from Brazoria and Fort Bend Counties northward, mostly in heavy, moist, black, clayey soils.

Bothriochloa hybrida (Gould) Gould **HYBRID BLUESTEM** Perennial bunchgrasses. Similar to *B. barbinodis.* Culms slender and fewer than *B. barbinodis.* Leaf blades narrower. Panicles with shorter inflorescence axis and culm nodes with fewer branches, glabrous or minutely puberulent. Sessile spikelets with glandular pit above center of first glumes.

Occasional in lowland areas along lower and mid Gulf Coast. Especially well adapted to ditches, roadways, and similar sites. Fair forage.

Bothriochloa ischaemum (L.) Keng var. *songarica* (Fisch. & Mey.) Celarier & Harlan **KING RANCH BLUESTEM** (Figure 31) Tufted perennials. Culms to 100 cm long, erect or decumbent, slender, becoming stoloniferous under close grazing or cutting; nodes bearded. Leaf sheaths glabrous; ligules 1 mm or shorter, a truncate membrane; blades 4–20 cm long, 2–4 mm wide, uppermost reduced. Panicles 4–10 cm long, exserted, branches two to eight, 3–9 cm long, pedicels with narrow medial groove. Sessile spikelets 3.0–4.5 mm long, narrowly ovate; first glumes glabrous, never with glandular pit or depression; upper lemma awns 1.0–1.5 mm long, geniculate and twisted. Pediceled spikelets staminate, awnless, about as long as sessile one but narrower.

Introduced from Asia to King Ranch near Kingsville. Has spread by seeding along roadsides throughout Gulf Coast; an aggressive weed in many situations. Poor to fair forage.

Bothriochloa laguroides (DC.) Herter subsp. *torreyana* (Steud.) Allred & Gould **SILVER BLUESTEM** (Figure 32) Perennial bunchgrasses. Culms to 80 cm tall, unbranched. Leaf blades 3–6 mm wide, apex attenuate. Panicles contracted; branches numerous, racemose, shorter than central axis. Spikelets commonly glaucous, maturing bronze or reddish; glumes ovate, apex truncate or acute; upper lemma of sessile spikelets with a geniculate, twisted awn 8–18 mm long.

Figure 31. *Bothriochloa ischaemum* var. *songarica* inflorescence (Gould and Box 1965).

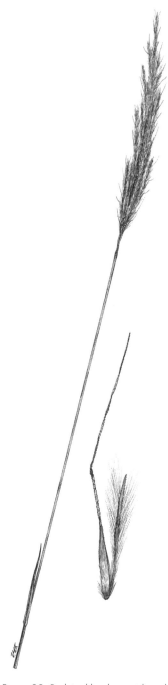

Relatively frequent on sand and sandy loam sites and other well-drained, moderately disturbed soils throughout Gulf Coast. Good forage.

Bothriochloa longipaniculata (Gould) Allred & Gould **LONGSPIKE SILVER BLUESTEM** Perennial bunchgrasses. Culms to 115 cm tall, erect or geniculate, branched near base. Leaf blades 15–25 cm long, 4–6 mm wide, glabrous. Panicles 10–17 cm long, contracted; peduncles with long pilose hairs to 1 cm long. Sessile spikelets 4.0–4.4 mm long with silky hairs; glumes equal the length of spikelets; upper lemmas membranous, awn 1.0–1.8 cm long, geniculate near base.

Shade tolerant grass frequent on fine-textured upland soils with good drainage. Common along roadsides and field borders of lower and mid Gulf Coast. Good livestock forage but does not persist in overgrazed pastures. Provides nesting cover for birds, escape cover for rodents and rabbits, foraging habitat for raptors and canids, and fawning cover for deer.

12. **BOUTELOUA** Lag. mut. Lag. • Grama Culms solid. Leaves basal and/or cauline; sheaths round or keeled; ligules membranous or a ring of hairs; blades flat or folded, narrow. Panicles of one to numerous short spicate primary unilateral branches, these bearing one to numerous closely placed, sessile or subsessile spikelets on either side of a flattened branch. Spikelets with one fertile floret and one to three reduced or rudimentary florets above; glumes 1-veined; lemmas 3-veined, awned.

Figure 32. *Bothriochloa laguroides* subsp. *torreyana*
inflorescence, sessile and pedicellate spikelets (Gould and Box 1965).

1. Spikelets not pectinately arranged, one tonine per primary unilateral branch **2**
1. Spikelets pectinately arranged, 15–60 per primary unilateral branch **3**
2(1). Primary branches 20–50 per inflorescence; lemma awns inconspicuous, 0–3 mm long .... ***B. curtipendula*** var. ***curtipendula***
2. Primary branches less than 15 per inflorescence; lemma awns conspicuous, usually 4 mm or longer .... ***B. rigidiseta*** var. ***rigidiseta***
3(1). Plants annual .... ***B. barbata***
3. Plants perennial **4**
4(3). Second glumes without papilla-based hairs; primary branch not prolonged beyond spikelets; branches terminating with spikelet .... ***B. trifida***
4. Second glumes with papilla-based hairs; primary branch prolonged beyond spikelets; branches not terminating with spikelet .... ***B. hirsuta***

Bouteloua barbata Lag. **SIXWEEKS GRAMA** Annuals. Culms to 35 cm tall, geniculate, numerous, spreading. Leaves basal; ligules 1 mm long, a ciliate membrane; blades 2–7 cm long, flat or involute. Panicles of three to eight spicate primary unilateral branches; branches 1–3 cm long, bearing numerous small, closely placed, pectinate spikelets. Spikelets 2.5–4.0 mm long; florets three; lower lemmas pilose toward base, 3-awned, awn to 3.5 mm long.

Inconspicuous, short-lived weedy grass of the Southwest; occurs sparingly along southern portion of Gulf Coast. Poor forage for livestock; poor value for wildlife.

Bouteloua curtipendula (Michx.) Torr. var. ***curtipendula*** **SIDEOATS GRAMA** (Figure 33) Rhizomatous perennial bunchgrasses. Culms to 90 cm tall, erect. Leaves basal and cauline; blades 3–7 mm wide, flat, lower margins with a few papilla-based hairs. Panicles with 40–70 spicate primary unilateral branches; central axis zigzagged; branches about 1 cm long, usually bearing two to nine spikelets, alternate, reflexed. Spikelets with glumes and lemmas typically purple-tinged.

Occasional throughout mid and upper Gulf Coast on several soil types; most frequent on clay and sandy loam sites. Official state grass of Texas. Good forage for livestock; poor wildlife value.

Bouteloua hirsuta Lag. **HAIRY GRAMA** (Figure 34) Tufted short-lived perennials. Culms to 70 cm tall, erect to spreading. Leaves basal and cauline; blades narrow, flat. Panicles of one to four spicate primary unilateral branches, each bearing 20 to 40 or more closely placed, pectinately-spreading spikelets; primary branches conspicuously extended beyond terminal spikelet as a naked pointed

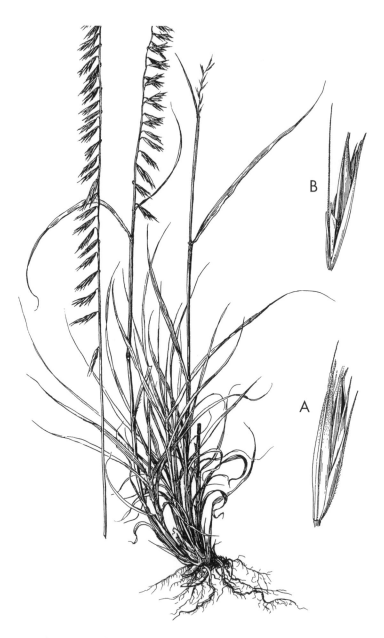

Figure 33. *Bouteloua curtipendula* var. *curtipendula*
plant, (A) spikelet, (B) florets (Hitchcock 1951).

stipe. Spikelets to 6 mm long; glumes unequal, hispid; second glumes with papilla-based hairs; lower lemmas 3-veined.

Grows best on sandy or sandy loam soils; most frequent in well-drained sites.
Name "hairy grama" apparently derives from stiff, papilla-based hairs on the
glumes. Fair livestock forage, it increases with heavy grazing; poor wildlife value.

Bouteloua rigidiseta (Steud.) A. S. Hitchc. var. ***rigidiseta*** **TEXAS GRAMA** (Figure 35) Tufted perennials. Culms to 40 cm tall, slender. Leaves basal; blades flat,

Figure 34. *Bouteloua hirsuta* plant (Gould and Box 1965) and spikelet (Hitchcock 1951).

short, narrow. Panicles of three to five spicate primary unilateral branches; branches deciduous, short, bearing three to five spikelets in bristly, wedge-shaped clusters. Spikelets with two florets; glumes unequal; upper florets reduced to three awns, awns 5–10 mm long.

Frequent on clay and clay loam soils; most abundant in disturbed sites. Poor forage value, it increases under heavy grazing; poor wildlife value.

Bouteloua trifida Thurb. **RED GRAMA** (Figure 36) Low, tufted perennials. Culms to 40 cm tall, spreading. Leaves basal; blades usually 10 cm or shorter, 1.5 mm wide or less. Panicles of three to seven spicate primary unilateral branches; branches 1.0–2.5 cm long, appressed. Spikelets reddish; lemmas 2–3 mm long, bearing three awns 4–9 mm long; rudimentary lemmas about 1 mm long with awns about as long as those of lower lemmas.

Typically found on dry rocky or sandy sites in the Southwest; only sparingly present on Gulf Coast. Fair to poor forage. Persists under heavy grazing and in very dry sites; poor wildlife value.

13. **BRIZA** L. • Quakinggrass
Culms hollow. Leaves cauline; sheaths open; ligules membranous; blades flat, midvein absent. Panicles open, one to several branches per node. Spikelets laterally compressed, disarticulation above the glumes; florets 3–12, widely spreading from the rachilla; reduced floret at apex; glumes subequal; lemmas rounded at apex; paleas rounded, veins widely spaced.

1. Spikelets 2–6 mm long; lemmas indistinctly veined .... ***B. minor***
1. Spikelets 12 mm or longer; lemmas 5- to 7-veined .... ***B. maxima***

Briza maxima L. **BIG QUAKINGGRASS** Annuals. Culms to 60 cm tall, erect or decumbent. Leaves with ligules to 10 mm long; blades 5–15 cm long, 2–8 mm wide. Panicles open, usually with about 12 spikelets. Spikelets 12–25 mm long, 8–12 mm wide; pedicels long, slender; glumes, and often lemmas, with purple or brown margins; lemmas with five to seven greenish veins, usually hirsute.

Garden ornamental established as an occasional weed in a few localities. Poor livestock and wildlife values.

Briza minor L. **LITTLE QUAKINGGRASS** (Figure 37) Delicate, short-lived, tufted annuals. Culms to 50 cm tall, single or in small clumps. Leaves with ligules 5–10 mm long, widely pointed with an inverted V-shaped area of attachment;

blades 4–18 cm long, mostly 2–8 mm wide. Panicles 3–15 cm long, typically much-branched, open. Spikelets 2–6 mm long, about as wide; florets 3–12, glabrous, awnless, somewhat pyramidal; glumes longer than successive lemmas; lemmas with firm, shiny, more or less pustulate or rugose central portion. Caryopses light brown, orbicular, flattened on one side.

Figure 35. *Bouteloua rigidiseta* var. *rigidiseta* inflorescence (Gould and Box 1965) and spikelet (Hitchcock 1951).

Grasses of the Texas Gulf Prairies and Marshes

Figure 36. *Bouteloua trifida*
plant and spikelet with glumes and florets separated (Gould and Box 1965).

Rare in moist woodland clearings and semi-disturbed soils of roadsides and ditch banks throughout Gulf Coast. Poor livestock and wildlife values.

14. **BROMUS** L. • Brome

Culms hollow. Leaf sheath margins connate nearly to apex; ligules membranous; blades flat or involute. Panicles open or contracted with several-floreted spike-

Figure 37. *Briza minor*
plant, (A) spikelet, and (B) floret (Hitchcock 1951).

lets. Spikelets large, pedicellate, reduced florets at the apex; glumes unequal, shorter than first floret; lemmas awned from between lobes of bifid apex or awnless; paleas frequently adnate to caryopsis.

1. Spikelets strongly compressed laterally; lemmas keeled, V-shaped, awnless or awn to 3 mm long .... *B. catharticus*

1. Spikelets terete or slightly flattened; lemmas not keeled, U-shaped, awn 4 mm or longer 2

2(1). First glumes usually 1-veined with slender acuminate apex .. *B. texensis*

2. First glumes 3- to 7-veined with acute to obtuse apex 3

3(2). Paleas 1–2 mm shorter than lemma; lemma awn 8–13 mm long, divergent at maturity; basal sheaths retrorsely hispid .... *B. japonicus*

3. Paleas less than 1 mm shorter than lemma awn; lemma awn 4–9 mm long, straight to slightly wavy at maturity; basal sheaths glabrous or nearly so .... *B. secalinus*

Bromus catharticus M. A. Vahl **RESCUEGRASS** (Figure 38) Annuals. Culms to 80 cm tall, in small clumps, rather thick and succulent. Leaf sheaths glabrous or pubescent, connate nearly to apex. Panicles 6–20 cm long, drooping with few to numerous large, flattened spikelets. Spikelets with 6–12 florets; glumes awnless; lemmas laterally flattened and keeled, V-shaped, awnless or with awn to 3 mm long.

Locally abundant on sandy soils; frequent to occasional on heavier soils. Good early spring forage for livestock and white-tailed deer. Seeds eaten by a number of birds and rodents.

Bromus japonicus Thunb. *ex* Murray **JAPANESE BROME** Annuals. Culms to 60 cm tall, slender, weak. Leaves cauline; sheaths, at least lowermost, typically shaggy-pilose with spreading or reflexed hairs; blades 2–7 mm wide, pilose or puberulent. Panicles 8–20 cm long; branches and pedicels slender, flexuous, often kinked. Spikelets 1.5–3.0 cm long excluding awns; florets 6–11; glumes wide, glabrous, awnless; lower lemmas mostly 7–9 mm long, with most apical teeth 1.5–2.0 mm long; awn 8–15 mm long, slender, divergent or straight; palea veins ciliate.

Occurs as a common weed of roadsides, field borders, and pastures of upper Gulf Coast. Poor forage.

Bromus secalinus L. **RYE BROME** (Figure 39) Annuals. Culms to 90 cm tall, relatively thick. Leaves cauline; sheaths glabrous or inconspicuously hirsute; blades 3–8 mm wide. Panicles 10–18 cm long; branches slender, erect or spreading. Spike-

Figure 38. *Bromus catharticus*
plant, (A) spikelet, and (B) floret (Gould and Box 1965).

lets 1.5–2.5 cm long, excluding awns; florets 6–11; glumes short, wide, stiff, awnless; lower lemmas mostly 6.0–7.5 mm long, 7- to 11-veined with apical teeth about 1 mm long, awns usually 4–9 mm long; palea often longer than lemmas, keels ciliate.

Found as a common weed of roadsides, field borders, and pastures of upper Gulf Coast. Poor forage.

Bromus texensis (Shear) A. S. Hitchc. **TEXAS BROME** (Figure 40) Short-lived annuals. Culms to 60 cm tall. Leaf sheaths, and usually blades, densely pubescent. Panicles 8–12 cm long, branches drooping. Spikelets to 2 cm long, florets six to eight; lower lemmas 9–12 mm long, awn 6–10 mm long; paleas about the length of lemmas.

Grows in the protection of shrubs on sandy loam soils along mid and upper Gulf Coast. Provides fair to poor early spring forage and some seed for birds.

15. BUCHLOË Engelm.

Plants usually dioecious. Culms solid, much-branched. Leaves basal and cauline; sheaths rounded; ligules a ciliate membrane; blades flat to inrolled. Pistillate inflorescences in burlike clusters, usually within the upper sheaths, with burs not exserted above the leaves; spikelet with one floret; lemmas 3-veined. Staminate inflorescences exserted above the leaves with one to four spicate primary unilateral branches. Spikelets with glumes unequal; florets two, staminate.

Buchloë dactyloides (Nutt.) Engelm. **BUFFALOGRASS** (Figure 41) Low, sodforming perennials, usually dioecious, sometimes monoecious with widely spreading stolons. Culms usually not over 20 cm tall, erect. Leaves with ligules about 1 mm long, ciliate membranes; blades mostly 2 mm wide or less, short, with a few long hairs near base. Staminate plants with panicle inflorescence of one to four spicate primary unilateral branches; pistillate plants with spikelets in burlike clusters enclosed by leaf sheath.

Occasional throughout Gulf Coast, commonly on clay soils. Often occurs with the vegetatively similar *Hilaria belangeri*, from which it may be distinguished by inflorescence characters and by lack of hairy nodes on stolons characteristic of the latter. Palatable, but rated only fair as forage, because of low production. Seeds eaten by birds and rodents. Used as a lawn grass.

16. CENCHRUS L. · Sandbur

Culms hollow or solid, branching. Leaves basal and cauline; sheaths open, keeled;

Figure 39. *Bromus secalinus*
plant, (A) spikelet, and (B) floret (palea view) (Gould and Box 1965).

ligules membranous or a ring of hairs; blades flat or folded. Panicles spikelike
with spikelets borne in deciduous fascicles (burs); fascicles of two to four spikelets subtended or surrounded and enclosed by a series of flattened spines or bristles
or both. Spikelets dorsally compressed, florets two, lower floret reduced, upper
floret perfect, disarticulation below the spines and/or bristles; first glumes reduced;

Figure 40. *Bromus texensis*
inflorescence and spikelet (Gould and Box 1965).

Grasses of the Texas Gulf Prairies and Marshes
96 –

Figure 41. *Buchloë dactyloides*
(A) pistillate plant, (B) pistillate inflorescence, (C) pistillate floret, (D) staminate plant, and
(E) staminate spikelet (Hitchcock 1951).

second glumes, lower and upper lemmas similar in size and texture. In the genus *Setaria*, the bristles represent reduced sterile inflorescence branches, and the spines of *Cenchrus* apparently are more highly modified branch axes.

1. Plants perennial; spine bases of burs not flattened .... ***C. myosuroides***
1. Plants annual; spine bases of burs flattened 2

2(1).   Burs with one whorl of fused, flattened spines, subtended by one or more whorls of bristles .... *C. echinatus*

2.   Burs with two or more whorls of fused, flattened spines, subtended by irregularly spaced spines .... *C. spinifex*

Cenchrus echinatus L. **SOUTHERN SANDBUR** (Figure 42) Annuals. Culms to 65 cm tall, geniculate, branching toward the base. Leaf sheaths about three-fourths the length of internodes; blades 4–9 mm wide. Panicles 5–10 cm long; central axis winged and grooved. Spikelets 5–7 mm long, two to four per bur, enclosed in tough burs about 1 cm long. Bur spines flattened near base, retrorsely barbed.

Occasional in sand and sand-shell mixtures throughout Gulf Coast. Poor forage; poor wildlife value.

Cenchrus myosuroides Kunth in H.B.K. **BIG CENCHRUS** (Figure 43) Perennials. Culms to 2 m tall, stiff, stout, usually in large, dense clumps. Leaf blades 12–40 cm long, 4–13 mm wide, scabrous. Panicles 8–12 cm long. Spikelets 4–5 mm long, one per bur. Bur spines and bristles not flattened, inner ones about the length of spikelets, outer ones shorter.

Occasional along streams and in river bottoms of mid Gulf Coast. Highly pre-

Figure 42. *Cenchrus echinatus*
bur with enclosed spikelets (Gould and Box 1965).

ferred by cattle but limited to fair forage value because of low abundance; poor wildlife value.

Cenchrus spinifex A. Cavanilles **COMMON SANDBUR** (Figure 44) Annuals or short-lived perennials. Culms to 80 cm long, usually geniculate-spreading or stoloniferous at the base. Leaf sheaths about one-half the length of internodes; blades 1.2–6.0 mm wide, glabrous or with papilla-based hairs. Panicles 3–6 cm long. Spikelets 3.5–4.5 mm long, two to four per bur. Burs globose; spines 8–40 per bur, flattened, retrorsely barbed.

Widespread disturbance species throughout Gulf Coast; most abundant on sandy or sandy loam soils. Noxious weed of lawns and overgrazed pastures. Poor forage; poor wildlife value.

17. CHASMANTHIUM Link • Woodoats

Culms solid, pithy, or hollow. Leaves cauline; sheath rounded; ligules a ciliate membrane or ring of hairs; blades flat. Panicles open or contracted, spikelets long- or short-pedicelled. Spikelets laterally compressed, disarticulation above the glumes; florets two to many, reduced florets one to four at spikelet base and again at apex; glumes unequal, awnless, shorter than first floret; lemmas 5- to 15-veined.

1. Panicles lax, nodding or drooping; spikelets with eight or more florets .... *C. latifolium*
1. Panicles erect, not lax or drooping; spikelets with less than seven florets .... *C. laxum*

Chasmanthium latifolium (Michx.) Yates **BROADLEAF WOODOATS** (Figure 45) Rhizomatous perennials forming small clumps. Culms to 150 cm tall; nodes glabrous, purplish. Leaf blades 1–2 cm wide, thin, glabrous. Panicles open, drooping with large, flat spikelets borne on slender branches. Spikelets 2–5 cm long, 0.6–1.8 cm wide, mostly with florets 8–20; glumes and lemmas keeled; lower one or two florets neuter; upper florets neuter or sterile.

Occasional to abundant in shade of moist sandy woods; most frequent along stream banks of mid and upper Gulf Coast. Good forage. Highly sensitive to grazing; disappears rapidly under grazing pressure. Seeds eaten by birds and rodents.

Chasmanthium laxum (L.) Yates **NARROWLEAF WOODOATS** Loosely tufted perennials with short rhizomes. Culms to 1.5 m tall, erect, unbranched. Leaves basal and cauline; sheaths glabrous to densely hispid; collar glabrous or pubes-

Figure 43. *Cenchrus myosuroides*
inflorescence (Hitchcock 1951) and bur with spikelet (Gould and Box 1965).

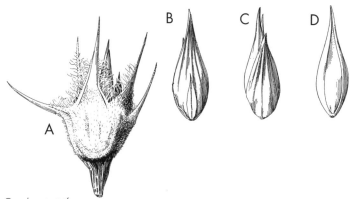

Figure 44. *Cenchrus spinifiex*
(A) inflorescence, (B) spikelet (first glume view), (C) spikelet (second glume view), and (D) upper floret (palea view) (Hitchcock 1951).

cent; blades 5–10 mm wide, long, narrow, tapering toward base. Inflorescence a panicle or spikelike raceme, contracted, few-spikeleted, exserted on a long peduncle. Spikelets 5–8 mm long, sessile or short-pedicellate; florets three to six, lower one or two florets neuter; glumes 1.0–2.5 mm long, about equal, awnless; upper lemmas 3–5 mm long, some beaked at apex. Caryopses exposed at maturity by widely spreading lemmas and paleas. Synonymous with *C. sessiliflorum*.

Occurs in moist pine and deciduous forests, and adjacent prairie openings; often a dominant woodland grass in east Texas and along upper Gulf Coast. Fair to poor forage; fair seed producer.

18. **CHLORIS** Sw. • Windmillgrass
Culms solid, branched or unbranched. Leaves usually basal and cauline; sheaths rounded or keeled; ligules a ciliate membrane; blades flat, folded or involute. Panicles of few to several spicate primary unilateral branches, these verticillate, digitate or aggregated on the upper portion of the central axis. Spikelets usually with 1 fertile floret and one rudiment above; disarticulation above the glumes; glumes 1-veined; lemmas 3-veined, awned from the apex or between the lobes of the apex.

1. Panicle branches in several whorls along central axis for a distance of 2 cm or more .... *C. verticillata*
1. Panicle branches in 1 whorl or if in several whorls, then whorls of central axis in an area less than 2 cm long 2

Figure 45. *Chasmanthium latifolium*
plant, (A) spikelet, and (B) floret (Hitchcock 1951).

2(1).	Lowermost lemmas awned from between 2 lobes .... *C. divaricata*
2.	Lowermost lemmas not awned from between 2 lobes 3
3(2).	Reduced florets 1 per spikelet 4
3.	Reduced florets 2 or more per spikelet 8
4(3).	Primary branches spikelet bearing to base; spikelets less than 3 mm apart at branch base 5
4.	Primary branches not spikelet bearing to base; spikelets 3 mm apart at branch base 7
5(4).	Lowermost lemmas 2 mm or less long, awn less than 1.5 mm long....... .... *C. cucullata*
5.	Lowermost lemmas 2.1 mm or more long, awn more than 1.5 mm long 6
6(5).	Plants annual; lowermost lemma gibbous .... *C. virgata*
6.	Plants perennial; lowermost lemma not gibbous . *C. x subdolichostachya*
7(4).	Lowermost lemmas 3 mm or less long; primary branches bearing spikelets to base .... *C. andropogonoides*
7.	Lowermost lemmas 3.5 mm or more long; primary branches not spikelet bearing on lower one-fourth .... *C. texensis*
8(3).	Plants stoloniferous; lowermost staminate or neuter floret 2 mm or more long .... *C. gayana*
8.	Plants tufted; lowermost staminate or neuter floret usually less than 2 mm long.. 9
9(8).	Inflorescence branches 7–14 cm long; upper floret awns 1.4–3.7 mm long .... *C. canterai*
9.	Inflorescence branches 2–7 cm long; upper floret awnless or awns less than 1.4 mm long .... *C. ciliata*

Chloris andropogonoides Fourn. **SLIMSPIKE WINDMILLGRASS** (Fig. 46)
Tufted perennials spreading by stout stolons. Culms to 30 cm tall, base flattened.
Leaves with lower sheaths strongly keeled, margins white and membranous; ligules
a fringe of hairs 0.5–0.7 mm long. Panicles of 6–13 spicate primary unilateral
branches; branches most commonly in 1 digitate whorl, branches with swollen
hirsute pulvini, disarticulating at base. Spikelets 2–3 mm long; glumes lanceolate,
scabrous midvein; lowermost lemmas about 5 mm long with awn about 4 mm
long; paleas about as long as lemmas, awnless.

Occasional to frequent on sandy loams, loams, and clay loams in mid and lower
Coast. Poor forage.

Chloris canterai Arech. (Fig. 47) Tufted perennials. Culms to 1 m tall, erect. Leaf sheaths keeled; ligules ciliate membranes with hairs to 7 mm long; blades to 25 cm long, 1–5 mm wide, often inrolled. Panicles with 3–6 spicate primary unilateral branches; branches each 4–14 cm long, digitate. Spikelets brown, florets 3, dense, overlapping; first glumes 1.6–2.4 mm long; second glumes 2.3–3.8 mm long; lowermost lemmas 2.4–2.7 mm long, keel densely ciliate, awns 2.4–5.5 mm long.

Naturalized on sandy to clay or loam soils, especially on low-lying rights-of-way in mid and lower Coast.

Chloris ciliata Swartz **FRINGED CHLORIS** (Fig. 48) Tufted perennials. Culms to 60 cm tall, glabrous, erect. Leaf blades about 5 mm wide. Panicles with 3-7 digitate spicate primary unilateral branches, branches spreading. Spikelets 3.0-3.8 mm long, florets 2-3, brown, branches appressed to scabrous; glumes with scabrous midvein, margins hyaline, awnless; lower lemmas 1.8-2.8 mm long, strongly flattened, margins and keels strongly ciliate, awn 0.9-2.7 mm long; sterile florets truncate with an awn 0.9-1.4 mm long; upper florets awnless.

Figure 46. *Chloris andropogonoides* inflorescence and spikelet (Gould and Box 1965).

Occasional on well-drained sites of mid and lower Coast. Usually grows on soils with slightly higher clay content than those that support *C. cucullata*.

Chloris cucullata Bisch. **HOODED WINDMILLGRASS** (Fig. 49) Tufted perennials. Culms to 60 cm tall, erect, glabrous. Leaf sheaths keeled; blades 2–4 mm wide. Panicles with 10–20 spicate primary unilateral branches; branches digitate, borne in several closely-radiating verticils at culm apex. Spikelets about 2 mm long, tawny, dense, widely divergent from branch; glumes awnless, midvein glabrous; first glumes one-half the length of the second; lower lemmas widely elliptic, apex obtuse, awns 0.3–1.5 mm long; upper florets markedly inflated, sometimes with delicate awn to 1.5 mm long.

Occasional to frequent on sandy and sandy loam soils, especially those in a disturbed condition. Fair forage; increases under heavy livestock grazing. Typically the inflorescence of has relatively thick, short panicle branches and dark, almost black spikelets at maturity.

Chloris divaricata R. Br. Stoloniferous perennials, sometimes mat-forming. Culms to 50 cm tall. Leaves cauline; blades 5–10 cm long, 1.0–1.5 mm wide. Panicles with 3–9 widely diverging spicate primary unilateral branches; branches each 4–17 cm long. Spikelets widely spaced, 3–7 per cm of branch, appressed, tawny; glumes narrowly lan-

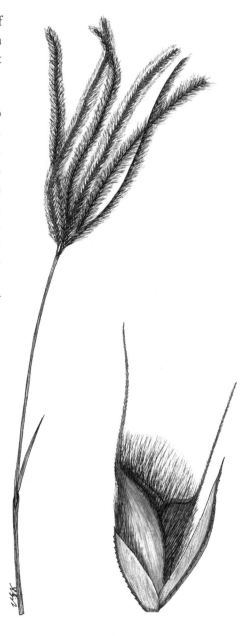

Figure 47. *Chloris canterai* inflorescence and spikelet (Gould and Box 1965).

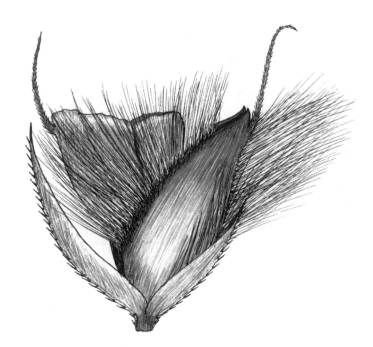

Figure 48. *Chloris ciliata*
spikelet (Gould and Box 1965).

Figure 49. *Chloris cucullata*
inflorescence and spikelet (Gould and Box 1965).

Grasses of the Texas Gulf Prairies and Marshes
106 –

ceolate, glabrous except for scabrous midvein; first glumes 0.9–1.8 mm long; second glumes 2.0–2.9 mm long; lower lemmas 2.9–4.0 mm long, linear to narrowly lanceolate, bilobed with awn 7.5–17.0 mm long; upper florets sterile, narrowly elliptic, bilobed, lobes to one-half the floret length with awn 4.5–9.5 mm long.

Rare along mid Coast.

Chloris gayana Kunth **RHODESGRASS** (Fig. 50) Tufted perennials with stout stolons. Culms to 110 cm tall, erect. Leaf blades 1.5 cm wide, scabrous. Panicles with 9–30 spicate primary unilateral branches, branches each 8–15 cm long, digitate, spreading. Spikelets 6.5–7.5 mm long, imbricate, tawny; glumes unequal, awnless, scabrous on veins; lower lemmas 2.5–3.2 mm long, ovate to elliptic, somewhat swollen on one side, awns 1.5–6.5 mm long; sterile florets 2–4, smaller than fertile florets.

Frequent as a roadside and pasture grass throughout mid and lower Coast. Good forage producer.

Chloris x subdolichostachya C. Muell. **SHORTSPIKE WINDMILLGRASS** (Fig. 51) Stoloniferous perennials. Culms to 70 cm tall, erect, bases flattened. Leaf sheaths laterally compressed; ligules 1 mm or more long, a ciliate membrane; collars brown; blades flat or folded. Panicles of 5 or more spicate primary unilateral branches; branches nearly digitate with hirsute reddish pulvini. Spikelets with 2 florets, including a single rudiment; mature florets often black at maturity; glumes awnless; lower lemmas 2.2–2.9 mm long, pilose with an awn 2–5 mm long.

Found on sandy and sandy loam sites throughout Coast. Fair to poor forage. The x before the specific epithet denotes a hybrid; this one is highly fertile.

Chloris texensis Nash **TEXAS WINDMILLGRASS** (Fig. 52) Tufted perennials. Culms to 45 cm tall, erect, glabrous. Leaves basal; blades to 15 cm long, 4 mm wide, scabrous. Panicles of 6–10 spicate primary unilateral branches with widely spaced spikelets on distal one-half to three-fourths portion only. Spikelets tawny, lanceolate; glumes awnless, midvein scabrous; lower lemmas with awn 7–11 mm long; awn of second lemmas 4.5–6.5 mm long; sterile florets elliptic, glabrous with awns 2.0–2.5 mm long.

Rare on sandy and sandy loam soils along mid Coast. Poor forage.

Chloris verticillata Nutt. **TUMBLE WINDMILLGRASS** (Fig. 53) Perennials. Culms to 40 cm tall, erect to decumbent. Leaves with ligules of ciliate membranes with hairs to 2 mm long; blades to 15 cm long, 2–3 mm wide. Panicles with 10–16

Figure 50. *Chloris gayana*
plant and spikelet (Gould and Box 1965).

spicate primary unilateral branches, distributed in 2–5 verticels, branches to 20 cm long without spikelets at the base. Spikelets appressed, widely spaced; glumes scabrous on midvein; lower lemmas with awn 4.8–9.0 mm long; sterile floret 1, oblong, inflated, truncate with an awn 3–7 mm long.

Frequent throughout Coast, especially on disturbed soils or in heavily grazed areas. Similar to the closely related *C. cucullata*. Poor to fair forage.

Chloris virgata Sw. **SHOWY CHLORIS** (Fig. 54) Tufted or stoloniferous annuals. Culms 5 cm to 100 cm tall, erect, decumbent, glabrous. Leaf sheaths glabrous; ligules ciliate membranes or lacking; blades to 1.5 cm wide. Panicles of 4–20 spicate primary unilateral branches; branches each 5–10 cm long, digitate, erect to ascending with numerous crowded spikelets. Spikelets tawny; first glumes 1.5–2.5 mm long; second glumes 2.5–4.3 mm long; lower lemmas 3-veined, awn to 15 mm long, ovate, gibbous; midvein and lower margin pubescent, the upper margin long ciliate.

Figure 51. *Chloris* x *subdolichostachya* spikelet (Gould and Box 1965).

Figure 52. *Chloris texensis*
inflorescence and spikelet (Gould and Box 1965).

Found on clay soils of roadsides and prairies as a weed, upper Coast. Poor forage.

19. **CHRYSOPOGON** Trin.

Culms solid. Leaves mostly basal and cauline; sheaths rounded; ligules a ciliate membrane. Panicles with whorl of racemose branches; branches with three spike-lets, one spikelet sessile and fertile, two spikelets pedicellate and staminate. Spike-lets more or less laterally compressed, disarticulation below glumes; florets two, lower sterile, upper perfect; glumes cartilaginous; lemmas hyaline, upper lemma awned; paleas present in upper floret.

Chrysopogon pauciflorus (Chapm.) Benth. *ex* Vasey (Figure 55) Annuals. Culms 60–120 cm tall, erect, sometimes decumbent. Leaf blades 4–8 mm wide, flat. Panicles loose, branches few, very slender. Sessile spikelets 1.5 cm long, including slender villous callus to 7 mm long; glumes coriaceous; lemmas hyaline; upper lemmas with awn to about 15 cm long; awn stout, brown, geniculate, twisted below.

Found in sandy piney woods, open ground, and fields of upper Gulf Coast.

20. **COELORACHIS** Brongn. • Jointtail

Culms solid. Leaves basal and cauline; sheaths rounded; ligules a ciliate membrane; blades flat. Spicate racemes terminal and axillary upon culms. Spikelets dorsally compressed, appearing embedded in rachis, disarticulation below glumes; spikelets paired, sessile one perfect, pedicellate one sterile, awnless. Sessile spikelet glumes indurate; lemmas hyaline.

1. Sheaths rounded to slightly keeled; first glumes pitted ...... *C. cylindrica*
1. Sheaths strongly keeled; first glumes with transverse ridges ... *C. rugosa*

Figure 53. *Chloris verticillata*
partial inflorescence and florets (Hitchcock 1951).

Figure 54. *Chloris virgata*
plant, (A) glumes, and (B) florets (Hitchcock 1951).

Coelorachis cylindrica (Michx.) Nash **CAROLINA JOINTTAIL** (Figure 56)
Tufted or rhizomatous perennials. Culms to 100 cm tall, erect. Leaves glabrous;
blades flat or folded. Spicate racemes 6–15 cm long, spikelets appear embedded
in rachis. Sessile spikelets 4–5 mm long, perfect, awnless. Pedicellate spikelets reduced, one-half pedicel length.

Widespread but infrequent throughout Gulf Coast. Highly palatable but of
poor livestock value due to limited abundance.

Figure 55. *Chrysopogon
pauciflorus* plant and spikelet
(Hitchcock 1951).

Coelorachis rugosa (Nutt.) Nash **WRINKLED JOINTTAIL** Coarse glabrous perennials. Culms to 130 cm tall, stout, branching and rebranching above. Lower leaf sheaths to 2 cm wide at base; blades to 35 cm or longer, 2–8 mm wide. Spicate racemes 4–8 cm long. Sessile spikelets 3.5–5.0 mm long; first glumes coarsely and irregularly transversely ridged. Pedicels thickened above, bearing a much reduced, rudimentary spikelet.

Infrequent, mostly in moist soil along streams, swales, and lakes of upper Gulf Coast.

21. **CORTADERIA** • Stapf
Culms mostly solid. Leaves mainly basal; ligules a ring of hairs; blades flat. Panicles large, open. Spikelets laterally compressed, disarticulation above glumes; florets three to five, reduced floret above; glumes awnless; lemmas awned.

Cortaderia selloana (Schult. & Schult.) Aschers. & Graebn. **PAMPASGRASS** Coarse, tufted, dioecious perennials. Culms to 3 m tall, erect. Leaves forming clumps to 1 m in diameter; blades to 100 cm long, margins and midvein sharply serrate. Panicles to 1 m long, dense, silvery white. Spikelets with two or three florets; glumes longer than lower florets; lemmas of pistillate inflorescences with long, silky hairs; lemmas of staminate inflorescences glabrous.

Introduced as a lawn ornamental. Relatively hardy but infrequent outside of cultivated areas.

22. **CYNODON** • L. Rich.
Culms hollow or pithy, much-branched. Leaves basal and cauline; ligules a ring of hairs; blades flat or involute. Panicles of several spicate primary unilateral branches, branches digitate or toward the culm apex. Spikelets laterally compressed, awnless, disarticulation above the glumes; florets one; glumes unequal; lemmas 3-veined; paleas subequal to lemma length; rachilla prolonged above floret.

Cynodon dactylon (L.) Pers. **BERMUDAGRASS** (Figure 57) Stoloniferous, rhizomatous, sod-forming perennials. Culms to 50 cm tall, weak. Leaves conspicuously distichous. Panicles of three to five spicate primary unilateral branches; branches digitate. Spikelets with one perfect floret, purple, awnless; lemmas shiny, firm; paleas 2-veined.

Improved hybrid strains widely established as pasture grasses throughout Gulf Coast. Highly salt- and alkali-tolerant. Common bermuda can be an aggressive weed. Both common and hybrid bermudas are good livestock forage, especially in fertilized pastures; poor wildlife value.

Figure 56. *Coelorachis cylindrica*
plant, (A) sessile spikelet and rachis, and (B) pedicel, pedicellate spikelet, and rachis (Hitchcock 1951).

23. **DACTYLIS** L. • Orchardgrass

Culms hollow. Leaves basal and cauline; sheaths keeled; ligules membranous; blades flat or folded. Panicles with a few branches; branches one-sided with compact fascicles of spikelets at apex. Spikelets laterally compressed, disarticulation above the glumes; florets two to five, reduced floret apical; glumes and lemmas with short awns; paleas well developed.

Dactylis glomerata L. ORCHARDGRASS (Figure 58) Culms to 100 cm tall, erect, slender. Leaf blades flat or folded. Panicles 3–20 cm long. Spikelets clustered on short pedicels at apex of main axis and on upper portion of a few other branches. Spikelets with two to five florets, disarticulation above glumes; glumes unequal to nearly equal, keeled, 1- to 3-veined, acute to acuminate or short-awned; lemmas mostly 5–8 mm long, apex acute, acuminate or short-awned; paleas slightly shorter than lemmas, veins scabrous-ciliate.

Infrequent adventive found mostly in shade and on field borders along upper Gulf Coast. Valuable pasture grass in more temperate climates.

24. DACTYLOCTENIUM · Willd.
Culms solid. Leaves basal and cauline; sheath margins connate; ligules a ciliate membrane; blades flat. Panicles of three to nine spicate primary unilateral branches; branches digitate, terminating in a bare point. Spikelets laterally compressed with two to seven florets, reduced florets above, disarticulation above glumes; glumes 1-veined; lemmas 3-veined, glabrous, awned, or mucronate.

Dactyloctenium aegyptium (L.) Beauv. DURBAN CROWFOOTGRASS (Figure 59) Annuals. Culms to 60 cm tall, erect or spreading, unbranched, occasionally rooting at nodes. Leaf blades 3–7 cm long; margins slightly crisp. Panicles with two to several spicate primary unilateral branches; branches short, thick, paired to digitate, projecting beyond last spikelet. Spikelets with two to five florets, laterally flattened; glumes unequal, apex truncate, extending into awn 1.0–1.5 mm long; lemmas similar to glumes, 3-veined with short, crooked awn; palea veins minutely scabrous.

Occurs as an occasional weed of ditches, roadsides, and other moist sites throughout Gulf Coast. Preferred by cattle but of poor forage value due to limited productivity.

25. DESMAZERIA Dumort.
Culms hollow. Leaves basal and cauline; sheaths rounded; ligules membranous; blades flat. Panicles of spicate primary branches, occasionally reduced to a raceme. Spikelets laterally compressed, disarticulation above the glumes; florets two to several, reduced florets apical; glumes unequal; lemmas rounded, obscurely 5-veined, glabrous, scarious margins; paleas about equal to lemmas.

Desmazeria rigida (L.) T. Tutin STIFFGRASS (Figure 60) Low, tufted annuals. Culms to 45 cm tall, slender, erect. Leaves glabrous; ligules 1.5–4.0 mm long, membranous, lacerate; blades 1–4 mm wide, thin. Panicles 3–10 cm long, con-

Figure 57. *Cynodon dactylon*
plant, (A) spikelet, (B) floret with elongated rachilla, and (C) lemma (Hitchcock 1951).

tracted. Spikelets with four to seven florets, glabrous; glumes awnless, subequal, slightly shorter than lemmas; lemmas about 2 mm long, awnless, rounded on back.

Adventive from Europe. Occasional along field borders, in disturbed sites, and on dunes of mid and upper Gulf Coast.

Figure 58. *Dactylis glomerata*
plant, (A) spikelet, and (B) floret (Hitchcock 1951).

Figure 59. *Dactyloctenium aegyptium*
plant, (A) spikelet, (B) floret, and (C) caryopsis (Hitchcock 1951).

Figure 60. *Desmazeria rigida*
plant, (A) floret, and (B) rachilla (Hitchcock 1951).

26. **DICHANTHELIUM** (A. S. Hitchc. & Chase) Gould • Rosettegrass (adapted from Gould and Clark 1978)

Culms hollow, vernal form unbranched, autumnal form much-branched. Leaves basal and cauline, most with basal rosette; sheaths rounded; ligules absent, membranous, or a ring of hairs; blades flat. Panicles terminal (vernal) and axillary (autumnal), open. Spikelets dorsally compressed, disarticulation below glumes; florets two, lower sterile, upper fertile; first glumes reduced; second glumes and lower lemmas similar in size and texture; upper floret indurate, smooth; lemma margins clasping paleas.

1.	Leaf blades linear, narrow, 20 times as long as wide .. ***D. linearifolium***
1.	Leaf blades lanceolate, usually much less than 20 times longer than wide 2
2(1).	Spikelets 3.3–5.4 mm long 3
2.	Spikelets 0.8–3.2 mm long 9
3(2).	Culm leaf blades, at least some, 13–35 mm wide 4
3.	Culm leaf blades less than 12 mm wide 6
4(3).	Spikelets broadly elliptic to obovate, turgid with conspicuous veins ... 5

4.	Spikelets narrowly elliptic to obovate, not turgid nor conspicuously veined .... *D. ravenelii*
5(4).	Ligules 1.6 mm or longer .... *D. oligosanthes* var. *oligosanthes*
5.	Ligules shorter than 1.6 mm .... *D. oligosanthes* var. *scribnerianum*
6(3).	Spikelets broadly elliptic to obovate; first glume one-fifth to one-fourth spikelet length 7
6.	Spikelets narrowly ovate or elliptic or obovate; first glume long or short 8
7(6).	Ligules 1.6 mm or longer .... *D. oligosanthes* var. *oligosanthes*
7.	Ligules shorter than 1.6 mm .... *D. oligosanthes* var. *scribnerianum*
8(6).	Spikelets 3.5–4.3 mm long, obpyriform; second glume bases attenuate .... *D. nodatum*
8.	Spikelets 3.2–3.9 mm long, ovate, elliptic, obovate or obpyriform; second glume bases not attenuate .... *D. aciculare*
9(2).	Spikelets 2.1–3.2 mm long 10
9.	Spikelets 0.8–2.0 mm long 20
10(9).	Leaf blades, at least some, 13–25 mm wide 11
10.	Leaf blades less than 12 (15) mm wide 12
11(10).	Spikelets 2.3–3.2 mm long, narrowly ovate to elliptic *D. commutatum*
11.	Spikelets 2.1–2.3 mm long, broadly elliptic to suborbicular .... *D. sphaerocarpon* var. *sphaerocarpon*
12(10).	Leaf blades cordate or subcordate at base 13
12.	Leaf blades not cordate or subcordate at base 14
13(12).	Spikelets 2.1–3.3 mm long, elliptical .... *D. commutatum*
13.	Spikelets 2.0–2.2 mm long, subspherical .... *D. sphaerocarpon* var. *sphaerocarpon*
14(12).	Ligule hairs 2–5 mm long 15
14.	Ligule hairs shorter than 2 mm 18
15(14).	Sheaths glabrous, pubescent or with hairs shorter than 1.5 mm .... *D. oligosanthes* var. *oligosanthes*
15.	Sheaths with hairs 2–4 mm long 16
16(15).	Culms pubescent to hairy; lower sheaths puberulent to villous .... *D. acuminatum* var. *acuminatum*
16.	Culms glabrous; lower sheaths generally glabrous 17
17(16).	Panicles 5–8 cm long, wide, width two-thirds length .... *D. acuminatum* var. *lindheimeri*
17.	Panicles 8–13 cm long, narrow, width one-third length .... *D. acuminatum* var. *densiflorum*

18(14). Culm nodes bearded .... *D. dichotomum* var. *ensifolium*

18. Culm nodes sparsely hairy or puberulent but not bearded **19**

19(18). Mid-culm leaf blades stiff, linear to linear-lanceolate, and acuminate
.... *D. aciculare*

19. Mid-culm leaf blades thin or firm but not stiff, lanceolate, acute ....
.... *D. oligosanthes* var. *scribnerianum*

20(9). Ligule hairs 2–5 mm long .... *D. acuminatum*

20. Ligule hairs shorter than 1.5 mm **21**

21(20). Culm internodes pubescent to villous .... *D. aciculare*

21. Culm internodes glabrous **22**

22(21). Leaf blades thick and glabrous, spikelets 1.4–2.0 mm long **23**

22. Leaf blades thin and glabrous; spikelets 1.2–2.0 mm long ....
.... *D. dichotomum*

23(22). Lower culm blades less than 6 mm wide at base .... *D. aciculare*

23. Lower culm blades 7–30 mm wide at base ....
.... *D. sphaerocarpon* var. *sphaerocarpon*

Dichanthelium aciculare (Poir.) Gould & Clark **NARROW-LEAF ROSETTEGRASS**
Tufted perennials. Culms to 75 cm tall, erect; secondary branches (autumnal) with
reduced fascicled leaves at upper nodes. Leaves with basal rosette of short, wide
blades, glabrous or hairy; mid-culm blades 5–18 mm long. Pani cles 4–9 mm long,
small, few spikelets on erect or spreading branches. Secondary inflorescences
greatly reduced with five to ten spikelets. Spikelets 2.0–3.6 mm long, elliptical or
obovate, usually pubescent.
   Common in woodlands and prairies of upper Gulf Coast.

Dichanthelium acuminatum (Sw.) Gould & Clark var. *acuminatum* **WOOLLY
ROSETTEGRASS** (Figure 61) Tufted perennials. Culms to 60 cm tall in large
clumps; nodes bearded with erect or spreading hairs; culms branching in the fall
to produce fascicles of reduced leaves and delicate few-spikeleted panicles. Basal
leaves in rosette, variously pubescent to glabrous; sheaths villous to puberulent;
blades thickened. Panicles 5–8 cm long. Spikelets 1.6–2.6 mm long, obovate.
   var. *densiflorum* (Rand & Redf.) Gould & Clark Variety has glabrous sheaths;
panicles 7–12 cm long; spikelets 1.4–1.8 mm long.
   var. *lindheimeri* (Nash) Gould & Clark **LINDHEIMER ROSETTEGRASS**
Variety differs from var. *acuminatum* in having glabrous culms, glabrous sheaths,
sheath margins pubescent-ciliate, and dense ligular hairs 2–6 mm long.
   Frequent in woodlands and wooded borders of upper Gulf Coast.

Dichanthelium commutatum (Schult.) Gould **VARIABLE ROSETTEGRASS** Tufted perennials from knotty bases. Culms to 75 cm tall, glabrous, branching with age at upper nodes to produce branchlets with moderately reduced, fascicled leaves. Leaves with basal rosette; blades 6–9 cm long, 9–25 mm wide, occasionally to 15 cm long and 35 mm wide; wider blades cordate at base. Panicles 6–12 cm long, open, branches spreading to erect; pedicels slender. Spikelets 2.4–3.3 mm long, narrowly elliptic, slightly pointed, puberulent or glabrous; first glumes thin, obtuse or widely acute, about 1 mm long; lemma of upper florets often spiculate.

Found in sandy woodlands, often in shade, along upper Gulf Coast.

Dichanthelium dichotomum (L.) Gould var. *dichotomum* Slender perennials. Culms to 100 cm tall, usually tufted from compact, often knotty crown; nodes often bearded; culms becoming much-branched ("bushy") with fascicled leafy branches (autumnal phase). Leaves of basal rosette and lower cauline leaves short and wide; blades of main culms 4–15 cm long, 3–13 mm wide, margins often sparsely ciliate near base; "autumnal" branches with blades commonly 3–7 cm long. Panicles well exserted, open; branches, branchlets, and pedicels tend to spread; late-formed panicles greatly reduced. Spikelets 1.5–2.4 mm long, glumes rounded at apex; first glumes 0.3–0.5 mm long, elliptic; second glumes and lower lemmas strongly 7- to 9-veined, pubescent; upper floret apex rounded.

Found on sandy soils, usually in or along woodlands, throughout Gulf Coast. Good

Figure 61. *Dichanthelium acuminatum* var. *acuminatum* plant and spikelet (Gould and Box 1965).

livestock forage but low productivity. Large seeds valuable to birds; utilized by deer early in growing season.

var. ***ensifolium*** (Baldwin) Gould & Clark Culms to 40 cm tall, fragile/delicate, glabrous. Leaf sheaths glabrous or ciliate on margins; ligules 0.5 mm or less; blades short, spreading, often reflexed. Panicles to 5 cm long with few spikelets. Spikelets 1.0–1.5 mm long, oblong to obovate.

Occurs in marshy seep areas and acid soil of bogs throughout upper Gulf Coast.

Dichanthelium linearifolium (Scribn.) Gould **SLIMLEAF ROSETTEGRASS** Densely tufted perennials. Vernal phase with culms several to many, densely pilose. Leaves with a basal rosette, pilose or hispid; blades 8–20 cm long, linear. Panicles 4–8 cm long, branches spreading to erect, narrow. Spikelets 2.7–3.2 mm long, oval, blunt; second glumes and lower lemmas shorter than upper florets. Autumnal phase similar, axillary panicles numerous.

Found on sandy or gravelly soils in open grassland along upper Gulf Coast.

Dichanthelium nodatum (A. S. Hitchc. & Chase) Gould **SARITA ROSETTEGRASS** (Figure 62) Subrhizomatous perennials. Culms to 65 cm tall, wiry, geniculate to erect, scabrous to puberulent to short-hispid. Leaf ligules dense tufts of hairs; blades 3–9 cm long, 4–9 mm wide. Vernal panicles not widely spreading. Spikelets 3.5–4.3 mm long, obovate.

Occasional on sandy sites of lower and mid Gulf Coast. Good livestock forage but low productivity. Large seeds valuable to birds. Utilized by deer early in growing season.

Dichanthelium oligosanthes (Schult.) Gould var. ***oligosanthes*** (Figure 63) Loosely tufted perennials. Culms to 80 cm tall, pubescent; autumnal culms muchbranched. Leaf blades of vernal phase 8–12 cm long, 6 mm wide, pubescent above, margins scabrous. Panicles 5–12 cm long on vernal culms; lowermost internodes of panicle axis villous or tomentose. Spikelets 3.2–3.7 mm long; glumes awnless; lemmas of fertile florets about the length of spikelets.

Found in sandy woodlands and brushy areas throughout Gulf Coast. Good livestock forage but limited productivity. Large seeds valuable to birds. Utilized by deer early in growing season.

var. ***scribnerianum*** (Nash) Gould **SCRIBNER'S ROSETTEGRASS** Similar to var. *oligosanthes,* but with smaller spikelets and nearly glabrous herbage. Spikelets 2.7–3.8 mm long, glabrous; lemma of fertile florets indurate, ovate, as long as spikelets, glabrous, apex rounded.

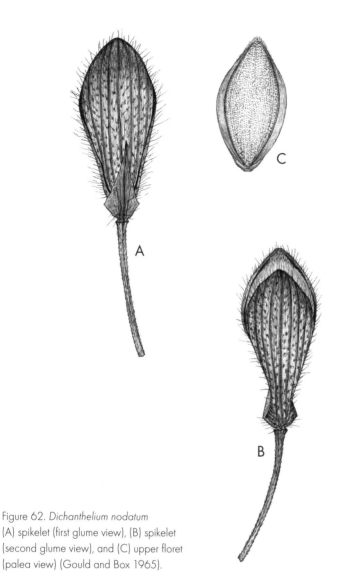

Figure 62. *Dichanthelium nodatum*
(A) spikelet (first glume view), (B) spikelet
(second glume view), and (C) upper floret
(palea view) (Gould and Box 1965).

Found throughout Gulf Coast, usually on loamy clay sites in open or brushy
areas. Good livestock forage but limited productivity. Large seeds valuable to birds;
utilized by deer early in growing season.

Dichanthelium ravenelii (Scribn.) Gould Stout perennials. Culms to 75 cm tall,
pubescent with erect or spreading hairs; nodes bearded, usually with wide glabrous band below bearded portion; culms branching with age at upper nodes to

Figure 63. *Dichanthelium oligosanthes* var. *oligosanthes*
(A) plant (autumnal form), (B) inflorescence (vernal form), and (C) spikelet (Gould and Box 1965).

produce clusters of short-leaved, lateral branches. Leaf sheaths, at least of lower leaves, pubescent; hairs coarse, erect or spreading, often papilla-based; blades 8–15 cm long, 10–25 mm wide, abruptly narrowing at base, typically glabrous on upper surface, tomentose or puberulent below. Panicles 7–13 cm long, open, usually few-spikeleted, axis puberulent. Spikelets 3.5–5.0 mm long, pubescent; first glumes mostly 1.8–2.2 mm long.

Found in sandy woodlands of upper Gulf Coast.

Dichanthelium sphaerocarpon (Ell.) Gould & Clark var. ***sphaerocarpon*** **ROUNDSEED ROSETTEGRASS** (Figure 64) Tufted perennials. Culms to 80 cm tall, sparingly branched in autumnal form. Leaves of basal rosette short and wide with white margins; sheaths usually pubescent, margins with fine soft hairs; blades 6–11 mm wide, glabrous on upper surface, ciliate below, base cordate-clasping.

Figure 64. *Dichanthelium sphaerocarpon* plant and spikelet (Gould and Box 1965).

Panicles open with many spikelets; central axis and branches glabrous. Spikelets 1.4–2.0 mm long, nearly spherical at maturity.

Occasional in sandy soil, usually in open woodlands or brushy pastures, throughout Gulf Coast. Good livestock forage but limited productivity. Large seeds valuable to birds; utilized by deer early in growing season.

27. DICHANTHIUM Willem. • Bluestem

Culms solid, nodes densely bearded. Leaves basal and cauline; ligules membranous; blades flat. Panicles of one or two to several racemose branches; branches digitate, ascending to spreading. Spikelets dorsally compressed, paired, one spikelet sessile and fertile, one spikelet pedicellate and sterile, disarticulation below glumes; glumes subequal; lemmas of sessile spikelet membranous, upper lemmas awned.

1.	First glumes with line of long hairs near apex, hairs to 3 mm long; plants without stolons; ligules 1.6–2.0 mm long	*D. sericeum*
1.	First glumes without line of long hairs near apex, pubescent; plants may develop stolons; ligules 1.0–1.3 mm long	2
2(1).	Inflorescence axis and branch bases pubescent	*D. aristatum*
2.	Inflorescence axis and branch bases glabrous	*D. annulatum*

Dichanthium annulatum (Forssk.) Stapf **KLEBERG BLUESTEM** (Figure 65) Stoloniferous perennials. Culms to 1 m tall, prostrate becoming erect, glabrous except for a ring of densely tufted hairs at nodes. Leaf sheaths about two-fifths length of internodes; collars yellow; blades 3–5 mm wide. Panicles with one to three branches; axis glabrous; branches racemose, densely pilose with paired spikelets. Sessile spikelets 3.0–3.3 mm long. Pedicellate spikelets 3.7–4.0 mm long, pedicels pilose.

Occurs as an escapee from pasture plantings, roadsides, and lawns throughout Gulf Coast. Poor forage for livestock and wildlife. Good bird nesting and fawning cover for deer.

Dichanthium aristatum (Poir.) C. E. Hubb. **ANGLETON BLUESTEM** Tufted or stoloniferous perennials. Culms to 80 cm tall, prostrate becoming erect, glabrous; nodes densely pubescent. Differentiated from *D. annulatum* by pubescent inflorescence axis and branch bases.

Found persisting in some native pastures; well established in many pastures, along roadways, and in ditches. An introduced grass, widely seeded all along Gulf Coast. Poor forage for livestock and wildlife. Good bird nesting and fawning cover.

Figure 65. *Dichanthium annulatum*
inflorescence with sessile and pedicellate spikelets (Gould and Box 1965).

Dichanthium sericeum (R. Br.) A. Camus **SILKY BLUESTEM** (Figure 66) Perennial bunchgrasses. Culms to 1 m tall, nodes densely bearded with silvery, spreading hairs 1–5 mm long; collars purple-fringed. Leaves glabrous. Panicles mostly terminal with two to seven branches; branches racemose with long villous hairs. Sessile spikelets 2.5–4.2 mm long; first glume apex subacute with line of hairs across tip; upper lemma awns 2.2–3.5 mm long, dark brown, twisted. Pedicellate spikelets about as large as sessile ones, awnless.

Planted as forage grass on prairie soil along lower to mid Gulf Coast. Poor to fair forage for livestock and wildlife. Good bird nesting and deer fawning cover.

Figure 66. *Dichanthium sericeum*
inflorescence with sessile and pedicellate spikelets (Gould and Box 1965).

28. **DIGITARIA** Fabr. • Crabgrass, Cottontop

Culms solid, usually branching. Leaves basal and cauline; ligules a ciliate membrane; blades flat. Panicles of numerous spicate primary branches or open panicles; branches winged or not winged. Spikelets dorsally compressed; florets two, lower florets sterile, upper florets fertile, disarticulation below glumes; first glumes highly reduced or absent; second glumes well developed; upper lemma margins membranous and folded over palea (rather than clasping).

1. Pedicels three times or more spikelet length 2
1. Pedicals two times or less spikelet length 4
2(1). Spikelets 3.5–4.6 mm long; second glumes 5- to 7- veined .. **D. arenicola**
   2. Spikelets 2.2–3.3 mm long; second glumes 3- (rarely 5-) veined 3
3(2). Lemma of lowermost florets 5-veined; second glume and lowermost lemma pubescent; rhizomes present or absent .... **D. cognata** ssp. **pubiflora**
   3. Lemma of lowermost florets 7-veined; second glume and lowermost lemma glabrous to pubescent; rhizomes absent .... **D. cognata** ssp. **cognata**
4(1). Primary branches winged, wing as wide as main body of branch; plants annual 5
   4. Primary branches not winged, or slightly so; plants annual or perennial 6
5(4). Lemmas of lowermost florets on sessile or subsessile spikelets with equi distant veins .... **D. bicornis**
   5. Lemmas of lowermost florets on sessile or subsessile spikelets with veins crowded to margins .... **D. sanguinalis**
6(4). Spikelets with long hairs tinged white to silvery to purple; plants perennial 7
   6. Spikelets pubescent but not with long hairs tinged white to silvery to purple; plants annual or perennial 8
7(6). Inflorescences contracted, branches appressed; upper floret apex acute .... **D. californica**
   7. Inflorescences open, branches stiffly spreading to erect; upper floret apex acuminate .... **D. patens**
8(6). Lemma of lowermost florets with hairs 2–4 mm long .... **D. insularis**
   8. Lemma of lowermost florets with hairs shorter than 1 mm 9
9(8). Upper floret lemmas light brown to gray when mature; plants often stoloniferous .... **D. texana**
   9. Upper floret lemmas dark brown when mature; plants not stoloniferous 10

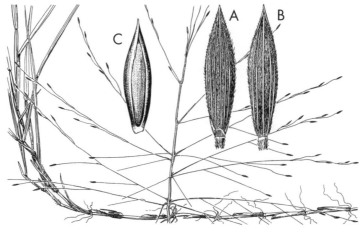

Figure 67. *Digitaria arenicola*
plant with rhizome and partial inflorescence, (A) spikelet (first glume view), (B) spikelet (second glume view), and (C) upper floret (palea view) (Hitchcock 1951).

10(9). Plants perennial; second glume and lowermost lemma margins densely villous .... *D. patens*

10. Plants annual; second glume and lowermost lemma margins puberulent **11**

11(10). Spikelets 1.5–1.9 mm long; panicle branches 8–13 cm long .. *D. filiformis*

11. Spikelets 2.0–2.6 mm long; panicle branches 13–28 cm long .... *D. villosa*

Digitaria arenicola (Swallen) Beetle **SAND WITCHGRASS** (Figure 67) Rhizomatous perennials. Culms to 60 cm tall, erect, glabrous; internodes solid, round. Leaf collars purple; blades 3–7 mm wide. Panicles open, disarticulation at base to become a tumbleweed; branches ascending to spreading; pedicels long, antrorsely scabrous. Spikelets about 4 mm long, widely spaced, dorsally compressed; glumes awnless; lower lemmas pubescent on margins, similar to second glumes; upper lemmas about 3 mm long, dark brown, indurate, densely villous.

Found on sands of dunes, islands, and adjacent inland prairies of mid and upper Gulf Coast. Fair forage for livestock; poor for wildlife.

Digitaria bicornis (Lam.) Roem. & Schult. **CRABGRASS** Spreading to decumbent annuals. Culms to 60 cm tall, appearing stoloniferous at base and rooting at lower nodes. Leaves cauline; blades 5–12 mm wide. Generally similar to *D. sanguinalis* but inflorescence branches digitate. Panicles of digitate spicate primary branches. Spikelets paired on branches, dorsally compressed; glumes awnless; first glumes scalelike; second glumes about half spikelet length; lower lemmas awnless; upper lemmas light brown.

Found as a common weed in lawns, gardens, and along roadsides throughout Gulf Coast.

Figure 68. *Digitaria californica*
plant base, inflorescence, and spikelet (Gould and Box 1965).

Digitaria californica (Benth.) Henr. **ARIZONA COTTONTOP** (Figure 68)
Tufted perennials. Culms to 100 cm tall, erect or geniculate, bases knotty. Leaves glabrous, except for pubescent lower sheaths; collars brown; blades 10–15 cm long, 2.0–4.5 mm wide, flat. Panicles contracted, of silvery pubescent spikelets; branches ascending, one per node with spikelets to the base. Spikelets 3–4 mm

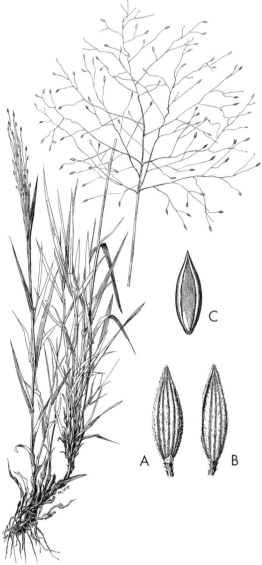

Figure 69. *Digitaria cognata* ssp. *pubiflora*
plant, (A) spikelet (first glume view), (B) spikelet (second glume view), and (C) upper floret (palea view) (Hitchcock 1951).

long with long silky hairs; second glumes and lower lemmas densely hirsute, hairs 2–4 mm long and tinged silvery or purple; upper lemmas narrowing to a short awn tip.

Found on well-drained soils, generally in the protection of brush throughout lower and mid Gulf Coast; increases under grazing pressure on upland sites. Fair forage for livestock; poor for wildlife.

Digitaria cognata (Schult.) Pilger ssp. ***cognata*** **FALL WITCHGRASS**
Tufted perennials. Culms to 60 cm tall, slender, wiry; bases knotty, usually densely hairy. Leaves with ligules membranous, truncate. Panicles open with long-pedicelled spikelets. Spikelets 2.5–3.0 mm long; second glume veins and lower lemmas glabrous; lower lemmas 7-veined, glabrous; upper lemmas dark brown, apex acute.

Occasional on well-drained sandy or sandy loam sites, usually in moderately disturbed open prairies throughout Gulf Coast. Similar to *D. arenicola*, but with shorter spikelets. Fair livestock value; poor wildlife value.

ssp. ***pubiflora*** (Vasey *ex* L. H. Dewey) Wipff **FALL WITCHGRASS** (Figure 69) Variety is similar to var. *cognata* except rhizomes may be present or absent; second glumes and lower lemmas pubescent; lower lemmas 5-veined.

Occasional throughout Gulf Coast on well-drained sandy sites. Fair livestock forage; poor wildlife value.

Figure 70. *Digitaria insularis* inflorescence and spikelet (Gould and Box 1965).

Digitaria filiformis (L.) Koel. **SLENDER CRABGRASS** Tufted annuals. Culms to 80 cm tall, slender, erect. Lower sheaths and blades sparsely to densely hirsute; upper culm leaves pubescent or glabrous; blades 10–25 cm or longer, 2–6 mm wide. Panicles of one to five spicate primary branches; branches 7–13 cm long, slender, erect, unbranched. Spikelets 1.5–1.9 mm long; first glumes absent; second glumes about three-fourths the length of spikelets; lower lemmas strongly 7-veined, margins puberulent, sometimes dorsally, hairs usually capitellate; upper lemmas dark brown, tapering to an acute apex.

Found in sandy soil and partial shade along upper Gulf Coast.

Digitaria insularis (L.) Mez *ex* Ekman **SOURGRASS** (Figure 70) Tufted perennials. Culms to 150 cm tall, stiffly erect, base knotty. Lowermost leaf sheaths densely pubescent, herbage otherwise glabrous; blades 4–10 mm wide. Panicles contracted, densely spikeleted. Spikelets 3.6–4.2 mm long, excluding hairs; first glumes minute; second glumes and lower lemmas densely shaggy, hirsute; hairs long, brownish, exceeding spikelets in length; lower lemmas pubescent; upper lemmas dark brown, tapering to a point or short awn.

Frequent in ditches and moist depressions along lower and mid Gulf Coast. Poor livestock and wildlife values.

Digitaria patens (Swallen) Henr. **TEXAS COTTONTOP** Tufted perennials. Culms to 75 cm tall. Panicles of spicate primary branches, open; branches to 12 cm long. Spikelets widely spaced on slender, silvery pubescent branches. Generally similar to *D. californica* but inflorescence branches stiffly spreading and spikelets widely spaced, barely if at all, overlapping.

Occasional on sandy and sandy loam soils of lower Gulf Coast; never abundant. Fair to good forage for livestock; poor for wildlife.

Digitaria sanguinalis (L.) Scop. **HAIRY CRABGRASS** (Figure 71) Decumbent to spreading annuals. Culms to 1 m long, branching at base. Leaves cauline, glabrous or sparsely pubescent with papilla-based hairs; ligules membranous. Panicles of four to nine spicate primary branches; branches digitate or subdigitate; branch axis flattened, scabrous. Spikelets 2.8–3.3 mm long; first glumes scalelike, minute; second glumes 1.0–2.7 mm long, awnless, pubescent, acute; lower lemmas similar to second glumes; upper lemmas about 3 mm long.

Frequent in ditches, fields, fencerows, and other disturbed sites throughout Gulf Coast. Poor livestock and wildlife values.

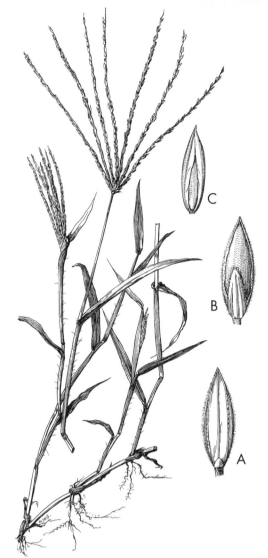

Figure 71. *Digitaria sanguinalis*
plant, (A) spikelet (first glume view), (B) spikelet (second glume view),
and (C) upper floret (palea view) (Hitchcock 1951).

Digitaria texana A. S. Hitchc. **TEXAS CRABGRASS** Rhizomatous, spreading to
decumbent perennials. Culms to 80 cm tall, often rooting at nodes. Leaf sheaths
villous-pubescent; ligules 1.5–2.0 mm long, membranous; blades 2–7 mm wide,
densely villous to hirsute to nearly glabrous. Panicles of 4–12 spicate primary
branches; branches 6–10 cm long, angled but not winged. Spikelets 2.0–3.6 mm

long, awnless; second glumes and lemmas of lower florets purple-tinged, pubescent with soft hairs on margins and back.

Known only from sandy coastal areas of lower and mid Gulf Coast. Poor to fair livestock forage; poor wildlife value.

Digitaria villosa (Walt.) Pers. **SHAGGY CRABGRASS** Tufted perennials. Culms to 150 cm tall, erect, from a much-branched base. Leaf sheaths and blades glabrous or pubescent; blades mostly 3–6 mm wide. Panicles of spicate primary branches; branches 15–25 cm long. Spikelets 2.0–2.6 mm long; second glumes and lower lemmas pubescent, hairs long. Similar in general aspect to *D. filiformis,* but larger in size, blades longer, and more pubescent.

Found on sandy soil in disturbed sites, especially along wooded edges of mid and upper Gulf Coast.

29. **DISTICHLIS** Raf. • Saltgrass
Plants dioecious. Culms solid. Leaves without auricles, conspicuously distichous; ligules a ciliate membrane. Panicles contracted, branches terminating in a spikelet. Spikelets unisexual, florets 4–16, awnless; pistillate spikelets, disarticulation above the glumes; glumes shorter than first floret; lemmas 5- to 11-veined, glabrous, entire.

Distichlis spicata (L.) Greene var. *spicata* **COASTAL SALTGRASS** (Figure 72) Low, dioecious perennials with stout, creeping rhizomes. Culms to 60 cm tall, nodes several to many; internodes short. Leaves overlapping, conspicuously distichous, lowermost reduced to scalelike sheaths; blades 2–10 cm long, 1–4 mm wide. Panicles to 10 cm long, contracted. Spikelets 6–18 mm long, florets 5–15; glumes unequal, awnless, acute; lemmas 3–6 mm long, acute, apex keeled; paleas slightly shorter than lemmas. Male and female plant inflorescences and spikelets similar in appearance.

Found in saline marshes, alkaline sites, and low, moist flats throughout Gulf Coast; often form extensive colonies in saline or brackish marshes. Good forage for livestock and geese.

30. **ECHINOCHLOA** Beauv. • Cockspur, Barnyardgrass
Culms solid. Leaves basal and cauline; sheaths rounded or keeled; ligules usually absent, rarely a ring of hairs; blades flat. Panicles of spicate branches, some of which rebranch; branches appressed or ascending. Spikelets dorsally compressed, disarticulation below the glumes; florets two, lower sterile, upper fertile; glumes

Figure 72. *Distichlis spicata* var. *spicata*
plant, (A) pistillate inflorescence, (B) pistillate floret,
(C) staminate spikelet, and (D) staminate floret (Hitchcock 1951).

unequal, awned or awnless; first glumes encircling the spikelets; second glume and lower lemma similar in size and texture; upper floret indurate.

1. Plants perennial; ligule a ring of yellow hairs on lower leaves ....
    .... ***E. polystachya***
1. Plants annual; ligule absent 2

2(1). Leaf sheaths hirsute or hispid .... *E. walteri*

2. Leaf sheaths glabrous **3**

3(2). Primary branches of panicle 1–2 (occasionally 3) cm long ... *E. colonum*

3. Primary branches of panicle 2.8–10.0 cm long **4**

4(3). Spikelets with some or all awns 15 mm or longer **5**

4. Spikelets all awnless or with awns shorter than 15 mm **8**

5(4). Lemma of upper florets obtuse to broadly acute .... *E. crusgalli*

5. Lemma of upper florets acuminate to narrowly acute **6**

6(5). Upper florets broadly ovate **7**

6. Upper florets oblong to narrowly ovate .... *E. walteri*

7(6). Spikelets shorter than 3.5 mm .... *E. muricata* var. *microstachya*

7. Spikelets 3.5 mm or longer .... *E. muricata* var. *muricata*

8(4). Panicles erect and stiff; spikelets conspicuously hispid **9**

8. Panicles soft and nodding; spikelets not conspicuously hispid **10**

9(8). Spikelets awnless, grayish-purple .... *E. crusgalli* var. *frumentacea*

9. Spikelets awned or awnless, straw colored or green ....
.... *E. crusgalli* var. *crusgalli*

10(8). Lemma of upper florets 2.5–2.8 mm long **11**

10. Lemma of upper florets 3.0 mm or longer .... *E. walteri*

11(10). Palea of lowermost florets present, well developed ....
.... *E. crus-pavonis* var. *crus-pavonis*

11. Palea of lowermost florets absent or rudimentary ....
.... *E. crus-pavonis* var. *macera*

Echinochloa colonum (L.) Link **JUNGLERICE** (Figure 73) Tufted annuals. Culms to 70 cm long, branching, succulent, usually decumbent, spreading. Leaves without ligules or auricles, commonly glabrous at junction of sheath and blade; blades flat, moderately wide, usually with transverse purple bands or markings. Panicle of spicate primary branches; branches 1–2 cm long. Spikelets 2.5–3.0 mm long, awnless; glumes 1.0–1.5 mm long, apex mucronate; upper lemmas elliptic; paleas of lower florets well developed.

Common weed of flower beds, ditches, and similar moist, disturbed habitats throughout Gulf Coast. Highly palatable to cattle, producing forage late in the hot summer period; good producer of seed for birds.

Echinochloa crusgalli (L.) Beauv. var. *crusgalli* **BARNYARDGRASS** (Figure 74) Large, succulent annuals with glabrous foliage. Culms to 2 m long, decumbent, spreading. Leaf blades 5–25 mm wide, flat, scabrous; margins finely serrate.

Figure 73. *Echinochloa colonum* inflorescence (Hitchcock 1951).

Panicles contracted, densely spikeleted with 5–25 spicate or nearly spicate primary branches. Spikelets 2.8–4.0 mm long; lower floret neuter; lower lemmas awnless, short-awned, or with an awn to over 5 cm long; paleas well developed; lemmas of upper florets obtuse with sharply differentiated apex, apex withering and membranous.

Locally abundant on poorly drained sites throughout mid and upper Gulf Coast. Highly palatable to cattle, producing forage late in the hot summer period; among the most important wetland plants for attracting upland game birds, songbirds, and waterfowl (ducks).

var. *frumentacea* (Link) W. F. Wight **JAPANESE MILLET** Similar in general appearance to var. *crusgalli*, but panicle branches more erect to appressed, more densely spikeleted with plump, awnless, usually grayish-purple spikelets.

Figure 74. *Echinochloa crusgalli* var. *crusgalli*
plant, (A) spikelet (first glume view), (B) spikelet (second glume view), and (C) upper floret (palea view) (Hitchcock 1951).

Figure 75. *Echinochloa crus-pavonis* inflorescence (Hitchcock 1951).

Often planted around ponds and wet areas for waterfowl; apparently does not persist without cultivation. Good seed producer.

Echinochloa crus-pavonis (Kunth) Schult. var. ***crus-pavonis*** **GULF COCKSPUR** (Figure 75) Large, coarse annuals. Culms to 1.5 m tall, glabrous; nodes often slightly swollen. Leaves cauline, glabrous; blades typically 1–2 cm wide. Panicles dense, nodding. Spikelets 2.8–3.1 mm long; lower florets neuter, lemmas awnless or with awn to 11 mm long; awn, when developed, present on all spikelets and uniform in size; paleas of lower florets well developed; upper florets narrowly elliptic, apex acute or obtuse, well differentiated, withering, membranous, coriaceous.

var. *macera* (Wieg.) Gould Differs from var. *crus-pavonis* in that plants are mostly less than 1 m tall, leaf blades 0.7–1.5 cm wide, and panicles stiffly erect on a relatively stout central axis. Spikelets usually awnless, or lemmas of lower florets minutely awn-tipped; paleas of lower florets absent or rudimentary.

Most common *Echinochloa* in Texas found all along Gulf Coast in swamps and swales, ditches, waste places, and field borders; often in shallow water during rainy periods. Highly palatable to cattle, producing forage late in the hot summer period; among the most important wetland plants for attracting upland game birds, songbirds, and waterfowl (ducks).

Echinochloa muricata (Beauv.) Fern. var. *muricata* Large annuals. Culms to 150 cm tall, generally erect but occasionally spreading from base. Leaves cauline; blades 1.0–2.5 mm wide, glabrous; margins minutely serrate. Panicles 10–30 cm long, typically with spreading, somewhat distant, spicate primary branches; branches 2–8 cm long. Spikelets 3.5 mm or longer, widely ovate, awned or awnless, usually conspicuously prickly with stout, papilla-based hairs; second glumes and lower lemmas about equal in length, usually hispid with papilla-based hairs; lower lemmas awnless or with awn 25 mm long; paleas well developed; upper florets widely ovate, abruptly narrowing to acuminate, non-withering apex.

var. *microstachya* Wieg. Differs in that spikelets are less than 3.5 mm long to base of awn or mucronate awn of lower lemmas; lower florets awnless or with awn to 6 mm long or less (infrequently to 10 mm).

Both varieties occur occasionally in moist open habitats along swales, ponds, and ditches of mid and upper Gulf Coast; var. *microstachya* is the most common. Highly palatable to cattle, producing forage late in the hot summer period; among the most important wetland plants for attracting upland game birds, songbirds, and waterfowl (ducks).

Echinochloa polystachya (Kunth in H.B.K.) A. S. Hitchc. Coarse perennials. Culms to 2 m long, stout, frequently decumbent, and rooting at lower nodes. Leaves with ligules of stiff, yellowish hairs, only at lower nodes; blades to 40 cm long, to 3 cm wide. Panicles 15–30 cm long, contracted; axis and branches sharply angled with stout papilla-based setae along ridges. Spikelets 4.5–6.5 mm long, excluding awn; second glumes acuminate or awn-tipped; lower lemma awns 2–15 mm long; upper lemmas narrowly ovate or elliptic, apex coriaceous, obtuse; apex well differentiated and withering.

Found in wet ditches and swales along lower Gulf Coast. Highly palatable to cattle, producing forage late in the hot summer period; among the most impor-

Figure 76. *Echinochloa walteri* inflorescence (Gould and Box 1965).

tant wetland plants for attracting upland game birds, songbirds, and waterfowl (ducks).

Echinochloa walteri (Pursh) Heller **COAST COCKSPUR** (Figure 76) Coarse annuals. Culms to 2 m tall, forming large clumps. Leaf sheaths typically hirsute. Panicles 10–40 cm long, branches erect to appressed, dense. Spikelets 3–5 mm long, narrowly ovate; glumes and lower lemmas scabrous; lower lemmas awned, occasionally awnless; upper florets coriaceous, apex acute to acuminate.

Figure 77. *Eleusine indica*
plant, (A) spikelet, (B) floret, and (C) caryopsis (Gould and Box 1965).

Found along mid and upper Gulf Coast. Highly palatable to cattle, producing forage late in the hot summer period; among the most important wetland plants for attracting upland game birds, songbirds, and waterfowl (ducks).

31. ELEUSINE Gaertn.

Culms solid, flattened. Leaves basal and cauline; sheaths without auricles; ligules a ciliate membrane; blades flat. Panicles of several spicate primary unilateral branches; branches ascending to spreading, digitate, with one or two branches below the whorl. Spikelets laterally compressed, disarticulation above the glumes; florets three to five, reduced florets apical; glumes awnless; lemmas 3-veined, awnless.

Eleusine indica (L.) Gaertn. **GOOSEGRASS** (Figure 77) Tufted or stoloniferous annuals. Culms to 70 cm tall, erect or spreading, somewhat succulent. Leaf sheaths laterally compressed, strongly keeled; ligules ciliate membranes, about 1 mm long; blades 3–8 cm wide. Panicles of spicate primary unilateral branches, digitate or with one or two branches subdigitate; branches flattened, winged, bearing closely

Figure 78. *Elionurus tripsacoides* plant, (A) partial inflorescence, and (B) spikelet pair with sessile and pedicellate spikelets (Hitchcock collection).

spaced spikelets in two rows. Spikelets 3–6 mm long, florets three to six, laterally compressed, glabrous, awnless.

Common to occasional widespread weed of roadsides, gardens, and other disturbed sites throughout Gulf Coast. Poor livestock and wildlife values.

32. ELIONURUS Willd. • Balsamscale

Culms solid. Leaves basal and cauline; ligules a ring of hairs; blades involute or flat. Spicate racemes with the rachis densely pilose. Spikelets dorsally compressed, paired, sessile one fertile, pedicellate one sterile, disarticulation below glumes; glumes indurate, subequal; lemmas membranous, awnless; paleas absent, vestigial or the length of lemmas.

Elionurus tripsacoides Humb. & Bonpl. *ex* Willd. **PAN AMERICAN BALSAMSCALE** (Figure 78) Tufted perennials, usually developing short rhizomes. Culms to 100 cm tall, branching above, sometimes geniculate. Leaf sheaths pubescent, margins densely pilose; blades 1.5–2.5 mm wide with papillose-based hairs above. Spicate racemes with paired spikelets; sessile spikelets 6.5–7.5 mm long, fertile; glumes indurate, awnless; lemmas and paleas awnless. Caryopses 3.7–4.2 mm long. Pedicellate spikelets 4.5–5.5 mm long, staminate.

Occasional to locally abundant on sandy and sandy loam sites. Fair to poor forage. Provides good bird nesting and deer fawning cover. Large seeds provide food for birds and rodents.

33. ELYMUS L. • Wildrye

Culms hollow. Leaf sheaths round; auricles pointed; ligules membranous; blades flat or involute. Spike with two or three spikelets per node, occasionally one or as many as six; rachis continuous. Spikelets with two to six florets, upper florets reduced, disarticulation above the glumes; glume widths variable; lemmas 5-veined.

1. Lemma awns divergently curved when dry; glumes only slightly bowed at base .... *E. canadensis* var. *canadensis*
1. Lemma awns straight when dry; glumes strongly bowed at base ....
.... *E. virginicus*

Elymus canadensis L. var. *canadensis* **CANADA WILDRYE** (Figure 79) Tufted perennials. Culms to 150 cm tall, decumbent. Leaves basal and cauline; auricles fragile, usually developed on either side of sheath and blade junction; blades 4–12 mm wide, glabrous or pubescent. Spikes 8–20 cm long, drooping; spikelets

Figure 79. *Elymus canadensis* var. *canadensis*
plant, (A) spikelet, and (B) floret (palea view) (Hitchcock 1951).

paired or in threes at each node; florets mostly three to five; glumes about equal, slightly broadened and tapering to an awn; lemmas mostly 0.8–1.0 cm long or more with divergent awns 1.5–5 cm long (usually outwardly curving at maturity).

Found throughout mid and upper Gulf Coast, mostly in shaded sites; frequently along fencerows, wooded borders, and in moist ravines on sandy and sandy loam soils of river floodplains. Provides good cool season forage for livestock; young plants valuable forage for deer. Provides nesting cover and seed for birds and fawning cover for deer.

Elymus virginicus L. **VIRGINIA WILDRYE** Tufted perennials. Culms to 120 cm tall, erect or decumbent. Leaves basal and cauline; blades 5–15 mm wide, glaucous, scabrous or minutely pubescent. Spikes usually stiffly erect, often partly enclosed by upper sheath. Spikelets two or three per node; glumes strongly veined, indurate, yellowish, bowed out at base, apex somewhat curved, tapering into a straight awn; lemma awns 5–25 mm long, straight or slightly curved.

Similar in appearance, distribution, and habitat to *E. canadensis*. Both are highly palatable to livestock and wildlife, but being weak perennials, are eliminated from heavily grazed areas.

34. ENTEROPOGON Nees • Windmillgrass

Culms erect, solid or hollow. Leaves basal and cauline; sheaths round; ligules a ciliate membrane; blades flat, linear. Panicles of several verticillate (occasionally single) spicate primary unilateral branches. Spikelets dorsally compressed, disarticulation above the glumes; florets two, the lower fertile, the upper staminate; rachilla extending into an awn; glumes lanceolate, acute, short-awned; lemmas 3-veined, midvein prominent, apex bifid, awned. Caryopsis narrowly elliptic, pericarp free.

Enteropogon chlorideus (J. Presl) W. Clayton **BURYSEED WINDMILLGRASS** (Figure 80) Rhizomatous perennials. Culms to 1 m tall, erect, glabrous. Leaves glabrous; ligules ciliate membranes; blades to 1 cm wide. Panicles of 3–12 spicate primary unilateral branches; branches 8–15 cm long, verticillate. Large cleistogamous spikelets borne on slender underground rhizomes. Aerial spikelets 7–15 mm long, tawny, four per cm of branch; glumes unequal; lower lemmas dorsally compressed, acuminate, margins ciliate, awned from between setaceous teeth, awn 6–15 mm long.

Infrequent in dune areas of lower to mid Gulf Coast. Poor forage.

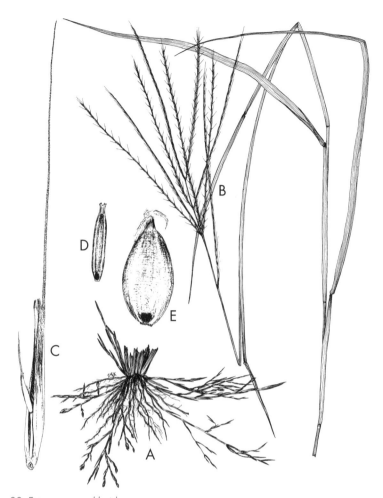

Figure 80. *Enteropogon chlorideus*
(A) plant base with cleistogamous spikelet on the rhizomes, (B) inflorescence with aerial spikelets,
(C) florets of aerial spikelets (glumes not illustrated), (D) caryopsis of aerial spikelet, and
(E) caryopsis of cleistogamous spikelet (Gould and Box 1965).

35. **ERAGROSTIS** Wolf · Lovegrass

Culms hollow. Leaves basal and cauline, sheaths without auricles, ligules a ciliate membrane or ring of hairs (rarely membranous). Panicles open or contracted, or rarely, with spicate primary unilateral branches. Spikelets with 3–30 florets, awnless, disarticulation above glumes; sterile florets above fertile florets, or absent; glumes shorter than first floret; lemmas 3-veined, usually conspicuous, entire, glabrous to scabrous; paleas may persist on rachilla.

1. Plants annual, without buds in basal sheaths 2
1. Plants perennial, with buds in basal sheaths 9
2(1). Plants with all florets unisexual, dioecious .... *E. reptans*
2. Plants with some perfect florets 3
3(2). Palea keels with cilia 0.5–0.8 mm long .... *E. ciliaris*
3. Palea keels scabrous or with cilia shorter than 0.1 mm 4
4(3). Plants prostrate, mat-forming and rooting at nodes .... *E. hypnoides*
4. Plants erect, or if decumbent, not prostrate and rooting at nodes 5
5(4). Spikelets 2.0–3.4 mm long .... *E. capillaris*
5. Spikelets 4 mm or longer, or if shorter, panicle less than one-half plant height 6
6(5). Keel of lemmas with glandular projections; panicle branches with glandular areas .... *E. cilianensis*
6. Keel of lemmas without glandular projections; panicle branches without glandular areas 7
7(6). Culms with glandular ring below nodes .... *E. barrelieri*
7. Culms without glandular ring below nodes 8
8(7). Pedicels appressed to panicle branches .... *E. pectinacea* var. *pectinacea*
8. Pedicels spreading (in part) from panicle branches ....
.... *E. pectinacea* var. *miserrima*
9(1). Spikelets sessile or with pedicels shorter than 1 mm (except for terminal spikelets on each branch) 10
9. Spikelets with at least some pedicels longer than 1 mm (excluding terminal spikelets in each branch) 13
10(9). Spikelets 3–5 mm wide .... *E. secundiflora* ssp. *oxylepis*
10. Spikelets less than 3 mm wide 11
11(10). Second glumes 3–6 mm long .... *E. sessilispica*
11. Second glumes 1.2–2.5 mm long 12
12(11). Inflorescence branches capillary; first glumes 1.1 mm or shorter ....
.... *E. refracta*
12. Inflorescence branches stiff, not capillary; first glumes 1.2 mm or longer
.... *E. curtipedicellata*
13(9). Lateral veins of lemma obscure 14
13. Lateral veins of lemma prominent 16
14(13). Spikelets with two to six florets .... *E. hirsuta*
14. Spikelets with 5–11 florets 15
15(14). Lower panicle branches verticillate; spikelets linear, 1 mm wide or less

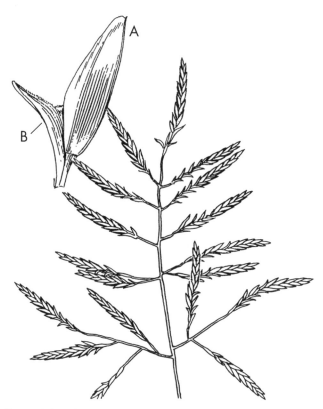

Figure 81. *Eragrostis barrelieri*
inflorescence, (A) floret (lemma), and (B) persistent palea from a lower floret (Hitchcock 1951).

Grasses of the Texas Gulf Prairies and Marshes

Eragrostis barrelieri Daveau **MEDITERRANEAN LOVEGRASS** (Figure 81) Low, tufted annuals. Culms to 50 cm tall, ascending to decumbent, branching at lower nodes; nodes with glandular ring below. Leaf sheaths pilose at throat; blades to 10 cm long. Panicles 5–16 cm long, little-branched. Spikelets 5–11 mm long; florets 6–15, linear to oblong, rachilla persistent; glumes unequal; lemmas membranous, gray-green; paleas hyaline.

Usually grows as a weed on disturbed sites, especially graded roadsides of mid and lower Gulf Coast. Poor livestock and wildlife values.

Eragrostis capillaris (L). Nees **LACEGRASS** Tufted annuals. Culms to 50 cm tall. Leaf sheaths overlapping, throat and margins hispid; blades 15–30 cm long, 2–4 mm wide, scattered papillose-hispid above. Panicles 5–15 cm long, branches capillary, ascending to spreading. Spikelets about 2 mm long, 1 mm wide, florets two to five, pedicellate, lanceolate to ovate, laterally compressed, rachilla persistent; glumes unequal, hyaline, acuminate, awnless; lower lemmas about 1.5 m long, membranous, greenish to plumbeous, lateral veins inconspicuous; paleas hyaline, about one-half the length of lemmas, persistent, keels ciliolate.

Infrequent in dry wooded openings of upper Gulf Coast. Frequently confused with small, early flowering plants of *E. lugens*. Poor livestock and wildlife values.

Eragrostis cilianensis (All.) Janchen **STINKGRASS** (Figure 82) Low, weedy annuals. Culms to 60 cm tall, branching at base and above, frequently geniculate, usually with ring of glands below nodes. Leaf sheaths with glandular pits or projections on or near keel; blades 2.5–7.0 mm wide, glabrous with glandular pits or projections in midrib on lower surfaces. Panicles 5.5–16.0 cm long, open, densely spikeleted. Spikelets 6–20 mm long, florets 12–40, gray-green, slightly compressed; glumes membranous, broadly to narrowly ovate, acute to subacute, keels with glandular pits or projections; lower lemmas 2–3 mm long, lateral veins conspicuous, usually glandular pits or projections on keels; paleas persistent, hyaline, keels ciliolate.

Old World species widely established as a weed of roadsides and other disturbed sites throughout Gulf Coast; especially well adapted to loamy clay bottomlands. Poor livestock and wildlife values.

Eragrostis ciliaris (L.) R. Br. **GOPHERTAIL LOVEGRASS** (Figure 83) Tufted annuals. Culms to 55 cm tall. Leaf sheaths pilose at throat; blades flat, 4–10 cm long, 2 mm wide with hairs above ligule. Panicles 4–10 cm long, dense to somewhat open, interrupted at base and occasionally above. Spikelets 2–3 mm long,

Figure 82. *Eragrostis cilianensis*
plant, (A) spikelet, (B) floret (lemma), and (C) palea of a lower floret (Hitchcock 1951).

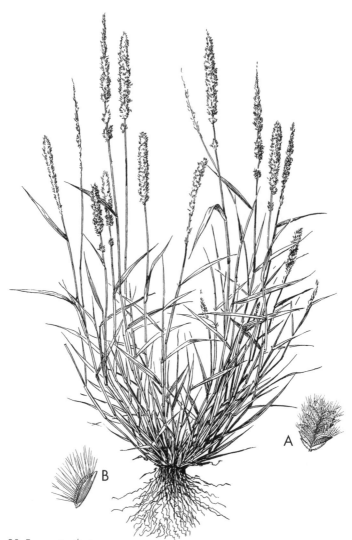

Figure 83. *Eragrostis ciliaris*
plant, (A) spikelet, and (B) floret (Hitchcock 1951).

florets 6–12, subsessile, broadly ovate; glumes hyaline; lower lemmas 1–2 mm long, hyaline, loosely overlapping, greenish-white, linear-oblong, blunt; paleas long-ciliate, keel hairs 0.4–0.8 mm long.

Infrequent along upper Gulf Coast. Poor livestock and wildlife values.

Eragrostis curtipedicellata Buckl. **GUMMY LOVEGRASS** (Figure 84) Tufted perennials. Culms to 60 cm tall, viscid. Leaf sheaths overlapping, pilose at throat, frequently viscid; blades about 10 cm long, 4 mm wide, flat, glabrous. Panicles 30–45 cm long, open; branches and pedicels viscid, scabrous. Spikelets 4–5 mm long, florets four to ten, subsessile, compressed, rachilla disarticulating; first glumes 1.2–1.5 mm long, second glumes 1.8–2.0 mm long; lower lemmas about 2 mm long, membranous, tinged greenish to reddish to straw colored, ovate, acute, lateral veins conspicuous; paleas membranous, keels ciliate.

Occasional in tight sandy clay and sandy loam soils throughout Gulf Coast. Poor livestock and wildlife values.

Figure 84. *Eragrostis curtipedicellata*
inflorescence and spikelet (Gould and Box 1965).

Eragrostis curvula (Schrad.) Nees **WEEPING LOVEGRASS** (Figure 85) Large, tufted perennials. Culms to 150 cm tall. Leaves with basal sheaths densely villous on back near base; blades involute, bristly; basal blades much longer and arching toward ground; culm blades 20–30 cm long, 1.0–1.4 mm wide. Panicles 25–40 cm long, open, nodding; branches slender, ascending to spreading. Spikelets with

Figure 85. *Eragrostis curvula*
plant base, inflorescence, and spikelet (Gould 1978).

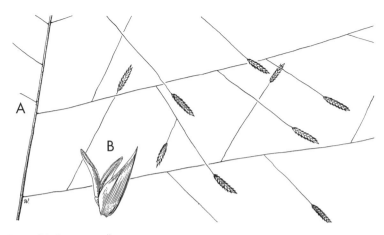

Figure 86. *Eragrostis elliottii*
(A) inflorescence and (B) floret (lemma and palea, and a persistent palea of an upper floret)
(Hitchcock 1951).

6–12 florets, rachilla disarticulating; first glumes about 1.8 mm long; second glumes about 2.8 mm long; lower lemmas 2.2–2.7 mm long, gray-green, acute, lateral veins conspicuous; paleas hyaline, keels scabrous. Caryopses about 1.4 mm long.

Common reclamation and pasture species especially adapted to sandy soils. Good forage producer but low palatability when mature. Good wildlife nesting cover and seed producer.

Eragrostis elliottii S. Wats. **ELLIOTT LOVEGRASS** (Figure 86) Tufted perennials. Culms to 75 cm tall, ascending. Leaf sheaths overlapping, pilose at throat, otherwise glabrous; blades 6–30 cm long, 2–4 mm wide, glabrous. Panicles 30–60 cm long, open; branches capillary, scabrous, stiffly ascending to spreading, fragile. Spikelets 4.5–18.0 mm long, florets 6–30, pedicellate, linear-oblong, strongly compressed; glumes acuminate; lateral veins of lemmas conspicuous; paleas scabrous on keels, persistent.

Found in sandy, piney woods of upper Gulf Coast.

Eragrostis hirsuta (Michx.) Nees **BIGTOP LOVEGRASS** Tufted perennials. Culms to 1 m tall, ascending. Leaf sheaths hirsute on margins; blades 20–40 cm long, attenuate. Panicles 20–55 cm long, 10–25 cm wide, ovate, open. Spikelets 2–4 mm long, florets two to six; glumes unequal, acuminate; lower lemmas 2.0–2.5 mm long with inconspicuous lateral nerves; paleas ciliolate on keels, persistent.

Found on sand and sandy loam soils in woodlands of upper Gulf Coast.

Figure 87. *Eragrostis lugens*
(A) plant base, (B) inflorescence branches, and (C) floret with palea of an upper floret (Gould and Box 1965).

Eragrostis hypnoides (Lam.) B.S.P. **TEAL LOVEGRASS** Mat-forming annuals. Culms to 25 cm tall, rooting at nodes, creeping. Leaf sheaths much shorter than culm internodes, usually with a ring of hairs at base, throat and margins pilose; blades 0.5–2.5 cm long, 0.5–1.5 mm wide, flat. Panicles 2–5 cm long, open. Spikelets 5–12 mm long; florets 8–22, short-pedicellate, compressed, rachilla persistent; first glumes about one-half the length of second glumes; lower lemmas 1.8–2.0 mm long, lateral veins conspicuous; paleas hyaline, persistent, keels ciliolate.

Occasional along upper Gulf Coast on mud and sandbars in streams, rivers, lakes, and pond margins. Spikelets eaten by ducks.

Eragrostis intermedia A. S. Hitchc. **PLAINS LOVEGRASS** Strongly tufted perennials. Culms to 90 cm tall, unbranched. Leaf sheaths glabrous except for pilose throat, margins usually pilose; blades to 40 cm long, 2.0–5.5 mm wide. Panicles 20–40 cm long, open; branches 10–25 cm long, ascending to spreading, scabrous. Spikelets 4–7 mm long, 1.4–1.8 mm wide; florets 5–11; glumes membranous, first glumes 1.2–1.8 mm long; second glumes 1.4–2.0 mm long; lower lemmas 1.8–2.2 mm long, loosely imbricate, lateral veins inconspicuous; paleas ciliolate on keels, persistent on rachilla.

Common throughout Gulf Coast, often in disturbed sites. Good to fair forage; provides bird nesting cover.

Eragrostis lugens Nees **MOURNING LOVEGRASS** (Figure 87) Perennial bunchgrasses. Culms to 70 cm tall, erect or ascending. Leaf sheaths overlapping, pilose at throat; blades 8–20 cm long, 1–2 mm wide, involute, attenuate. Panicles 18–28 cm long, open, many-spikeleted; branches 9–15 cm long, slender, lower ones mostly verticillate. Spikelets 3.0–4.5 mm long, 0.5–1.0 mm wide; florets five to seven, pedicellate, longer than pedicels, linear-lanceolate, compressed; glumes hyaline, unequal, ovate, acute to subacuminate; first glumes 0.6–1.0 mm long; second glumes 1.1–1.4 mm long; lower lemmas 1.5–1.6 mm long, membranous, usually shiny-plumbeous, ovate, acute; paleas persistent on rachilla, hyaline, keels cililate.

Frequent on many sites throughout Gulf Coast; best adapted to sandy soils. Flowering as early as January, and almost continuously, throughout the year. Fair forage; provides bird nesting cover.

Eragrostis pectinacea (Michx.) Nees *ex* Steud. var. *pectinacea* **SPREADING LOVEGRASS** Tufted annuals. Culms to 55 cm tall, geniculate, branching at lower nodes. Leaf sheaths shorter than internodes; blades 8–18 cm long, 3–7 mm wide, flat. Panicles 12–30 cm long, much-branched, open. Spikelets 5–8 mm long, 1–2 mm wide; florets 8–14, narrowly lanceolate or linear; glumes hyaline, unequal; lower lemmas 0.8–2.2 mm long, gray-green; paleas hyaline, keels ciliolate, persistent. Caryopses about 1 mm long, ellipsoidal.

Found along mid to upper Gulf Coast in disturbed sites.

var. *miserrima* (Fourn.) J. Reeder Distinguished from var. *pectinacea* by smaller size and less imbricate lemmas.

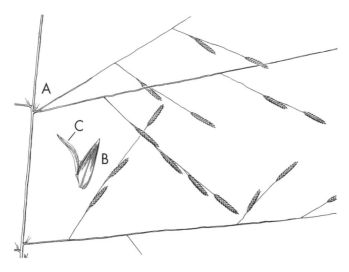

Figure 88. *Eragrostis refracta*
(A) inflorescence, (B) floret (lemma), and (C) palea of an upper floret (Hitchcock 1951).

Eragrostis refracta (Ell.) Scribn. **COASTAL LOVEGRASS** (Figure 88) Tufted perennials. Culms to 80 cm tall, ascending. Leaves basal and cauline; blades 10–25 cm long, 2–5 mm wide, dense hair above ligule. Panicles 30–60 cm long, open, few-spikeleted; branches 10–20 cm long, capillary, stiff but not straight, scabrous, spreading to reflexed. Spikelets 5–16 mm long, 1.5–2.0 mm wide, sessile to subsessile, strongly compressed; florets 10–28; glumes unequal, acuminate; lower lemmas 1.4–2.2 mm long, tinged greenish- to reddish-purple, lateral veins conspicuous; paleas scabrous on keel.

Found in sandy, piney woods of upper Gulf Coast.

Eragrostis reptans (Michx.) Nees **CREEPING LOVEGRASS** (Figure 89) Stoloniferous, dioecious, mat-forming, annuals. Culms to 20 cm tall, rooting at lower nodes. Leaves cauline, minutely puberulent; sheaths short, membranous on margins; ligules a minute fringe of hairs; blades 1–4 cm, flat or folded. Pistillate and staminate panicles similar, capitate, central axis short. Spikelets 8–20 mm long, laterally compressed, borne in irregular clusters; florets 15–35 on zigzag rachilla; glumes unequal, awnless, first glumes one-third to two-thirds the length of second glumes; lower lemmas 2–3 mm long, awnless, apex acute; paleas membranous, margins pubescent.

Locally abundant throughout Gulf Coast on poorly drained sites with fine-textured soils. Frequently present in solid stands of "hog wallows" and drying lake beds.

Eragrostis secundiflora Presl ssp. *oxylepis* (Torr.) S. D. Koch **RED LOVEGRASS** (Figure 90) Tufted perennials, highly variable in size, color, and general aspect. Culms 10–90 cm long, coarse, few in clusters. Foliage glabrous except for a few long hairs on the blades. Panicles 5–15 cm or longer, dense; spikelets crowded. Spikelets with 10–26 florets, laterally flattened, pale green or violet to reddish-brown; glumes and lemmas glabrous, sharply keeled; lower lemmas 3–4 mm long, strongly 3-veined; paleas membranous, not persistent on rachilla.

Occasional to frequent on deep sands and sandy loam sites throughout Gulf Coast. Poor livestock and wildlife values.

Eragrostis sessilispica Buckl. **TUMBLE LOVEGRASS** (Figure 91) Tufted perennials. Culms 30–90 cm tall, wiry. Leaf sheaths overlapping below; ligules 2–3 mm long, a ring of hairs. Panicles 15–30 cm or longer, over one-half the length of the culms, breaking off at maturity to become a tumbleweed; spikelets sessile on and appressed to stiff, curving inflorescence branches; branches not viscid. Spikelets 5.0–12.5 mm long, florets 5–12; glumes persistent, unequal; lower lemmas 3–5 mm long, lateral veins conspicuous; paleas indurate.

Most frequent on heavily grazed, open sandy prairies throughout Gulf Coast; increases under heavy grazing. Poor livestock and wildlife values.

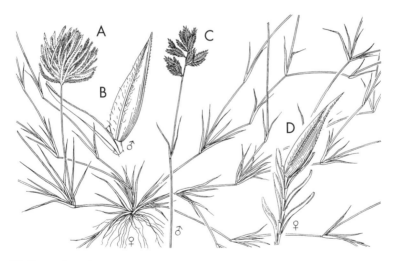

Figure 89. *Eragrostis reptans*
plant, (A) pistillate inflorescence, (B) pistillate floret, (C) staminate inflorescence, and (D) staminate floret (Hitchcock 1951).

Figure 90. *Eragrostis secundiflora* ssp. *oxylepis* inflorescence and spikelet (Gould and Box 1965).

Eragrostis silveana Swallen **SILVEUS LOVEGRASS** Tufted perennials from knotty, rhizomatous bases. Culms to 60 cm tall, usually viscid. Leaf sheaths overlapping, viscid, upper margins pilose; blades 8–25 cm long, 2–4 mm wide. Panicles 20–30 cm long, open, commonly viscid above; branches 6–12 cm long, capillary, ascending to spreading. Spikelets 3.5–5.0 mm long, about 1 mm wide, florets four to nine, pedicellate, linear to oblong, compressed; glumes chartaceous, unequal; lower lemmas about 1.4 mm long, chartaceous, reddish-purple, lateral veins conspicuous and sometimes double; paleas hyaline, keels ciliate. Caryopses about 0.6 mm long, broadly ellipsoidal.

Infrequent, usually associated with buffalograss and other short grasses on open prairie sites of mid Gulf Coast.

Eragrostis spectabilis (Pursh) Steud. **PURPLE LOVEGRASS** (Figure 92) Perennial bunchgrasses from a knotty, rhizomatous base. Culms to 55 cm tall, erect, unbranched. Leaf blades 1.5–2.5 mm wide, flat. Panicles 25–45 cm long, open, ovate, readily breaking off at base to become a tumbleweed at maturity. Spikelets 4–7 mm long, purple-tinged, florets 7–11, linear-oblong, pedicellate; glumes unequal; lower lemmas 1.8–2.2 mm long, lateral veins conspicuous; palea keels ciliolate.

Occasional on sandy sites, especially in open woodlands, throughout Gulf Coast. Poor livestock and wildlife values.

Figure 91. *Eragrostis sessilispica* inflorescence and spikelet (Gould and Box 1965).

Eragrostis swallenii A. S. Hitchc. **SWALLEN LOVEGRASS** Tufted perennials. Culms to 70 cm tall with a glandular band below the nodes. Leaf blades 10–20 cm long, 2–4 mm wide. Panicles 20–35 cm long, open; branches mostly simple, ascending to spreading, stiffly flexuous; pedicels frequently with a glandular band. Spikelets 6–16 mm long; florets 8–25, pedicellate, laterally compressed; first glumes about 1.4 mm long; second glumes about 1.8 mm long; lower lemmas about 2 mm long, lateral veins conspicuous, dull green; palea keels scabrous.

Occurs on sandy soils of lower and mid Gulf Coast.

36. **ERIOCHLOA** Kunth in H.B.K. • Cupgrass
(adapted from Shaw and Webster 1987)
Culms solid, terete. Leaves basal and/or cauline; ligules a ring of hairs; blades flat or involute. Panicles of a few to several, short spicate primary unilateral branches; branches usually appressed. Spikelets dorsally compressed, disarticulation below the glumes; florets two, lower reduced, upper perfect; first glumes reduced to a cup or disk; second glumes and sterile lemmas similar in size and texture, acuminate; upper lemmas indurate, minutely rugose, apiculate or short-awned.

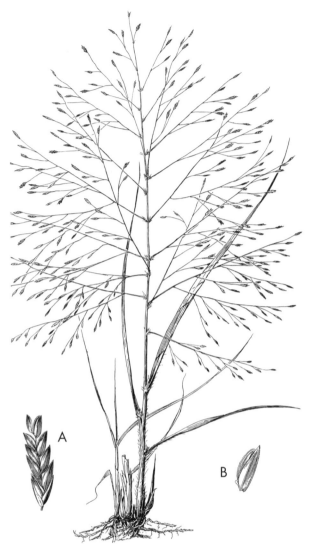

Figure 92. *Eragrostis spectabilis*
plant, (A) spikelet, and (B) floret (lemma view) (Hitchcock 1951).

1. Lemma of upper florets with mucro shorter than 0.2 mm, second glume awnless .... ***E. sericea***
1. Lemma of upper florets with awn longer than 0.2 mm, or with second glume awned 2
2(1). Pedicel apex with long, straight hairs .... ***E. pseudoacrotricha***
2. Pedicel apex without long, straight hairs 3

3(2).　Plants perennial; spikelets 4–5 mm long; upper lemma awn 1.0–1.5 mm long .... ***E. punctata***

　　3.　Plants annual; spikelets 3.5–4.0 mm long; upper lemma awn 0.5–0.8 mm long .... ***E. contracta***

Eriochloa contracta A. S. Hitchc. **PRAIRIE CUPGRASS** (Figure 93) Tufted annuals. Culms to 80 cm tall, erect or geniculate, nodes puberulent. Leaves basal

Figure 93. *Eriochloa contracta*
plant, (A) spikelet, and (B) floret (palea view)
(Gould and Box 1965).

Grasses of the Texas Gulf Prairies and Marshes

and cauline; sheaths and blades, at least the lower, pubescent with minute, spreading or reflexed hairs; blades 2–7 mm wide, usually not more than 5 mm. Panicles 6–15 cm long with 6–15 erect to appressed spicate primary unilateral branches; branches 1–2 cm long, densely hirsute with short, stiff hairs. Spikelets 3.5–4.0 mm long; first glumes absent; second glumes and lemma of lower florets appressed-hispid, short awn-tipped; lemma of upper florets mucronate with an awn usually 0.5–0.8 mm long.

Occasional in moist sandy sites, often occurring along ditches, swales, and watercourses of mid and upper Gulf Coast. Poor forage.

Eriochloa pseudoacrotricha (Stapf *ex* Thell.) C. E. Hubb. *ex* S. T. Blake Tufted perennials. Culms 40–80 cm tall, erect, nodes hairy. Leaves cauline; sheaths smooth, glabrous; ligules 0.4–1.0 mm long; blades 2–4 mm wide, flat. Panicles of two to eight spicate primary unilateral branches; branches 25–50 mm long, winged, glabrous with loosely arranged spikelets. Spikelets 3.5–5.5 mm long; first glumes absent; second glumes 0.5–1.5 mm long, hairy, acuminate, awned; lower florets neuter; upper floret lemmas 2.1–3.8 mm long, elliptic, awned; upper lemma awns 0.4–1.0 mm long.

Found in roadsides and ditches of Cameron, Kenedy, and Kleberg Counties. Probably introduced from Australia by accident.

Eriochloa punctata (L.) Desv. *ex* Hamilton **LOUISIANA CUPGRASS** Coarse tufted perennials. Culms to 110 cm or longer, decumbent. Leaf blades mostly 5–10 mm wide, flat. Panicles 8–18 cm long; spicate primary unilateral branches 8–15; branches 2–6 cm long, erect, appressed; axis, branches and pedicels puberulent or pubescent. Spikelets 4–5 mm long, first glumes absent; second glumes and lemma of lower florets sparsely appressed-pilose, second glumes often short-awned; lemma of upper florets awn-tipped, awn 1.0–1.5 mm long.

Occasional in swales, ditches, and moist habitats of lower and mid Gulf Coast.

Eriochloa sericea (Scheele) Munro *ex* Vasey **TEXAS CUPGRASS** (Figure 94) Moderately tall, tufted perennials. Culms 50–100 cm tall; nodes, at least the lower, densely white-pubescent. Leaves basal and cauline, puberulent near hairy ligule and collar; blades 10–20 cm long, 3–6 mm wide, involute upon drying. Panicles narrow, contracted; spicate primary unilateral branches four to ten, widely spaced, erect; axis and branches ciliate or villous; glumes and lemma of lower florets appressed-hirsute, awnless; lower lemmas 3.6–4.2 mm long; upper lemmas awn-tipped, rugose.

Figure 94. *Eriochloa sericea*
plant, (A) spikelet, and (B) floret (palea view) (Gould and Box 1965).

Frequent to locally abundant on clay and clay loam prairie sites throughout Gulf Coast. Good forage, persisting in overgrazed pastures only under the protection of shrubs.

37. **ERIONEURON** Nash • Erioneuron

Culms solid, slightly flattened. Leaves basal; sheaths keeled; auricles absent; ligules a ciliate membrane; blades often involute with a white cartilaginous margin. Panicles or racemes short and capitate or contracted. Spikelets laterally compressed, disarticulation above the glumes; florets six to ten; reduced florets at apex;

Figure 95. *Erioneuron pilosum* plant and floret (Hitchcock 1951).

glumes shorter than florets; lemmas 3-veined, emarginate or lobed, veins ciliate basally, awned from midvein.

Erioneuron pilosum (Buckl.) Nash **HAIRY ERIONEURON** (Figure 95) Low tufted or stoloniferous perennials. Culms to 30 cm tall, typically with only one node elevated above basal leaves. Leaf blades 2–8 cm long, 1–2 mm wide, thick, flat, glabrous, abruptly pointed; margins thick and white. Panicles or racemes mostly 2–3 cm long, contracted with four to nine large, pale spikelets. Spikelets mostly 10–16 mm long; florets 7–18; glumes 4.5–6.0 mm long; lower lemmas densely ciliate, 3-veined, pubescent with long, silvery hairs on veins, margins, and interveins near base; lemma awn 1–2 mm long from notched apex.

In dry, open sites on sandy or caliche soils of lower and mid Gulf Coast. Poor forage for both wildlife and livestock.

38. **EUSTACHYS** Desv.

Culms solid. Leaves mostly basal; sheaths keeled; ligules a ring of hairs; blades flat or folded. Panicles of several spicate primary branches; branches digitate or subdigitate. Spikelets laterally compressed, disarticulation above the glumes; florets two, lower fertile, upper sterile; glumes unequal, second glumes mucronate; lemmas pubescent on keels.

1. Upper (sterile) lemmas 1.3–1.5 mm long; spikelets pale brown to golden; lower lemma margins pubescent throughout .... *E. caribea*
1. Upper (sterile) lemmas 0.8–1.2 mm long; spikelets dark brown to blackish (when mature); lower lemma margins glabrous on lower one-half to two-thirds .... *E. petraea*

Eustachys caribea (Spreng.) Herter Tufted, rhizomatous perennials. Culms to 70 cm tall. Leaf sheaths keeled, usually glabrous; ligules 0.5–1.0 mm long, a ciliate membrane; blades to 20 cm long, 6–10 mm wide, glabrous, folded. Panicles of four to nine spicate primary unilateral branches; branches 4–9 cm long, digitate, ascending with spikelets in two rows. Spikelets with two florets; first glumes 1.0–1.3 mm long, acute; second glumes 2.0–2.6 mm long, apex lobed, awn 0.5–0.8 mm long; lower lemmas 2.5–3.2 mm long, 3-veined, margins pilose; upper lemma obconic, truncate.

Infrequent along upper Gulf Coast.

Eustachys petraea (Sw.) Desv. **STIFFLEAF EUSTACHYS** (Figure 96) Stoloniferous or tufted perennials. Culms to 120 cm tall, glabrous. Leaf blades obtuse, scabrous. Panicles with two to eight spicate primary unilateral branches; branches 4–12 cm long, digitate to subdigitate. Spikelets 15–30 per cm, widely divergent, closely imbricate; glumes unequal, glabrous except for scabrous midvein; first glumes 0.9–1.5 mm long, narrowly lanceolate; second glumes 1.1–1.7 mm long, nearly linear, short-awned, apex lobed; lemma of lower florets 1.1–1.5 mm long, dark brown at maturity, pilose on upper one-half to three-fourths, apex awnless or mucronate; sterile florets 0.8–1.0 long, cylindrical, truncate, glabrous below, scabrous above, awnless or short-mucronate.

Figure 96. *Eustachys petraea* inflorescence and spikelet (Gould and Box 1965).

Occasional on sandy and sandy loam soils, usually in moist situations near permanent brackish water, islands, and dredge materials throughout Gulf Coast. Poor livestock and wildlife values.

39. **GLYCERIA** R. Br. • Mannagrass

Culms hollow. Leaves basal and cauline; sheath margins connate; ligules membranous; blades flat, folded or involute. Panicles open or contracted, branches usually flexuous. Spikelets laterally compressed, disarticulation above the glumes; florets two to several, reduced floret apical; glumes unequal, shorter than first lemma; lemmas (5-) 7- (9-)-veined, veins strongly and uniformly developed, parallel; paleas 2-veined.

Figure 97. *Glyceria septentrionalis* inflorescence and floret (lemma view) (Hitchcock 1951).

Glyceria septentrionalis A. S. Hitchc. **EASTERN MANNAGRASS** (Figure 97) Robust perennials. Culms to 1.8 m long, thick, often rooting at lower nodes. Leaves with ligules 3–6 mm long, membranous; blades 4–10 mm wide, elongate. Panicles 18–40 cm long; branches 3–12 cm long, stiff, usually erect. Spikelets 0.8–3.0 cm long; florets 7–20, widely spaced; glumes hyaline, margins thin, apex erose; first glumes 2–5 mm long; second glumes slightly longer; lower lemmas 3.5–5.0 mm long, scabrous, apex broad, erose.

Found usually in moist or marshy ground, often in woodlands of upper Gulf Coast.

40. GYMNOPOGON Beauv. • Skeletongrass

Culms solid. Leaves cauline, conspicuously distichous; sheaths rounded; ligules membranous, minute; blades flat or folded. Panicles open; branches spicate, widely spaced, stiffly spreading, one or two per node over the upper 20 cm of the culm apex. Spikelets laterally compressed, disarticulation above glumes; florets two, lower fertile, upper sterile; glumes subequal; lemmas 3-veined, shorter than glumes, lemmas awned from notched apex.

Gymnopogon ambiguus (Michx.) B.S.P. **BEARDED SKELETONGRASS** (Figure 98) Perennials from hard, knotty, rhizomatous bases. Culms to 60 cm tall, slender, branching; nodes many. Leaves numerous, short, overlapping; blades 3–10 cm long, 4–15 mm wide, stiff, spreading or deflexed, abruptly narrowed at base. Panicles 10–25 cm long, wider than long, large, open; spikelets appressed on numerous widely spreading spicate branches, slender, widely spaced. Lower spikelets of branches successively more widely spaced, lowermost one or two spikelets often rudimentary. Spikelets with two florets, lower perfect, upper rudimentary, usually reduced to a stipitate awn 2–5 mm long; glumes 4–6 mm long, about equal, narrow, 1-veined, vein scabrous, tapering to narrow point; lemmas 3-veined with long awns from minutely notched apex.

Found on sand or sandy clay soils, usually under shade trees along upper Gulf Coast.

41. HAINARDIA Greuter

Culms solid. Leaves cauline; sheath margins connate at base; ligules membranous; blades narrow. Spikes cylindrical with embedded spikelets. Spikelets solitary, dorsally compressed, disarticulation below spikelets; florets one; glumes one; lemmas awnless, 3-veined, membranous.

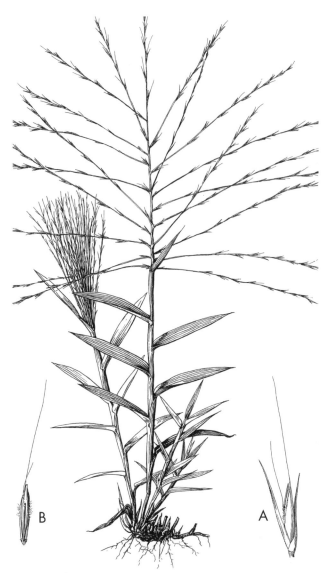

Figure 98. *Gymnopogon ambiguus*
plant, (A) spikelet, and (B) floret (palea view) (Hitchcock 1951).

Hainardia cylindrica (Willd.) Tutin **THINTAIL** (Figure 99) Tufted annuals.
Culms to 30 cm tall, erect to spreading to prostrate, much-branched. Leaves with
ligules truncate; blades to 7 cm long. Spikes to 25 cm long, straight or curved,
cylindrical, rachis disarticulating at maturity; spikelets appear embedded in rachis. Spikelets 3–8 mm long, floret one; first glumes absent, except on terminal

spikelet; second glumes about 6 mm long, indurate; lemmas 3-veined, hyaline; paleas shorter than lemmas, hyaline.

Occasional on clay loam banks along upper Gulf Coast.

42. **HEMARTHRIA** R. Br.

Culms solid. Leaves basal and cauline; sheaths rounded; ligules a ciliate membrane; blades usually flat. Spicate racemes terminal and axillary on culms with

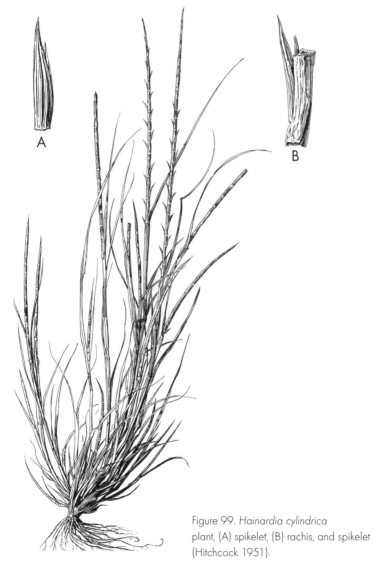

Figure 99. *Hainardia cylindrica* plant, (A) spikelet, (B) rachis, and spikelet (Hitchcock 1951).

paired spikelets; sessile spikelets fertile, pedicellate spikelets sterile. Sessile spike-lets dorsally compressed, disarticulation below sessile spikelets, awnless; sessile spikelets glumes subequal, lemmas membranous, paleas membranous.

Hemarthria altissima (Poir.) Stapf & Hubb. **AFRICAN JOINTTAIL** (Figure 100)
Coarse tufted perennials. Culms to 100 cm tall, decumbent at base, flattened, nodes numerous, internodes short. Leaves with ligules a ciliate membrane, lacerate; blades 3–5 mm wide. Spicate racemes 3–5 cm long, emerging from upper leaf sheaths. Spikelets paired, awnless; sessile spikelets 5–7 mm long; upper lemmas 4.5 mm long, awnless; upper paleas about 3.5 mm long. Caryopses to 2 mm long, brown.

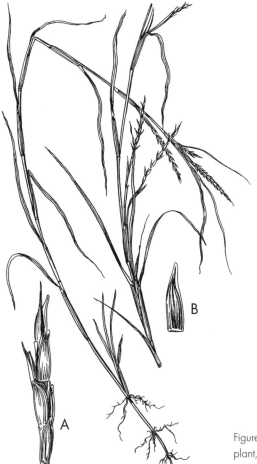

Figure 100. *Hemarthria altissima* plant, (A) partial inflorescence, and (B) sessile spikelet (first glume view) (Hitchcock 1951).

Infrequent on moist ditch banks and other disturbed areas of lower and mid Gulf Coast. Good livestock forage; poor wildlife value.

43. **HETEROPOGON** Pers.

Culms solid, flattened. Leaves basal and cauline; sheaths conspicuously keeled; ligules a ciliate membrane; blades flat or folded. Spicate racemes appearing one-sided; spikelets paired, sessile one fertile, pedicellate one sterile; basal spikelet pairs usually sterile, awnless; sessile spikelets with glumes equal; upper lemma awns twice-geniculate.

Heteropogon contortus (L.) Beauv. ex Roem. & Schult. **TANGLEHEAD** (Figure 101) Tufted perennials. Culms 20–80 cm tall, much-branched at base. Leaf sheaths flattened, keeled; blades 6–20 cm or longer, mostly 4–6 (rarely 10) mm wide. Spicate racemes mostly 4–7 cm long (excluding awns). Spikelets in pairs, one sessile and one pediceled, lower few to several pairs staminate or neuter, awnless; remaining sessile spikelets perfect; calluses sharp-pointed, bearded; lemma awns dark colored, geniculate, twisted. Staminate or neuter spikelets 7–10 mm long; glumes broad, thin, green, several-veined, glabrous or sparsely hispid. Perfect spikelets 5–8 mm long; glumes narrow, rounded, dark colored, several-veined, brownish-hispid; lemma awn of perfect florets 5–12 cm long, hispid, weakly twice-geniculate, dark brown.

Occasional to frequent along lower and mid Gulf Coast. Once common in coastal prairies, now persists only in well managed pastures; decreases under grazing. Good forage for livestock; good nesting cover for birds and fawning cover for deer.

44. **HILARIA** Kunth

Culms solid. Leaves basal and cauline; sheaths open; ligules a ciliate membrane or ring of hairs; blades flat or involute, narrow. Spikes with three sessile spikelets per node on a wavy or zigzag rachis. Spikelets disarticulating from rachis as a unit; lateral spikelets two, staminate with two florets; central spikelets one, perfect with one floret, lemma 3-veined.

Hilaria belangeri (Steud.) Nash **COMMON CURLYMESQUITE** (Figure 102) Low stoloniferous, sod-forming perennials. Culms to 130 cm tall, erect, wiry; nodes bearded. Leaves basal; ligules membranous, lacerate; blades 1–2 (–3) cm long, involute, scabrous to pilose. Spikes 2–4 cm long, exserted with three spikelets per node. Spikelet clusters 4–6 mm long; lateral spikelets with two florets, staminate;

Figure 101. *Heteropogon contortus* plant and spikelet (Hitchcock 1951).

central spikelets with one perfect floret. Glumes of central spikelets with awn to 5 mm long.

Frequent to locally abundant on clay prairie sites; increases with heavy grazing. Often associated with buffalograss and similar vegetatively, but can be distinguished by pubescent culm nodes. Palatable to livestock but only fair grazing value because of its short stature.

Figure 102. *Hilaria belangeri*
plant and (A and B) two views of three spikelet clusters (Gould and Box 1965).

45. HOLCUS L.

Culms hollow. Leaves mostly basal; sheaths open; ligules membranous; blades flat. Panicles contracted. Spikelets laterally compressed, disarticulation below the glumes; florets two, lower perfect, upper staminate; glumes longer than florets, subequal, keeled; lower lemma awnless; upper lemma with a hooked awn arising from between the apex lobes.

Holcus lanatus L. **COMMON VELVETGRASS** Weak perennials. Culms to 100 cm tall, thick, velvety pubescent. Leaves basal and cauline; blades 5–10 mm wide, soft, typically, sparsely hispid or hirsute. Panicles irregularly contracted, dense. Spikelets 4–6 mm long, florets two, disarticulation below glumes; glumes subequal, ciliate on midvein and often scabrous-hispid on back; first glumes 3.0–4.5 mm long; second glumes much wider; lower florets about 2 mm long, perfect, firm, smooth, shiny, awnless; upper florets usually staminate, about the length of lower florets but narrower; upper lemma awns short, hooked, exserted from back near apex.

Found along upper Gulf Coast. No voucher specimens located (Gould 1975). Introduced from Europe as a pasture grass.

46. HORDEUM L. • Barley

Culms hollow. Leaves cauline; sheaths open, auricles present or absent; ligules membranous; blades flat. Spicate raceme or spike (*H. vulgare*), usually with three spikelets per node, central spikelets perfect and sessile, lateral spikelets reduced and sterile except in the cultivated barley, *H. vulgare*. Rachis readily disarticulating. Spikelets with glumes subulate, much reduced, many appearing as awns; florets one; rachillas terminating in a bristle; lemmas awned.

1. Lemma of lateral spikelets absent or much smaller than lemma of central spikelet .... ***H. pusillum***
1. Lemma of lateral spikelets as large as lemma of central spikelet **2**
2(1). Lateral spikelets pedicellate; glumes of central spikelet ciliate ....
.... ***H. leporinum***
2. Lateral spikelets sessile; glumes of central spikelet glabrous to scabrous
.... ***H. vulgare***

Hordeum leporinum Link **HARE BARLEY** (Figure 103) Tufted annuals. Culms to 60 cm tall, succulent, usually geniculate-spreading below. Leaves cauline; auricles usually well developed, slender, pointed; blades 6–15 cm long, 3–8 mm wide, flat, weak. Spicate racemes 4–8 cm long, about 1 cm wide (excluding awns), often partially enclosed in expanded uppermost leaf sheath. Spikelets three per node; lateral spikelet florets large, usually equaling or exceeding that of central spikelets; outer glumes narrow, setaceous, long-awned, more or less broadened and flattened below, margins coarsely ciliate; central spikelet floret borne on elongated rachilla joint about the length of lateral spikelet pedicels; glume awns mostly 1.0–2.5 cm long, scabrous, lemma body 6–12 mm long, gradually tapering into awn 10–35 mm long; paleas pubescent.

Occurs along mid and upper Gulf Coast.

Hordeum pusillum Nutt. **LITTLE BARLEY** (Figure 104) Short-lived, low, slender annuals. Culms to 40 cm tall, usually geniculate at base; nodes glabrous, dark colored. Leaves cauline; blades mostly 3–12 cm long, 2–4 mm wide, flat, glabrous or pubescent. Spicate racemes 3–8 cm long, 4–8 mm wide (excluding awns), nar-

Figure 103. *Hordeum leporinum*
inflorescence and sessile spikelet with two pedicellate spikelets (Gould and Box 1965).

row and dense. Lateral spikelet glumes awnlike, without expanded bodies; central spikelet glumes broadened and flattened above base, scabrous with awns mostly 7–15 mm long; lemmas of lateral spikelets short-awned, irregularly reduced, body one-third to one-half the length of central spikelets. Central spikelets perfect, lemmas of central spikelet's body 4–6 mm long with awn 2–7 mm long.

Frequent locally along mid and upper Gulf Coast in early spring on roadways,

Figure 104. *Hordeum pusillum*
plant and sessile spikelet with two pedicellate spikelets
(Gould and Box 1965).

ant beds, and other disturbed sites; often associated with *Vulpia octoflora*. Poor forage; poor wildlife value.

Hordeum vulgare L. **BARLEY** (Figure 105) Annuals. Culms to 1.2 m tall, stout, erect, succulent. Leaves cauline; auricles well developed; blades 5–15 mm wide, flat, elongate. Spikes thick, dense, rachis non-disarticulating. Spikelets three per node, sessile; glumes flattened, slightly broadened at base, glabrous or variously pubescent, tapering to a short or long awn; lemmas mostly 8–12 mm long, shiny or glaucous; lemma awns scabrous, to 15 cm long.

Barley, the common cereal, is frequent along roadsides and field borders due to chance seedings, but is unable to persist without cultivation. Provides good forage; fair wildlife value because of large seeds.

Figure 105. *Hordeum vulgare*
plant, (A) three spikelet cluster, and (B) floret (palea view with extended rachilla) (Hitchcock 1951).

47. **LEERSIA** Sw. • Cutgrass

Culms hollow. Leaf sheaths open; ligules membranous; blades flat, midvein present, margin and surface scabrous. Panicles open, branches one per node. Spikelets laterally compressed, florets one; glumes absent; lemmas 5-veined, awnless, strongly keeled; paleas 3-veined, about the length of lemmas. Similar to the closely related cultivated rice, *Oryza sativa*. Cutgrasses derive their common name from the sharp leaf margins and scabrous epidermal surfaces that cut or adhere when touched.

1.	Basal panicle branches spikelet-bearing to near base	***L. hexandra***
1.	Basal panicle branches spikelet-bearing from at least 1.5 cm to one-half above base	**2**
2(1).	Spikelets 1.3–2.0 mm long, glabrous; plants tufted	***L. monandra***
2.	Spikelets 2.2 mm or longer; keel, or keel and veins, hispid to bristly ciliate; plants rhizomatous	**3**
3(2)	Spikelets 2.2–3.5 mm long	***L. virginica***
3.	Spikelets 4 mm or longer	**4**
4(3).	Spikelets 2 mm wide or less	***L. oryzoides***
4.	Spikelets 3–4 mm wide	***L. lenticularis***

Leersia hexandra Sw. **CLUBHEAD CUTGRASS** (Figure 106) Rhizomatous perennials. Culms to 1 m tall, erect, decumbent; nodes retrorsely hispid. Leaves cauline; blades 2–5 mm wide, scabrous. Panicles 5–8 cm long, loosely contracted; branches short, stiffly erect, bearing spikelets to near base. Spikelets 3.2–4.5 mm long, 1.0–1.5 mm wide; lemmas and paleas smooth to hispidulous.

Frequent locally along lower and mid Gulf Coast in moist, sandy soils and pond microsites; often growing in water around ponds, drainages, and creeks. Palatable to livestock but of low forage value due to limited abundance; provides seed for waterfowl (i.e., puddle ducks).

Leersia lenticularis Michx. **CATCHFLYGRASS** (Figure 107) Rhizomatous perennials. Culms to 150 cm long, decumbent. Leaves cauline; sheaths retrorsely hispid; blades 5–20 mm wide, flat, scabrous. Panicles 10–20 cm long, open; branches with spikelets clustered toward tips, flexuous, often drooping. Spikelets mostly 4–5 mm long, 3–4 mm wide, closely imbricate; keel and lateral veins of lemmas and keel of paleas bristly-ciliate with stiff, short hairs.

Found in wet or marshy soil along streams, lake shores, and swales of upper Gulf Coast.

Figure 106. *Leersia hexandra*
plant and spikelet (Gould and Box 1965).

Leersia monandra Sw. **BUNCH CUTGRASS** (Figure 108) Perennial bunchgrasses. Culms to 100 cm tall, stiffly erect, slender. Leaves basal and cauline,
retrorsely scabrous; blades 5–18 cm long, mostly 2–5 mm wide. Panicles 5–15 cm
long with small spikelets closely imbricate on terminal one-third or upper one-
half of branches, slender; branches widely spaced, erect, or spreading; basal
branches sometimes reflexed. Spikelets 1.3–2.0 mm long, broadly ovate, glabrous,
awnless.

Frequent in edges of chaparral mottes on heavy clay soils, in wet ditches and swales, along shallow lakes, and in moist, shaded woodland sites of lower and mid Gulf Coast. Palatable but poor forage for livestock, but decreases under grazing; poor wildlife value.

Leersia oryzoides (L.) Sw. **RICE CUTGRASS** (Figure 109) Rhizomatous perennials. Culms to 150 cm tall, bases often decumbent or stoloniferous; nodes retrorsely hispid. Leaves cauline; sheaths and blades retrorsely scabrous, margins and blade midvein sharply serrate; blades mostly 7–10 cm long. Panicles 10–20 cm long, drooping, often partially included in upper sheath; branch bases without spikelets. Spikelets about 5 mm long, narrowly oblong, asymmetrical; lemmas and paleas short-hispid or scabrous, keels bristly-ciliate.

Occasional throughout Gulf Coast, mostly on saturated soils along streams, lakes, marshes, and wet ditches. Seed utilized by ducks; occasionally eaten by muskrats.

Figure 107. *Leersia lenticularis* inflorescence and leaf (Hitchcock 1951).

Figure 108. *Leersia monandra*
inflorescence and leaves (Hitchcock 1951).

Leersia virginica Willd. **WHITEGRASS** (Figure 110) Perennials with stout rhizomes. Culms to 100 cm tall, slender, weak. Leaves cauline, retrorsely scabrous; blades 4–12 cm long, 3–8 mm wide. Panicles 5–20 cm long; branches widely spaced with few spikelets densely clustered on upper half. Spikelets 2.2–3.5 mm long, about 1 mm wide.

Occurs in low moist sites along upper Gulf Coast.

48. **LEPTOCHLOA** Beauv. • Sprangletop
Culms solid. Leaf sheaths open, terete or keeled; ligules a ciliate membrane; blades flat or folded. Panicles of few to numerous spicate primary unilateral branches along main axis or clustered near apex. Spikelets with 2–12 florets, overlapping and closely spaced on branches, disarticulation above glumes; glumes thin, 1-veined; second glume occasionally 3-veined, acute, awnless or mucronate, longer than the first; lemmas 3-veined, frequently puberulent on veins; paleas well developed, 2-veined, occasionally puberulent.

Figure 109. *Leersia oryzoides*
plant and spikelet (Hitchcock 1951).

4(1).	Lowermost lemma awns 0.5 mm or longer .... *L. fascicularis*
4.	Lowermost lemma awnless or awn shorter than 0.5 mm 5
5(4).	Panicle branches 15–30; spikelets 5.5 mm or longer 6
5.	Panicle branches 38–35; spikelets 2.0–5.3 mm long 7
6(5).	Panicle branches 3–6 cm long; second glumes shorter than 3 mm .... *L. uninervia*
6.	Panicle branches 4–12 cm long; second glumes longer than 3 mm .... *L. fascicularis*
7(5).	Lowermost lemmas 2–3 mm long .... *L. panicoides*
7.	Lowermost lemmas 1.0–1.7 mm long 8
8(7).	Panicle branches appressed to central axis .... *L. nealleyi*
8.	Panicle branches spreading to ascending .... *L. mucronata*

Figure 110. *Leersia virginica* inflorescence and leaves (Hitchcock 1951).

Leptochloa chloridiformis (Hack.) Parodi **ARGENTINE SPRANGLETOP** Robust perennials. Culms to 150 cm tall, stiffly erect. Leaves basal and cauline; ligules 1–2 mm long, a dense fringe of white hairs; blades 2–7 mm wide, scabrous. Panicles long-exserted with 5–20 spicate primary unilateral branches at culm apex. Spikelets about 4 mm long, florets three or four, short pedicellate; first glumes shorter than second glumes; lemma margins ciliate with rather long hairs, apex notched and usually with an awn to 0.6 mm long.

Found in disturbed soil on dry sites along lower Gulf Coast.

Leptochloa dubia (Kunth in H.B.K.) Nees **GREEN SPRANGLETOP** (Figure 111) Perennial bunchgrasses. Culms 30–120 cm tall, erect. Leaf sheaths glabrous; blades flat or somewhat involute. Panicles of three to several spicate primary unilateral branches; branches 4–12 cm or longer; cleistogamous spikelets produced in axils of lower leaf sheaths. Spikelets 5–10 mm long, subsessile, florets three or four; glumes unequal, lanceolate, awnless; first glumes slightly shorter; second glumes usually 4–5 mm long; lemmas broad, rounded on back, truncate to emarginate, apex usually notched, awnless.

Infrequent along Gulf Coast in sandy or sandy loam sites. Good forage; fair bird seed producer.

Leptochloa fascicularis (Lam.) Gray **BEARDED SPRANGLETOP** Tufted annuals. Culms to 100 cm tall; under adverse conditions flowering culms may be 10–15 cm tall. Leaves cauline, well developed, uppermost usually sheathing inflorescence base, a long blade often overtopping inflorescence; ligules 2–6 mm long, well developed, hyaline, lacerate but not ciliate, lateral lobes appearing as sheath auricles; blades 2–7 mm wide, firm, elongate. Panicles 10–30 cm long; spicate

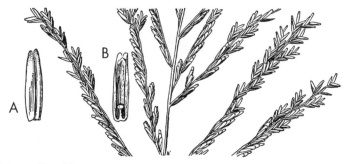

Figure 111. *Leptochloa dubia*
inflorescence, (A) lemma, and (B) floret (palea view) (Hitchcock 1951).

primary unilateral branches 8–35, stiffly erect or erect to spreading, scattered on upper culm axis. Spikelets 5–10 mm long with 6–12 florets maturing bluish-gray; glumes unequal, 1-veined; second glumes mostly 3.0–4.2 mm long, lower lemmas 0.5–1.5 mm long, pubescent on margins and midvein below middle, apex often slightly notched.

Found along mid and upper Gulf Coast in moist sites, commonly growing near the water's edge in brackish marshes, swales, streams, and ponds. Good forage; fair bird seed producer.

Leptochloa mucronata (Michx.) Kunth **RED SPRANGLETOP** (Figure 112) Decumbent, spreading annuals. Culms 10–80 cm tall. Leaves papillose-hispid or pilose; sheaths rounded; ligules 1–2 mm long, a ciliate membrane; blades flat. Panicles 8–35 cm long, one-third to one-half the length of culm; spicate primary unilateral branches numerous, slender, flexuous, widely spreading at maturity. Spikelets 1.5–3.0 mm long, florets two to four, widely spaced on branches; glumes unequal, acute, awnless; lower lemmas 1.0–1.6 mm long, awnless, apex truncate.

Occurs as a common weed of roadsides, barnyards, cropland, and other disturbed sites throughout Gulf Coast.

Leptochloa nealleyi Vasey **NEALLEY SPRANGLETOP** Robust annuals. Culms commonly 1 m or taller, stiffly erect. Leaf sheaths scaberulous, basal leaves sharply keeled; ligules 1–3 mm long, truncate, lacerate, glabrous; blades 3–10 mm wide, folded or involute, rather thick. Panicles 20–50 cm long; spicate primary unilateral branches 25–75 or more, each 2–6 cm long, stiffly erect or erect-spreading. Spikelets 2–3 mm long, florets three or four, laterally compressed; glumes 1.0–1.5 mm long; first glumes acute, second glumes longer and wider, apex broad, often slightly notched apex; lowermost lemmas 1.0–1.6 mm long, pubescent on veins, apex broad, awnless, occasionally slightly notched and apiculate; paleas broad, slightly shorter than lemmas, awnless.

Usually found growing in moist sandy or sandy loam sites; most frequent in roadside ditches, along ponds, and in swales of mid and upper Gulf Coast. Poor forage; fair bird seed producer.

Leptochloa panicoides (Presl) A. S. Hitchc. **AMAZON SPRANGLETOP** Coarse tufted annuals. Culms to 100 cm tall, stiffly erect, tightly compressed at base. Leaf sheaths glabrous; blades 6–12 mm wide, margins scabrous. Panicles 12–30 long with 40–100 spicate primary unilateral branches; branches erect to ascending to spreading. Spikelets 4–5 mm long, pediceled; florets four or five; second glumes

Figure 112. *Leptochloa mucronata*
plant, (A) spikelet, and (B) floret (Hitchcock 1951).

wider than first glumes, acute, awnless; lemmas awnless, broadly acute, apex minutely lobed.

Infrequent on muddy shores and in swamps and swales of upper Gulf Coast.

Leptochloa uninervia (Presl) A. S. Hitchc. & Chase **MEXICAN SPRANGLETOP**
(Figure 113) Generally similar to *L. fascicularis,* but with inflorescence branches

averaging 3–6 cm long; spikelets usually more darkly gray-green; lower lemmas 2–3 mm long, obtuse, awnless, or abruptly mucronate.

Usually found growing in moist or wet clay soils near water along lower and mid Gulf Coast.

Leptochloa virgata (L.) Beauv. **TROPIC SPRANGLETOP** Tufted perennials. Culms to 100 cm tall, erect, base sometimes geniculate. Leaves cauline; sheaths pilose; blades 3–10 mm wide. Panicles with 5–16 spicate primary unilateral branches; branches 3–14 cm long. Spikelets 2–4 mm long, florets three to eight; glumes awnless; lemmas 1.5–2.9 mm long, awns up to 3 mm long from slightly notched apex.

Occasional on sandy and sandy loam savannah sites, often in the shade of oaks but seldom in dense mottes along lower and mid Gulf Coast.

49. **LIMNODEA** Dewey
Culms hollow. Leaves cauline; sheaths rounded; ligules membranous; blades flat.

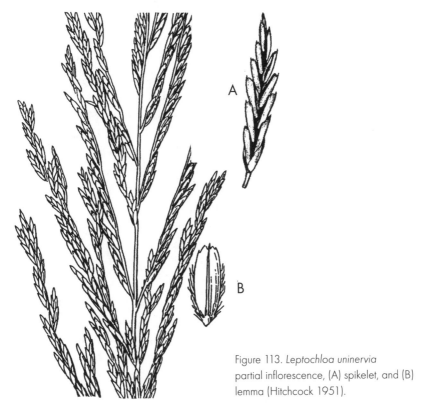

Figure 113. *Leptochloa uninervia* partial inflorescence, (A) spikelet, and (B) lemma (Hitchcock 1951).

Panicles loosely contracted, branches with spikelets to near the base. Spikelets disarticulating below the glumes; florets one; glumes equaling spikelet length; lemmas with twisted and geniculate awn from back of lemma.

Limnodea arkansana (Nutt.) L. H. Dewey **OZARKGRASS** (Figure 114) Short-lived annuals. Culms to 60 cm tall, erect. Leaves cauline; sheaths rounded; ligules a lacerate membrane; blades 3–12 cm long, glabrous. Spikelets 3.5–4.0 mm long, floret one, disarticulation below glumes; glumes firm, equal, as large as lemmas, awnless; lemmas membranous, apex 2-toothed, bearing a delicate awn between teeth; paleas awnless, about the length of lemmas.

Frequent in disturbed areas and margins of shallow ponds; occasional in micro-lows of heavy clay upland prairies along mid and upper Gulf Coast. Commonly associated with *Vulpia octoflora* and *Hordeum pusillum*. Poor forage for both livestock and wildlife.

Figure 114. *Limnodea arkansana* plant, (A) glumes, and (B) floret (Hitchcock 1951).

50. **LOLIUM** L. • Ryegrass

Culms hollow. Leaf sheaths open, auricles well developed; ligules membranous; blades flat or folded. Spikes elongated; spikelets solitary, attached edgewise with back of lemma toward rachis. Spikelets large, several-floreted, disarticulation above glumes; first glumes absent except on terminal spikelets; lemmas 5-veined, awned or awnless; paleas nearly equaling lemma length.

1. Second glumes as long or longer than spikelet ....
..... ***L. temulentum*** var. ***temulentum***
1. Second glumes shorter than spikelet ....***L. perenne***

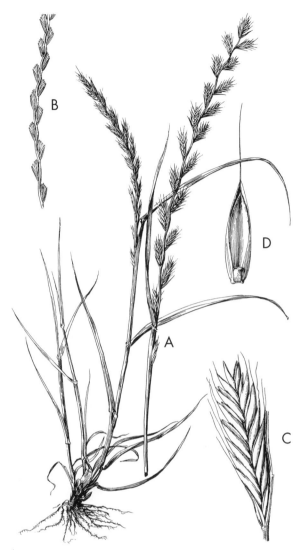

Figure 115. *Lolium perenne*
plant, (A) inflorescence (awned spikelets), (B) inflorescence (awnless spikelets), (C) spikelet, and
(D) floret (palea view) (Hitchcock 1951).

Lolium perenne L. **PERENNIAL RYEGRASS** (Figure 115) Annuals or weak perennials. Culms to 1 m tall, erect. Leaves bright green, rather succulent; blades 2–
10 mm wide, flat, glabrous. Spikes 10–20 cm long. Spikelets large, florets 5–12,
flattened; first glumes absent except on terminal spikelets; lemmas 5–7 mm long,
awnless or awn to 8 mm long; lemma awn lengths extremely variable and does
not appear to be correlated with other plant characters.

Seeded as a cool-season forage grass throughout Gulf Coast; also used for winter lawns and roadside stabilization. Good winter/spring forage for livestock and deer; provides nesting cover for birds.

Lolium temulentum L. var. *temulentum* **DARNEL RYEGRASS** Annuals. Culms to 70 cm tall. Leaf blades 2–8 mm wide, glabrous. Spikes 10–25 cm long, stiffly erect. Spikelets with five to nine florets; first glumes absent except on terminal spikelets; second glumes 1.5–2.0 cm long, apex acute or rounded, exceeding uppermost floret; lemmas 4–7 mm long, plump at maturity, awns 5–15 mm long.

Occasional along mid and upper Gulf Coast as a roadside weed.

51. LUZIOLA Juss.

Culms hollow. Leaf sheaths open, rounded; ligules hyaline; blades flat. Spikelets unisexual, disarticulation below floret, floret one; glumes absent; lemmas and paleas nearly equal. Staminate panicles terminal. Pistillate spikelets axillary, purplish.

Luziola peruviana Gmel. (Figure 116) Monoecious, stoloniferous perennials. Culms to 40 cm tall; culms and leaves ascending. Leaves cauline; sheaths rounded; ligules 5.5–12.0 mm long, hyaline with three to several acuminate divisions; blades 10–12 cm long, 1.0–3.1 mm wide. Staminate panicles narrow, terminal. Staminate spikelets 5.3–6.5 mm long, hyaline; lemmas 7-veined; paleas 5-veined; stamen six or more; anthers 3.0–3.2 mm long, yellow. Pistillate panicles axillary, diffuse. Pistillate spikelets 2.0–2.5 mm long, glabrous, purplish, ovoid, acuminate; lemmas 7-veined; paleas 5-veined; caryopsis 1.0–1.5 mm long, ovoid, yellow.

Recently collected along upper Gulf Coast in coastal wetlands.

52. MELICA L. • Melic

Culms hollow. Leaves basal and cauline; sheaths rounded, margins connate; ligules membranous; blades flat or folded. Panicles open or contracted or a raceme. Spikelets disarticulating above the glumes, with several perfect florets, reduced florets apical and rudimentary; glumes equal to subequal, margins scarious; lemmas obtuse, margins scarious, 7- to 13-veined and usually conspicuous; paleas with two submarginal veins.

Melica mutica Walt. **TWO-FLOWERED MELIC** (Figure 117) Tufted perennials from creeping rhizomes. Culms to 1 m tall, erect to ascending. Leaf sheaths scabrous to pubescent, margins connate; ligules membranous, to 1 mm long; blades to 7 mm wide, flat or folded. Panicles 4–15 cm long, primary branches ascending

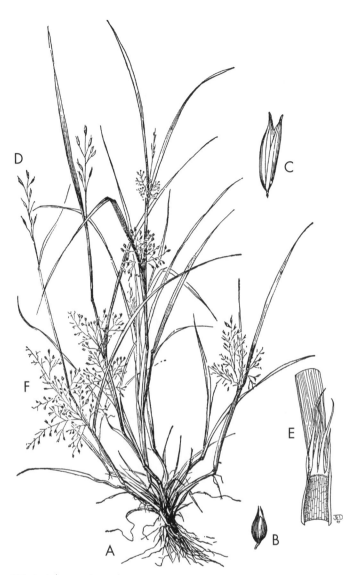

Figure 116. *Luziola peruviana*
(A) plant, (B) pistillate spikelet, (C) staminate spikelet, (D) staminate inflorescence (Hitchcock 1951), (E) ligule [Dawson], and (F) pistillate inflorescence (Hitchcock 1951).

and seldom rebranched, occasionally reduced to a raceme. Spikelets 6–12 mm long, awnless, florets two to four, somewhat triangular; glumes subequal, scarious to glabrous, thin; lower lemmas 6–11 mm long, 7-veined, apices and upper margins hyaline; paleas scabrous. Caryopses 2–3 mm long.

Frequent in moist open woods along upper Gulf Coast.

Figure 117. *Melica mutica*
plant, (A) spikelet, and (B) floret (palea view) (Hitchcock 1951).

53. **MELINIS** P. Beauv.

Culms solid. Leaves basal and cauline; sheaths open; ligules a ring of hairs or a ciliate membrane; blades flat. Panicles open, branches not spikelet-bearing to the base. Spikelets dorsally compressed, disarticulation below glumes; florets two, lower sterile, upper fertile; glume unequal, second glumes short-awned with long silky hairs; lower lemmas awned and with silky hairs; upper lemmas membranous, awnless.

Melinis repens (Willd.) Zizka **NATALGRASS** (Figure 118) Tufted perennials. Culms mostly 70–100 cm tall, geniculate to erect; nodes puberulent. Leaves hispid to nearly glabrous; ligules 0.5–1.0 mm long, a ciliate membrane; blades mostly 8–18 cm long, 2–5 mm wide, narrow, flat or folded. Panicles mostly 6–20 cm long, loosely contracted, slender, nodding; secondary branches and pedicels villous. Spikelets pinkish to silvery, disarticulation at base of spikelet; first glumes minute; second glumes and lower lemmas about equal, silky-villous with fine hairs, apex

Figure 118. *Melinis repens*
plant, (A) spikelet, and (B) upper floret (palea view) (Hitchcock 1951).

notched and minutely awned; lemmas of upper florets much shorter than second glumes and lower lemmas; upper lemma narrow, membranous, glabrous, margins thin, not inrolled over paleas.

Found along roadways, railways, ditch banks, and other areas of moderately disturbed, well-drained soils of lower and mid Gulf Coast. Poor forage for livestock and wildlife.

54. **MONANTHOCHLOË** Engelm.

Plants dioecious. Culms solid, much-branched. Leaves cauline, fascicled and clustered on short lateral shoots; sheath margins connate; ligules a ciliate membrane; blades inrolled, short. Spikelets occur singly in axils of fascicled leaves; florets three to five, uppermost much reduced; glumes absent; lemma texture leaflike.

Monanthochloë littoralis Engelm. **SHOREGRASS** (Figure 119) Low dioecious, mat-forming perennials. Culms to 15 cm tall, wiry, decumbent, stoloniferous. Leaves clustered on short lateral branches, distichous; sheaths mostly 0.4–0.6 mm long, rounded, glabrous or puberulent, smooth and shiny; blades 0.5–1.5 cm long, 1–2 mm wide, uniformly several-veined, bluish-green. Spikelets borne singly on axils of fascicled leaves, pistillate spikelets eventually disarticulating at lower rachilla node. Spikelets with three to five florets, uppermost florets rudimentary; glumes absent; lemmas rounded on back, several-veined, those of pistillate spikelets like leaf blades in texture; paleas narrow, enfolding caryopses.

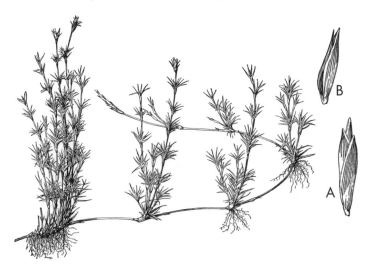

Figure 119. *Monanthochloë littoralis*
plant, (A) spikelet, and (B) floret (Hitchcock 1951).

Abundant locally on saline sites. The only grass in many of the salt flat areas throughout Gulf Coast and barrier islands; both have sandy and clay sites. Poor forage for livestock and wildlife.

55. MUHLENBERGIA Schreb. • Muhly

Culms solid. Leaf sheaths open; ligules membranous; blades flat or involute, midvein absent. Panicles open or contracted; branches one to several per node. Spikelets 1-floreted, laterally compressed, disarticulation above glumes; glumes usually unequal, 1-veined, shorter than the lemmas; lemmas 3-veined, awned from the apex or less frequently awnless; palea the length of lemma, indistinctly veined.

1.	Panicles contracted, branches ascending	*M. schreberi*
1.	Panicles open, branches spreading	2
2(1).	Plants annual	*M. fragilis*
2.	Plants perennial	3
3(2).	Second glume awn 5–20 mm long; lemma teeth setaceous, 0.5–2.5 mm long	*M. filipes*
3.	Second glume awn to 2.5 mm long; lemma without conspicuous setaceous teeth	*M. capillaris*

Muhlenbergia capillaris (Lam.) Trin. **HAIRYAWN MUHLY** (Figure 120) Densely tufted perennials. Culms to 100 cm tall, ascending. Leaves basal; ligules 2–5 mm long, prominent, firm, strongly decurrent; blades 20–50 cm long, 1–2 mm wide, becoming involute, often curved outward near base exposing ligule. Panicles to 40 cm long, diffused, branches capillary. Spikelets 3.5–4.5 mm long, purple; glumes 1.0–1.5 mm long, apex irregularly erose; second glumes frequently with awn 1.5–2.5 mm long; lemmas 3.0–4.5 mm long, reddish- purple, linear-lanceolate, 3.0–4.5 mm long, awns 5–13 mm long flexuous; palea apex acuminate.

Common on sandy soils in liveoak woodlands throughout Gulf Coast; rare on vegetational flats of South Padre Island, and rare also on North Padre Island. Poor forage.

Muhlenbergia filipes M. A. Curtis **GULF MUHLY** Densely tufted perennials. Culms to 160 cm tall, glabrous. Similar in vegetative characteristics to *M. capillaris* except longer throughout. Panicles 30–70 cm long. Spikelets 4–5 mm long, purplish; glumes awned; first glumes 0.5–1.0 mm long with awns 1–5 mm long; second glumes 1.0–1.5 mm long with awns 5–19 mm long; lemmas 3–4 mm long, awned from between two small setaceous teeth, awns 11–26 mm long and flexuous; paleas distinctly 2-veined, veins extended to short awns.

Figure 120. *Muhlenbergia capillaris*
plant, (A) glumes, and (B) floret (Hitchcock 1951).

Found in sand dunes and open coastal woodlands throughout Gulf Coast. Poor forage; good nesting cover for birds.

Muhlenbergia fragilis Swallen **DELICATE MUHLY** Tufted annuals. Culms to 35 cm tall. Leaves basal; sheaths with conspicuous auricles; ligules 1.5–2.5 mm long, hyaline; blades mostly 2–5 cm long, 1.5–2.0 mm wide, thin, margins whitish, thickened. Panicles open, diffuse, usually two-thirds to three-fourths entire height of plant, readily breaking off at maturity. Spikelets 0.9–1.3 mm long, awnless; glumes 0.6–0.9 mm long, obtuse to broadly acute; lemmas 0.9–1.2 mm long, usually acute; paleas the length of lemmas.

Infrequent on open, rocky slopes at medium to high elevations along upper Gulf Coast.

Muhlenbergia schreberi Gmel. **NIMBLE-WILL** (Figure 121) Weak, decumbent, usually stoloniferous perennials. Culms decumbent, much-branched and rooting at lower nodes. Flowering culms to 40 cm tall, slender. Leaves cauline; sheaths shorter than internode; blades 3–8 cm long, 1–3 mm wide, thin. Panicles 4–12 cm long, contracted; branches short, usually appressed. Spikelets 2.0–2.5 mm long; first glumes rudimentary or absent; second glumes 0.1–0.3 mm long; lemmas 2.0–2.5 mm long, more or less pubescent at base, awns 1.5–5.0 mm long; paleas scabrous, about the length of lemmas.

Infrequent on sandy soils in partial shade along mid and upper Gulf Coast. Poor forage.

56. NASSELLA Desv. • Needlegrass

Culms hollow or solid. Leaves mainly basal, enclosing cleistogamous spikelets in some species; sheaths open; ligules usually membranous; blades usually involute. Panicles open or contracted. Spikelets large, floret one, disarticulation above the glumes; glumes equaling or longer than lemma, equal or subequal; lemmas indurate, enclosing the paleas, callus sharp-pointed at the base; lemma awn apical, once- or twice-geniculate; paleas shorter than lemmas, hidden by overlapping lemma margins.

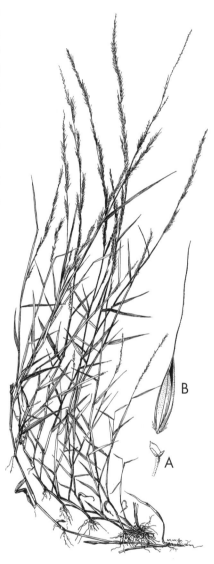

Figure 121. *Muhlenbergia schreberi* plant, (A) glumes, and (B) floret (palea view) (Hitchcock 1951).

Figure 122. *Nassella leucotricha*
(A) inflorescence, (B) spikelet (Gould and Box 1965), (C) cleistogamous spikelet, (D) basal leaf sheaths with enclosed cleistogamous spikelet (Leithead et al. 1976), and (E) crown of lemma (Hitchcock 1951).

Nassella leucotricha (Trin. & Rupr.) Pohl **TEXAS WINTERGRASS** (Figure 122) Tufted perennials. Culms to 70 cm tall, often geniculate-ascending base. Leaves basal and cauline; blades 10–30 cm long, 1–4 mm wide, basal blades pubescent to hirsute on one or both surfaces. Panicles 6–25 cm long, contracted; branches usually long, slender, flexuous. Spikelets 12–18 mm long; glumes thin, glabrous, attenuate, subequal; first glumes 3-veined; second glumes 3- to 5-veined; callus sharp-pointed, densely bearded; lemmas 9–12 mm long, light brown, base densely hairy, body rugose; neck 0.6–1.0 mm long, whitish, fringed; lemma awns 4.5–10.0 cm long, stout, loosely once- or twice-geniculate, scabrous on twisted lower portion.

Most common cool-season perennial throughout Gulf Coast, especially on clays and clay loams. High value as winter and early spring cattle and wildlife forage.

57. **OPLISMENUS** Beauv. • Basketgrass

Culm solid or hollow. Leaves basal and cauline; ligules a ciliate membrane; blades flat. Panicles of spicate primary branches with spikelets in two rows. Spikelets dorsally compressed, disarticulation below glumes; florets two, lower sterile, upper fertile; glumes subequal, awned; lower lemmas and second glumes similar in size and texture; lower lemmas awned; upper lemmas indurate.

Oplismenus hirtellus (L.) Beauv. **BASKETGRASS** (Figure 123) Stoloniferous annuals or weak perennials. Culms to 30 cm long, rooting at nodes. Leaf blades 1.0–1.5 cm wide, short, hirsute. Panicles of three to seven spicate primary branches. Spikelets subsessile, dorsally compressed, florets two; glumes about equal, pubescent, awned from midvein; first glumes 5–10 mm long; lowermost lemma awns about 0.8 mm long; upper lemmas indurate, awnless; paleas the length of upper lemmas.

Found in shady habitats of lower and mid Gulf Coast. Poor livestock and wildlife values.

58. **ORYZA** L. • Rice

Culms hollow. Leaves basal and cauline; sheaths rounded; ligules membranous; blades flat. Panicles open with pedicellate spikelets. Spikelets not compressed, disarticulation below spikelet; florets three, glumes absent, two lower bracts reduced florets, upper floret perfect with lemma and palea.

Oryza sativa L. **RICE** (Figure 124) Tall, tufted annuals. Culms to 1.5 m tall, succulent, erect, glabrous. Leaves with sheaths rounded; auricles well developed; ligules 2-lobed; blades 7–20 mm wide, flat. Panicles large, drooping. Spikelets 7–10 mm long, laterally flattened; glumes absent; two short bracts superficially-appearing to be glumes represent reduced lemmas of rudimentary florets; uppermost lemmas flattened, awnless or short-awned, caryopses tightly enclosed by thick firm lemmas.

Figure 123. *Oplismenus hirtellus* plant and spikelet (Gould and Box 1965).

Figure 124. *Oryza sativa*
plant and spikelet (Hitchcock 1951).

Occurs sparingly as an escapee along sloughs and marshy ditches; a major crop plant along upper Gulf Coast. Good forage and seed for livestock and waterfowl; can be used for shoreline stabilization.

59. PANICUM L. • Panicum

Culms usually solid. Leaf sheaths round or occasionally keeled; ligules a membrane, a ciliate membrane, or absent; blades flat. Panicle open or contracted. Spikelets dorsally compressed, disarticulation below glumes, awnless; florets two, lower neuter or staminate, upper perfect; first glumes usually reduced in size; second glumes and lower lemmas similar in size and texture; upper florets indurate, glabrous, lemma tightly clasping palea with inrolled margins.

1.	Plants annual	2
1.	Plants perennial	7
2(1).	Second glume and lowermost lemma tuberculate-hispid or verrucose	3
2.	Second glume and lowermost lemma not tuberculate-hispid or verrucose	4
3(2).	Spikelets 1.7–2.5 mm long, glabrous	*P. verrucosum*
3.	Spikelets 3.1–3.7 mm long, hispid	*P. brachyanthum*
4(2).	Spikelets 3.8 mm or longer	*P. miliaceum*
4.	Spikelets 3.7 mm or shorter	5
5(4).	Spikelets 1.0–1.4 mm long	*P. trichoides*
5.	Spikelets 1.8–3.0 mm long	6
6(5).	First glume one-fifth to one-fourth spikelet length, apex truncate to obtuse to rounded	*P. dichotomiflorum*
6.	First glume more than one-fourth spikelet length, apex acute to acuminate	*P. capillare*
7(1).	First glume the length of second glume, apex broad; plant stoloniferous	*P. obtusum*
7.	First glume shorter than second glume, or if longer, then apex acute to acuminate; plants stoloniferous, rhizomatous or caespitose	8
8(7).	Second glume 5.0–6.5 mm long, twice the length of upper floret	*P. capillarioides*
8.	Second glume shorter than 4 mm, less than twice the length of upper floret	9
9(8).	Spikelets 4–8 mm long	10
9.	Spikelets shorter than 3.7 mm	12
10(9).	Panicles contracted, narrow; plants with stout rhizomes	*P. amarum*

10. Panicles open, usually pyramidal; plant with rhizomes or stolons **11**

11(10). Spikelets 4–5 mm long; plants densely clumped with rhizomes .... *P. virgatum*

11. Spikelets 5.5–7.0 mm long; plants not densely clumped, without rhizomes, usually stoloniferous. .... *P. gymnocarpon*

12(9). Palea of lower florets appearing inflated or enlarged or firm and obovate .... *P. hians*

12. Palea of lower florets not appearing inflated or enlarged or firm and obovate **13**

13(12). Spikelets appressed and closely clustered on simple or nearly simple branches **14**

13. Spikelets not appressed and closely clustered on simple or nearly simple branches. **21**

14(13). Scaly rhizomes present **15**

14. Scaly rhizomes absent **16**

15(14). Spikelets 2.4–2.6 mm long; lower culm sheaths not strongly keeled .... *P. hemitomon*

15. Spikelets 2.8–3.6 mm long; lower culm sheaths strongly keeled .... *P. anceps*

16(14). Lower sheaths laterally keeled and compressed .... *P. rigidulum*

16. Lower sheaths rounded, not keeled **17**

17(16). Lower florets neuter **18**

17. Lower florets staminate **20**

18(17). Spikelets 2.2–2.8 mm long; panicle branches erect .... *P. tenerum*

18. Spikelets 2.8–3.9 mm long; panicle branches spreading **19**

19(18). Plants ascending to prostrate; spikelets 2.0–2.7 mm long .... *P. hallii* var. *filipes*

19. Plants erect; spikelets 2.8–3.5 mm long .... *P. hallii* var. *hallii*

20(17). Ligules 0.5–1.0 mm long; upper lemma smooth .... *P. antidotale*

20. Ligules 3–4 mm long; upper lemma rugose .... *P. maximum*

21(13). Rhizomes present **22**

21. Rhizomes absent **24**

22(21). First glume truncate to rounded .... *P. repens*

22. First glume acute **23**

23(22). First glume one-third to one-half spikelet length; ligule 0.5 mm or shorter .... *P. anceps*

23. First glume two-thirds to three-fourths spikelet length; ligule 1.5–3.0 mm long .... *P. virgatum*

24(21). Lower panicle branches pilose in axils; primary branches in verticils of three to five .... *P. pilcomayense*

24. Lower panicle branches glabrescent in axils; primary branches usually solitary **25**

25(24). Spikelets 2.0–2.8 mm long; culms ascending to prostrate ... *P. diffusum*

25. Spikelets 2.8–3.4 mm long; culms erect .... *P. ghiesbreghtii*

Panicum amarum Ell. **BITTER PANICUM** Coarse, rhizomatous perennials. Culms 0.5–2.0 m tall, glabrous, glaucous, in clumps or solitary. Leaves cauline; ligules 0.8–1.5 mm long, a ring of hairs; collars purple, glabrous; blades flat, 3–15 mm wide. Panicles 20–35 cm long, contracted. Spikelets 3.5–5.5 mm long; glumes acute at apex; second glumes the length of spikelets; upper lemmas 2.4–3.1 mm long, indurate, glabrous.

Occurs on barrier islands, sandy beaches, and dunes throughout Gulf Coast; important for stabilizing sand dunes. Highly palatable to cattle; produces large seeds in low numbers.

Panicum anceps Michx. **BEAKED PANICUM** Tufted perennials from stout, scaly rhizomes. Culms to 100 cm tall, bases flattened, often keeled. Leaves basal and cauline; blades 4–8 mm wide. Panicles 15–40 cm long, open to contracted. Spikelets 4.5–6.5 mm long, clustered on secondary branches, glabrous; first glumes one-third to one-half the length of spikelets; second glumes and lower lemmas about equal, narrowly acute, widely separated at maturity; upper florets smooth and shiny.

Frequent in forest or shaded grasslands of upper Gulf Coast; common name from beaklike appearance of spikelets. Good livestock and fair wildlife values; prolific seed producer.

Panicum antidotale Retz. **BLUE PANICUM** Robust perennials from hard, knotty bases. Culms to 3 m tall, firm or hard, often glaucous, becoming much-branched and bushlike with age; nodes pubescent, conspicuously swollen. Leaf blades 4–12 mm wide, flat. Panicles mostly 12–25 cm long, open or somewhat dense and contracted, much-branched. Spikelets 2.5–3.0 mm long, 1.2–1.5 mm wide; glumes greenish-white; first glumes thin, broadly rounded at apex, one-third to one-half the length of spikelet; lower florets equaling spikelet length; upper lemmas smooth, shiny, narrowly pointed, about the length of spikelet.

Infrequently persistent along lower and mid Gulf Coast after pasture planting. Fair to good forage for livestock and important as a seed producer for wildlife. Once widely used in seeding mixtures following mechanical brush control.

Panicum brachyanthum Steud. **PIMPLE PANICUM** (Figure 125) Glabrous annuals. Culms to 120 cm tall, wiry, decumbent, much-branched. Leaf blades bright green. Panicles with a few spikelets on short pedicels. Spikelets mostly 3.0-3.5 mm long, obovate. Similar to *P. verrucosum*, but blades 1–3 mm wide, spikelets larger, and second glumes and lower lemmas tuberculate-hispid.

Adapted to sandy soils and most frequently present in open woodlands and rights-of-way throughout Gulf Coast.

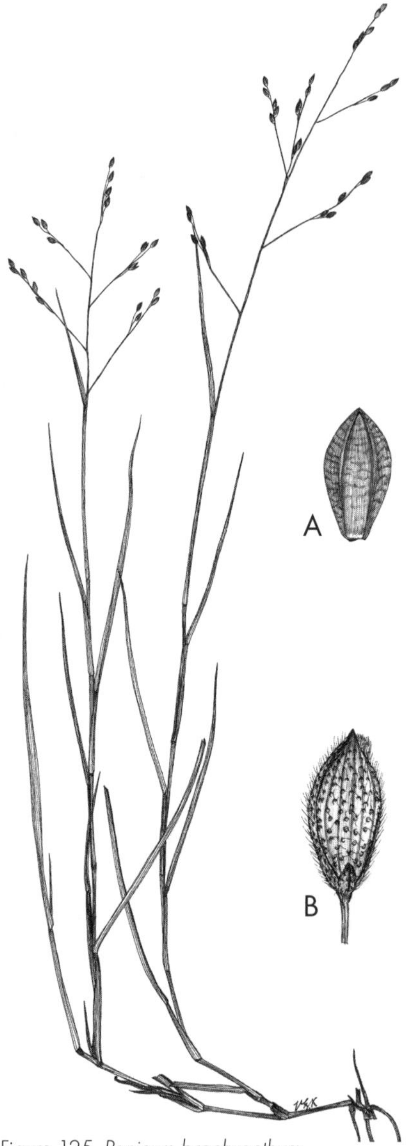

Panicum capillare L. **COMMON WITCHGRASS** (Figure 126) Tufted annuals. Culms to 80 cm long, usually much-branched, decumbent to spreading at base, nodes pubescent or hairy. Leaves cauline; sheaths papillose-hispid with spreading hairs; blades 5–20 mm wide, flat. Panicles 10–30 cm long, large, diffuse, usually one-half or more as wide as long and often one-half or more entire length of culm; branches scabrous, spreading widely; pulvini in branch axils well developed, pubescent; disarticulating at maturity. Spikelets 2.0–3.5 mm long, glabrous; second glume and lower lemma apices abruptly acuminate; first glumes one-third to two-thirds the length of spikelet; lemma of upper florets 1.3–2.3 mm long, smooth and shiny.

Common weed of disturbed soils, often in gardens, flower beds, and vacant lots along upper Gulf Coast. Poor livestock and wildlife forage.

Figure 125. *Panicum brachyanthum* plant, (A) spikelet (first glume view), and (B) upper floret (palea view) (Gould and Box 1965).

Panicum capillarioides Vasey **SOUTHERN WITCHGRASS** (Figure 127) Tufted perennials from knotty bases. Culms 30–70 cm tall, ascending, stiff, geniculate. Leaf blades to 1 cm wide, flat. Panicles 10–30 cm long, open with spikelets mostly at branch apices. Spikelets 5-7 mm long, narrow, glabrous; second glumes and lower lemmas long, prolonged beyond tip of caryopses; lemma of fertile florets 1.6–1.8 mm long, obtuse, brown.

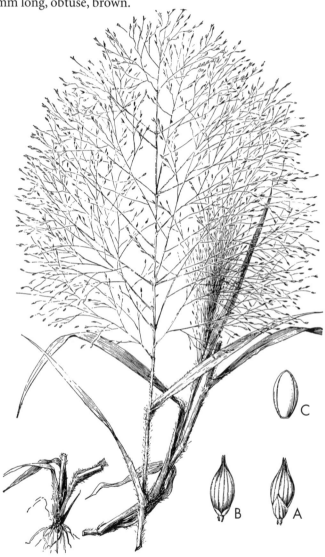

Figure 126. *Panicum capillare*
plant, (A) spikelet (first glume view), (B) spikelet (second glume view), and (C) upper floret (palea view) (Hitchcock 1951)

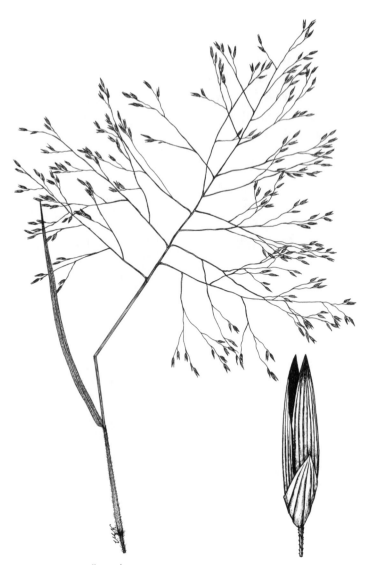

Figure 127. *Panicum capillarioides*
inflorescence and spikelet (Gould and Box 1965).

Frequent on deep sandy and sandy loam sites along lower and mid Gulf Coast; usually associated with soil disturbance or poor range condition. Poor livestock and wildlife forage.

Panicum dichotomiflorum Michx. **FALL PANICUM** (Figure 128) Coarse annuals. Culms often 1–2 m long, thick, weak, erect, or trailing; nodes glabrous. Leaf blades flat, glabrous. Panicles 12–40 cm long, (axillary panicles much smaller), large, open. Spikelets 2-3 mm long, glabrous, narrowly ovate, appressed to branchlets; first glumes one-fourth length of spikelet, obtuse or rounded at apex; second glumes and lower lemmas about the length of spikelet; upper lemmas shiny, narrow, acute.

Frequent on clay upland soils of low fields, ditches, swales, and moist disturbed sites of mid and upper Gulf Coast. Increases early in plant succession and may be found on heavily grazed ranges in an improving condition. Fair forage; poor to fair seed producer for wildlife.

Panicum diffusum Sw. **SPREADING PANICUM** Densely tufted perennials. Culms less than 30 cm long, wiry, frequently branching, nodes pubescent with both spreading and appressed hairs. Leaf sheath margins, especially the lower, ciliate with line of ascending hairs; ligules a ciliate membrane with hairs 1–2 mm long; blades 5–20 cm long, 1.0–4.5 mm wide, glabrous or occasionally spreading-pilose on both surfaces. Terminal panicles 5–25 cm long, exserted, pyramidal; branches ascending or stiffly spreading, scabrous with few short-pediceled spikelets toward ends; axillary panicles partially included in sheaths. Spikelets 2.1–2.7 long, 1.0 mm wide, glabrous, acute.

Frequent locally in dry lake beds and disturbed areas on sites along lower and mid Gulf Coast. Poor forage.

Panicum ghiesbreghtii Fourn. **GHIESBREGHT PANICUM** Tufted perennials. Culms to 80 cm tall, erect to ascending, rather robust, occasionally branching. Leaves cauline and basal; sheaths densely pubescent with papilla-based hairs; blades 20–30 cm long, 1.0–1.5 cm wide, midvein prominent. Panicles 20–30 cm long, open; terminal panicles short-exserted, often equaled by upper blades; axillary panicles partially included in sheaths. Spikelets 2.8–3.5 mm long, on short pedicels; glumes tinged purple; first glumes one-third to one-half the length of spikelet; second glumes and lower lemmas about the length of spikelet.

Occurs on sandy soils near Gulf Coast, around dense oak thickets along lower coastal region.

Panicum gymnocarpon Ell. **SAVANNAH PANICUM** Stout perennials from creeping, stoloniferous bases. Culms to 100 cm tall, erect to ascending, glabrous. Leaves cauline and basal; blades to 3 cm wide, long, flat. Panicles 15–40 cm long with several primary branches, spreading, stiffly erect. Spikelets 5.5–7.0 mm long, in small clusters on short pedicels; glumes with attenuate tips; second glumes exceeding lower lemmas; lemma of lower florets exceeding obovate upper florets.

Found in moist woodland habitats, ditches, and wooded riparian areas along upper Gulf Coast. Fair forage.

Panicum hallii Vasey var. ***hallii*** **HALLS PANICUM** (Figure 129) Tufted perennials. Culms to 60 cm tall, erect to ascending, glaucous. Leaves basal and cauline; blades 2-6 mm wide, flat, curling with age. Panicles 6–20 cm long, branches stiffly

Figure 128. *Panicum dichotomiflorum*
inflorescence and spikelet (Gould and Box 1965).

Figure 129. *Panicum hallii* var. *hallii*
plant, (A) spikelet, and (B) upper floret (palea view)
(Gould and Box 1965).

spreading, pyramidal, spikelets appressed to branchlets. Spikelets 2.2–3.7 mm long, glabrous; first glumes one-third to two-thirds the length of spikelet; upper florets dark brown, shiny, ovate-elliptic.

Usually found on calcareous soils all along Gulf Coast; primarily adapted to dry rocky or gravelly hill and valley sites. Provides fair livestock forage; produces seed for birds.

var. *filipes* (Scribn.) Waller **FILLY PANICUM** Tufted perennials differing from var. *hallii* by taller habit, lax rather than stiff or curled leaves, larger panicles with more branches and spikelets, and smaller spikelets.

Frequent on upland clay soils along mid and upper Gulf Coast, often in depressions receiving extra moisture. One of the first grasses to increase on heavily grazed pastures. Poor to fair forage; produces seed for birds. More productive than var. *hallii*.

Panicum hemitomon Schult. **MAIDENCANE** Robust perennials from creeping rhizomes and stoloniferous bases. Culms to 150 cm tall, numerous sterile shoots present. Leaf blades 12–30 cm long, 7–15 mm wide, typically glabrous. Panicles 8–32 cm long, contracted, spikelets closely clustered on primary branches and short, appressed secondary branches. Spikelets 2.0–2.6 mm long, subsessile; glume midveins scabrous; first glumes acute, about one-half the length of spikelet; second glumes equaling lower lemmas or slightly shorter; upper florets shiny.

Found in ditches and along canals, swales, riverbanks, and lake shores along upper Gulf Coast. Provides good forage; used for shoreline stabilization.

Panicum hians Ell. **GAPING PANICUM** (Figure 130) Slender tufted perennials. Culms to 75 cm tall, commonly decumbent at base, much-branched. Leaf blades 6–18 cm long, 2–5 mm wide, often pilose or hispid. Panicles mostly 6–20 cm long, small; primary branches slender, usually bare of spikelets on lower 1.5–3.0 cm. Spikelets 1.8–2.6 mm long, glabrous, oblong, widely gaping at apex between florets at maturity; lower floret paleas appear inflated, much larger and broader than associated lemmas; upper floret lemmas narrowly ovate, pointed, smooth, but not shiny.

Found in low, moist sites and deep sands throughout Gulf Coast.

Panicum hirsutum Sw. **HAIRY PANICUM** Stout perennials. Culms to 1.5 mm tall, erect or geniculate, unbranched; nodes with appressed pubescence, hairs to 4 mm long. Leaf sheaths densely hirsute; blades 50–85 cm long, 1.7–2.2 cm wide, flat, midvein prominent, minutely pubescent. Panicles 20–45 cm long, dense, short-exserted to included in sheath; branches scabrous, ascending or spreading. Spikelets 1.7–2.2 mm long, 1.0 mm wide; first glumes acute, one-third the length of spikelet; upper florets elliptic, smooth, shiny.

Occurs along lower Gulf Coast, growing mostly in low, moist soils, often in shaded habitat; rare to localized in abundance.

Figure 130. *Panicum hians*
plant and spikelet (Gould and Box 1965).

Panicum maximum Jacq. **GUINEAGRASS** (Figure 131) Stout, tufted to rhizomatous perennials. Culms to 2.5 m tall, nodes densely hirsute. Leaves basal and cauline; collars densely pubescent; ligules a short ciliate membrane with stiff hairs 3–4 mm long; blades 0.8–3.5 cm wide, long, flat, variously hispid or pubescent. Panicles 20–50 cm long, open with slender, wiry, primary branches, each 8–20 cm long. Spikelets 3.0–3.5 mm long, elliptic-lanceolate; glumes purple, apex blunt; second glumes and lemma of lower florets subequal; upper florets transverse rugose.

Abundant in plantings and as an escapee, recently increasing along mid Gulf Coast on roadsides, abandoned land, and lightly grazed ranges. Grows most robustly in shade of mature honey mesquite (*Prosopis glandulosa*), perhaps responding to the increased fertilization (nitrogen fixation) by this woody legume. Good livestock forage and seed producer for wildlife.

Panicum miliaceum L. **BROOMCORN MILLET** (Figure 132) Variable sized annuals. Culms to 1 m tall, erect or from a decumbent base. Leaves mainly cauline; sheaths with papillose-based hairs; ligules a ciliate membrane, about 1.5 mm long; blades to 20 cm long, to 12 mm wide with papilla-based hairs. Panicles 5–25 cm long, contracted, branches ascending. Spikelets 4–5 mm long, ovate to elliptic; glumes unequal, glumes and lower lemma with strongly developed veins; lower lemmas 9- to 11-veined; upper floret 3.0–3.5 mm long, shiny, smooth.

Found growing in scattered locations, especially in temperate areas throughout Gulf Coast; probably introduced into the United States from birdseed. Planted as a seed producer in wetlands managed for waterfowl.

Panicum obtusum Kunth in H.B.K. **VINE MESQUITE** (Figure 133) Stoloniferous perennials. Flowering culms to 80 cm tall, erect from creeping stolons with long internodes; nodes conspicuously hairy; erect culm nodes glabrous. Panicles 3-15 cm long, contracted with short, spicate branches. Spikelets 3.2–4.0 mm long, obovate, blunt, glabrous; first glumes about as large and long as second glumes and lower lemmas; upper florets lemmas smooth, shiny, minutely reticulate.

Frequent throughout Gulf Coast on fine-textured upland soils, usually growing in depressions and low places. One of the top four grasses in cattle diets along the mid Gulf Coast on mid-successional rangelands. Good forage for livestock; fair seed producer for wildlife.

Panicum pilcomayense Hack. Stout perennials. Culms to 100 cm tall, erect; nodes, at least the lower, with appressed pubescence. Sheaths longer than internodes, glabrous; ligules a ciliate membrane with hairs to 2.5 mm long; blades 20–60 cm

Figure 131. *Panicum maximum*
plant, (A) spikelet (first glume view), (B) spikelet (second glume view), and (C) upper floret (palea view) (Hitchcock 1951).

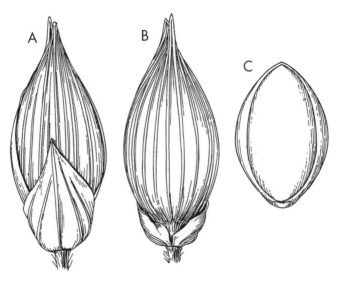

Figure 132. *Panicum miliaceum*
(A) spikelet (first glume view), (B) spikelet (second glume view), and (C) upper floret (palea view)
(Hitchcock 1951).

long, 4–10 mm wide, essentially glabrous except for some long hairs on upper surface and margins. Panicles 20–40 cm long, often included at base, often one-third to one-half height of plant, broadly pyramidal and diffuse; lower branches up to 30 cm long, in verticils of three to seven; upper branches scabrous, spikelets near ends of spreading branchlets; panicles disarticulating as a tumbleweed at maturity. Spikelets 2.4–3.0 mm long, acute or abruptly acuminate; first glumes acute, one-third to one-half the spikelet length; second glumes and lower lemmas about the length of spikelet; upper florets smooth, shiny, elliptic.

Occurs as a weed of ditches, low prairie sites, and field margins along mid and upper Gulf Coast. Similar to *P. filipes* but with larger and more widely branched panicle.

Panicum repens L. **TORPEDOGRASS** (Figure 134) Rhizomatous perennials. Culms to 75 cm tall, erect, widely spreading, branched. Leaf blades 5–25 cm long, 2–8 mm wide, commonly hispid on one or both surfaces. Panicles 7–15 cm long, open but narrow. Spikelets 2.2–2.7 mm long, plump, glabrous; glumes and lower lemmas thin, light colored; first glumes 0.6–0.8 mm long, truncate, collarlike; second glumes and lower lemmas equal, apex slightly beaked; upper florets smooth and shiny.
    Found in coastal sands along upper Gulf Coast.

Panicum rigidulum Nees **REDTOP PANICUM** (Figure 135) Tufted perennials. Culms to 100 cm tall, often rebranching at upper nodes and forming axillary panicles; lower culm internodes typically flat. Leaf sheaths laterally compressed, keeled, occasionally with line of hairs on collar; blades to 50 cm long, 4–12 mm wide. Panicles 10–40 cm long, pyramidal, loosely contracted or more frequently open; branches slender, spreading; spikelets clustered at branch tips and on short secondary branches. Spikelets 1.6–2.5 mm long, glabrous, erect on short pedicels,

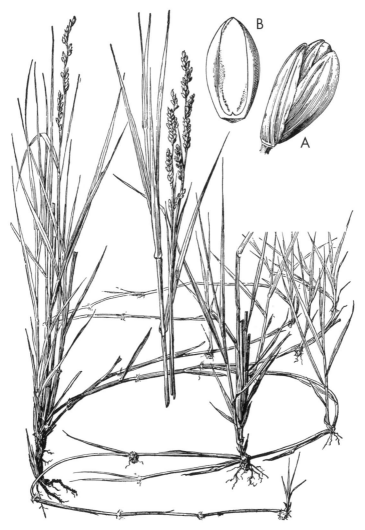

Figure 133. *Panicum obtusum*
plant, (A) spikelet, and (B) upper floret (palea view) (Hitchcock 1951).

not obliquely angled; first glumes acute, two-thirds or slightly less spikelet length; second glumes acute, slightly beaked, slightly longer than lemmas of lower florets; upper florets smooth, shiny, narrowly ovate with or without short stipe at base.

Locally abundant on mid and upper Gulf Coast along ponds, swales, and woodlands. Fair livestock forage; good producer of seeds for wildlife.

Figure 134. *Panicum repens*
plant, (A) spikelet (first glume view), (B) spikelet (second glume view), and (C) upper floret (palea view) (Hitchcock 1951).

Figure 135. *Panicum rigidulum*
inflorescence and spikelet (Gould and Box 1965).

Panicum tenerum Beyr. *ex* Trin. Slender perennials. Culms to 100 cm tall, wiry, stiffly erect from a firm, knotty base. Leaves basal and cauline; blades 4–18 cm long, 1.5–3.0 mm wide, firm. Panicles 3–8 cm long, contracted, sparsely branched. Spikelets 2.2–2.8 mm long; first glume apex broadly acute, about two-thirds the length of spikelet; second glume and lemma of lower florets nearly equal, narrowly acute, spreading at maturity.

Found in sandy soil of coastal prairies, margins of swamps, and wet places in piney woods along upper Gulf Coast.

Panicum trichoides Sw. Stoloniferous annuals. Culms to 40 cm tall, much-branched below. Leaf sheaths pubescent or hispid with papilla-based hairs; blades 2–7 cm long, 6–22 mm wide, base wide, cordate, asymmetrical; apex narrowly acute. Panicles 4–18 cm long, much-branched, usually two-thirds or more of plant height. Spikelets 1.0–1.4 mm long; glumes subequal; second glumes rounded at apex, slightly shorter than lemmas of lower florets; upper florets minutely rugose, light brown.

Infrequent along lower Gulf Coast.

Panicum verrucosum Muhl. **WARTY PANICUM** Sprawling annuals. Culms 120 cm or longer, slender, glabrous, becoming decumbent, much-branched at lower nodes. Leaves cauline; blades 5–20 cm long, 4–10 mm wide. Panicles few-spikeleted, one to three spikelets at apex of slender, stiffly spreading branches. Spikelets 1.7–2.1 mm long, elliptic to obovate; first glumes greatly reduced, one-fifth to one-fourth the length of spikelet; second glumes and lemmas of lower florets about equal in length, roughened with small warts; upper florets finely reticulate.

Usually occurs in moist or marshy sandy soil and often in open woodlands along upper Gulf Coast.

Panicum virgatum L. **SWITCHGRASS** (Figure 136) Coarse perennial bunch-grasses from hard, knotty rhizomatous bases. Culms to 2 m tall, unbranched, in large clumps. Leaves basal and cauline; blades 3–15 mm wide, flat, glabrous. Panicles to 50 cm long, open, pyramidal. Spikelets 3–5 mm long, glabrous; glumes narrowly acute to acuminate; lower florets staminate; upper florets narrowly ovate, smooth, shiny.

Occasional on all sites but most frequent on sandy and sandy loams of wet or swale sites receiving extra moisture; frequent along stream banks. Once a climax dominant on lowlands of coastal prairie. Good livestock forage and seed producer; good ground nesting bird cover. Also good for shoreline stabilization and as grass barrier wedges for wind and water erosion control.

60. PAPPOPHORUM Schreb. • Pappusgrass

Culms solid, unbranched. Leaf sheaths open; ligules a ring of hairs; blades flat or folded. Panicles contracted, spikelike. Spikelets dorsally compressed, disarticulation above the glumes; florets three to five with only the lower one to three fertile; glumes thin and 1-veined; lemmas broad, 11-veined, with each vein ending in short awn, awns unequal.

Figure 136. *Panicum virgatum*
plant, (A) spikelet (first glume view), (B) spikelet (second glume view), and (C) upper floret (palea view) (Hitchcock 1951).

1.   Spikelets pink or purplish-pink; panicle contracted, somewhat lobed
.... ***P. bicolor***

1.   Spikelets white to tawny; panicle contracted .... ***P. vaginatum***

Pappophorum bicolor Fourn. **PINK PAPPUSGRASS** (Figure 137) Perennial bunchgrasses. Culms to 80 cm tall, stiffly erect, glabrous. Leaf sheaths with a tuft of long hairs on either side of collar; ligules a ring of short hairs but a second group of hair at base of blade immediately above ligule, hairs 2–4 mm long; blades 10–20 cm long, 1.5–5.0 mm wide, adaxial surface scabrous. Panicles 12–20 cm long with short but somewhat erect to spreading branches, pink or purple-tinged

Figure 137. *Pappophorum bicolor*
plant, (A) spikelet, and (B) floret (palea view) (Gould and Box 1965).

Grasses of the Texas Gulf Prairies and Marshes

at maturity. Spikelets 6–8 mm long, short-pediceled, appressed, two or three perfect florets and two reduced florets above; glumes 3–4 mm long, apex minutely notched and mucronate; lower lemmas 3–4 mm long, midvein and margins pubescent from base to middle, apex dissected into 11–15 awns of irregular lengths, the longest 2.5–5.0 mm; paleas slightly longer than lemma body, 2-veined but tapering to acute or acuminate apex.

Occasional on open, sandy loam sites along lower Gulf Coast. Fair forage.

Pappophorum vaginatum Buckl. **WHIPLASH PAPPUSGRASS** Similar to *P. bicolor* but inflorescences more contracted, without pinkish coloration (whitish to tawny), and only three florets per spikelet.

Occurs on heavy clays near ship channels and on spoil islands of lower Gulf Coast. Fair forage.

61. **PARAPHOLIS** Hubb.

Culm hollow, much-branched. Leaves cauline; sheaths rounded; ligules membranous; blades weak. Spikes curved, cylindrical with embedded spikelets. Spikelets solitary, not compressed, disarticulation below the glumes; florets one, glumes subequal; lemmas hyaline, 3-veined, the lateral veins very short.

Parapholis incurva (L.) C. E. Hubb. **SICKLEGRASS** (Figure 138) Low, tufted, much-branched annuals. Culms 5–35 cm long, erect or decumbent. Leaves cauline; blades 2–8 mm long, 0.5–2.0 mm wide, thin, weak. Spikes 3–10 cm long, stiffly

Figure 138. *Parapholis incurva*
plant, (A) rachis, and (B) spikelet (Hitchcock 1951).

curved, cylindrical, disarticulation at rachis nodes. Spikelets with one floret, solitary at rachis nodes, partially embedded in and disarticulating with rachis sections; glumes 3–6 mm long, subequal, flattened but firm, asymmetrical, tapering to a point, placed in front of spikelet and appearing as halves of a single glume; lemmas thin and hyaline, 1-veined, awnless, shorter than glumes but longer than the narrow hyaline paleas.

Found throughout Gulf Coast in brackish swales, calciferous sites, and saline sites. Commonly associated with *Spartina* and *Distichlis* along ditches and coastal flats.

62. PASPALIDIUM Stapf

Culms solid. Leaves basal and cauline; sheaths rounded; ligules a ring of hairs; blades flat. Panicles of several spicate primary unilateral branches, branches appressed and terminating in a bristle; spikelets with second glume oriented toward the primary branch axis. Spikelets dorsally compressed, disarticulation below glumes; florets two, lower one sterile, upper one fertile; glumes unequal; first glumes short and broad; second glumes and lower lemmas similar in size and texture; upper florets rugose.

1. Lower lemma veins conspicuous; spikelets 2.8 mm or longer ....
.... *P. geminatum* var. *paludivagum*
1. Lower lemma veins inconspicuous; spikelets shorter than 2.7 mm ....
.... *P. geminatum* var. *geminatum*

Paspalidium geminatum (Forssk.) Stapf var. *geminatum* EGYPTIAN PASPALIDIUM (Figure 139) Clumped perennials from rhizomatous bases. Culms to 65 cm tall, glabrous. Leaves basal and cauline; blades 3–6 mm wide, flat, glabrous. Panicles of 7–20 spicate primary unilateral branches; branches appressed. Spikelets 2.2–3.0 mm long in two rows with first glumes oriented away from axis of branches; glumes awnless, first glumes one-fourth to one-third the length of spikelet; lower florets awnless, paleas well developed; upper florets finely rugose, acute.

Found mostly beside ditches and canal banks, often in shallow water along lower and mid Gulf Coast. Poor forage.

var. *paludivagum* (A. S. Hitchc. & Chase) Gould WATER PASPALIDIUM Similar to var. geminatum but culms stoloniferous and widely spreading. Spikelets 2.8–3.0 mm or slightly longer; glumes and lemmas of lower florets chartaceous, veins conspicuous.

Occasional in moist sites, often in temporary water.

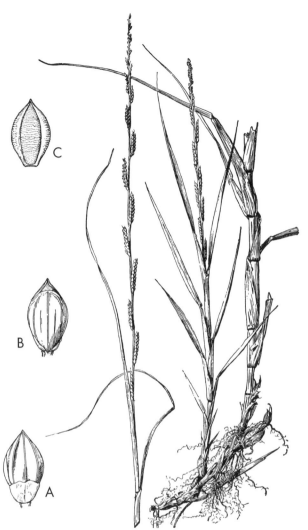

Figure 139. *Paspalidium geminatum* var. *geminatum*
plant, (A) spikelet (first glume view), (B) spikelet (second glume view), and (C) upper floret (palea view) (Hitchcock 1951).

63. PASPALUM L. • Paspalum (adapted from Gould 1975)

Culms solid. Leaf sheaths open; ligules membranous or a ring of hairs; blades usually flat. Panicles of one to many spicate primary unilateral branches; branches alternate, occasionally paired at the culm apex. Spikelets awnless, plano-convex, disarticulation below the glumes; florets two, lower sterile, upper fertile, first glumes usually absent (vestigial in a few species); second glumes and lower lemmas similar in size and texture; upper florets obtuse, indurate, lemma margin clasping palea.

1.	Primary branches broad and winged, leaflike, as wide or wider than two rows of spikelets **2**
1.	Primary branches narrow, not winged, not leaflike, not as wide as combined rows of spikelets **3**
2(1).	Primary branches extending beyond uppermost spikelet ... *P. fluitans*
2.	Primary branches not extending beyond uppermost spikelet .... *P. dissectum*
3(1).	Spicate primary unilateral branches two, paired (opposite) or less than 1 cm apart (rarely one or two additional branches below) **4**
3.	Spicate primary unilateral branches one to many, but alternate and not paired at culm apex **8**
4(3).	Spikelets broadly ovate, elliptic or obovate, apex obtuse or broadly acute **5**
4.	Spikelets narrowly ovate or elliptic, apex tapering **7**
5(4).	Spikelets 1.3–1.9 mm long .... *P. conjugatum*
5.	Spikelets 2–5 mm long **6**
6(5).	Spikelets 2.0–2.5 mm long .... *P. minus*
6.	Spikelets 2.8–5.0 mm long .... *P. notatum*
7(4).	Plants caespitose, without rhizomes .... *P. almum*
7.	Plants rhizomatous or stoloniferous .... *P. vaginatum*
8(3).	First glume present on some or all spikelets **9**
8.	First glume absent on all spikelets **12**
9(8).	Plants without rhizomes; spikelets shorter than 3 mm, pubescent .... *P. langei*
9.	Plants with creeping rhizomes; spikelets 3 mm or longer, glabrous **10**
10(9).	Leaf blades involute, 2 mm wide or less (as rolled). *P. monostachyum*
10.	Leaf blades flat, 5 mm wide or more **11**
11(10).	Inflorescence a single primary branch (or panicle, occasionally with two branches); spikelets 2.9–3.3 mm long .... *P. unispicatum*
11.	Inflorescence a panicle of three to five widely spaced primary branches; spikelets 3.3–4.0 mm long .... *P. bifidum*
12(8).	Margin of spikelets ciliate with long hairs **13**
12.	Margin of spikelets not ciliate with long hairs **14**
13(12).	Primary branches three to six .... *P. dilatatum*
13.	Primary branches 12–20 .... *P. urvillei*
14(12).	Upper florets dark brown and shiny **15**
14.	Upper florets green, light brown, or straw colored **17**
15(14).	Plants annual; lowermost lemma without transverse wrinkles .... *P. boscianum*

15.	Plants perennial; lowermost lemma with transverse wrinkles **16**
16(15).	Lower lemmas without transverse wrinkles; leaf blades 12–27 mm wide .... *P. virgatum*
16.	Lower lemmas with transverse wrinkles; leaf blades 3–8 mm wide .... *P. plicatulum*
17(14).	Spikelets 3.5–4.8 mm long **18**
17.	Spikelets shorter than 3.4 mm **19**
18(17).	Leaf blades hirsute, frequently dense hairs .... *P. floridanum* var. *floridanum*
18.	Leaf blades glabrous except near ligule .. *P. floridanum* var. *glabratum*
19(17).	Spikelets elliptic or obovate, 2.2–3.4 mm long **20**
19.	Spikelets suborbicular, broadly ovate or broadly obovate, 1.4–3.4 mm long **23**
20(19).	Spikelets 2.0–2.5 mm long, glabrous; panicle branches 1.5–4.0 cm long .... *P. lividum*
20.	Spikelets 2.7–3.4 mm long, pubescent or glabrous; panicle branches 4–11 cm long **21**
21(20).	Leaf blades 6–15 mm wide, flat, lanceolate .... *P. pubiflorum* var. *pubiflorum*
21.	Leaf blades mostly 2–5 mm wide, folded or involute, linear **22**
22(21).	Spikelets in four rows on primary branches, glabrous *P. hartwegianum*
22.	Spikelets in two rows on primary branches, pubescent .... *P. almum*
23(19).	Primary branches one or two; spikelets 1.4–2.6 mm long; axillary in- florescences developed in upper leaf sheaths **24**
23.	Primary branches three to many; spikelets 2.2–3.4 mm long; axillary inflorescences not developed in upper leaf sheaths **27**
24(23).	Leaf blades pilose **25**
24.	Leaf blades glabrous or nearly so **26**
25(24).	Midvein of lowermost lemmas absent .... *P. setaceum* var. *stramineum*
25.	Midvein of lowermost lemmas present . *P. setaceum* var. *muhlenbergii*
26(24).	Leaves yellow-green to dark green; leaf blades 3–15 mm wide; midvein of lowermost lemmas absent; spikelets 1.6–2.2 mm long .... *P. setaceum* var. *stramineum*
26.	Leaves dark green to purplish; leaf blades 3–20 mm wide; midvein of lowermost lemmas present or absent: spikelets 1.7–2.6 mm long .... *P. setaceum* var. *ciliatifolium*
27(23).	Spikelets paired or solitary and paired on each side of primary branch .... *P. praecox*

27.   Spikelets solitary on each side of primary branch **28**

28(27).   Spikelets 2.0–2.5 mm wide, ovate, oval, obovate ...... *P. laeve* var. *laeve*

28.   Spikelets 2.7–3.2 mm wide, orbicular to suborbicular ....
.... *P. laeve* var. *circulare*

Paspalum almum Chase **COMBS PASPALUM** Densely tufted perennials. Culms
to 50 cm tall. Leaves basal and cauline; ligules about 2 mm long, membranous;
blades 2–5 mm wide, flat, thin, margins ciliate with papilla-based hairs. Panicles
or racemes, commonly with terminal branch and second inserted 0.5–1.5 cm
below, occasionally one or two additional branches below; branches spicate. Spikelets 2.8–3.4 mm long, glabrous; upper florets straw colored, awnless.

Found on sandy or silty clay loam soils along upper Gulf Coast.

Paspalum bifidum (Bertol.) Nash **PITCHFORK PASPALUM** Perennials. Culms
to 120 cm tall, erect, from short, scaly, densely lanate-pubescent rhizomes. Leaves
basal and cauline, hirsute with long, silvery hairs; blades 15–40 cm or longer,
4–12 mm wide, flat. Panicles of three to five spicate primary unilateral branches;
branches 4–16 cm long, flattened, flexuous. Spikelets 3.3–4.0 mm long, widely
spaced, elliptical, paired, both pedicellate or on a common pedicel; first glumes
usually absent; second glumes and lemma of lower florets strongly 5- to 7-veined;
upper florets light brown.

Relatively infrequent in sandy woods along upper Gulf Coast.

Paspalum boscianum Flugge **BULL PASPALUM** Annuals. Culms to 70 cm tall,
succulent. Leaves basal and cauline; ligules 1.5–3.0 mm long, membranous; blades
6–15 mm wide, flat, glabrous. Panicles of 4–12 spicate primary unilateral branches;
branches 4–7 cm long and bearing crowded spikelets in four rows. Spikelets 2.0–
2.5 mm long, obovate to suborbicular, glabrous; second glumes and lemma of
lower florets brownish; upper florets becoming dark brown.

Infrequent in ditches, field borders, and cutover woodlands along upper Gulf
Coast.

Paspalum conjugatum Bergius **SOUR PASPALUM** Perennials with long, leafy
stolons. Culms to 50 cm tall, erect; stolon nodes pilose. Leaves basal and cauline;
ligules membranous with ring of stiff hairs immediately above; blades 8–12 cm
long, 5–15 mm wide, flat, thin, glabrous. Panicles of paired spicate primary unilateral branches at culm apex; branches 5–15 cm long, widely spreading. Spikelets 1.4–2.0 mm long, elliptic, closely imbricated on branch; glume margins
sparsely long-pilose; upper florets straw colored.

Infrequent along lower Gulf Coast.

Paspalum dilatatum Poir. **DALLISGRASS** (Figure 140) Tufted perennials from hard, knotty bases. Culms to 120 cm tall, ascending. Leaves basal and cauline; lowermost sheaths usually hirsute, upper sheaths glabrous; ligules 1.5–3.0 mm long, membranous, brownish; blades mostly 3–12 mm wide, firm, flat, tapering to narrow point. Panicles of two to seven spicate primary unilateral branches usually widely spaced on slender axis; spikelets in four rows, on wide, flat branches, branches 3–8 cm long. Spikelets widely ovate, tapering to short, acute apex; first glumes absent; second glumes and lower lemmas 3–4 mm long, distinctly 3- to 5-veined; margins pubescent with long, silky hairs; upper florets ovate to suborbicular, straw colored.

Occurs throughout Gulf Coast; best adapted to clay and loam soils of roadsides and bottomland sites. Seeded as a pasture grass in many areas. Provides good forage for livestock and seed for wildlife.

Paspalum dissectum (L.) L. **MUDBANK PASPALUM** Perennials with decumbent, creeping, mat-forming bases. Culms to 50 cm long. Leaves cauline; blades 3–6 cm long, 2–5 mm wide, thin. Panicles of two to four spicate primary unilateral branches; branches 1–3 cm long, 2–3 mm wide, bearing two rows of spikelets. Spikelets 1.8–2.2 mm long, glabrous, awnless.

Occasional in moist or marshy soil, usually on stream banks and lake shores along upper Gulf Coast.

Paspalum floridanum Michx. var. *floridanum* **FLORIDA PASPALUM** (Figure 141) Coarse perennial bunchgrasses from thick rhizomes. Culms to 2 m tall, erect to ascending. Leaves hirsute; ligules membranous; blades 4–10 mm wide, flat or folded with dense tuft of hairs above ligules. Panicles with two to five spicate primary unilateral branches; branches 4–13 cm long with spikelets closely spaced in four rows. Spikelets 3.6–4.8 mm long, glabrous, elliptic; lower floret lemmas with well developed midvein; upper florets light brown, minutely rugose.

var. *glabratum* Engelm. *ex* Vasey **FLORIDA PASPALUM** Similar to var. *floridanum* but with glabrous herbage, except conspicuously hirsute tuft of hairs immediately above ligules.

Both varieties occur along mid and upper Gulf Coast in sandy, woodland openings and grasslands where var. *glabratum* is much more frequent and widespread than var. *floridanum.* Fair to good livestock forage; good seed producers for wildlife.

Paspalum fluitans (Ell.) Kunth **WATER PASPALUM** Succulent annuals. Culms to 1 m long, usually decumbent, rooting at lower nodes. Leaves cauline; ligules

Figure 140. *Paspalum dilatatum*
plant, (A) spikelet (second glume view), (B) spikelet (lowermost lemma view), and (C) upper floret (palea view) (Hitchcock 1951).

1.5–2.0 mm long, decurrent, often forming pointed sheath auricles; blades 8–15 mm wide, short. Panicles of numerous spicate primary unilateral branches; branches 3–7 cm long, wide, leaflike, equaling or exceeding in width the two rows of short-pedicled spikelets and projecting as a point beyond uppermost spikelets, eventually disarticulating at base. Spikelets 1.2–1.7 mm long, oblong or ovate, apex acute.

Infrequent along upper Gulf Coast in moist or marshy soil of ditches, marshes, lakes, and stream banks, often with the culms floating.

Paspalum hartwegianum Fourn. **HARTWEG PASPALUM** Perennial bunch-grasses, similar in general aspect to *P. pubiflorum* but bases of plants less firm and

Figure 141. *Paspalum floridanum* var. *floridanum*
plant, (A) spikelet, and (B) upper floret (palea view) (Gould and Box 1965).

less knotty. Culms 30–80 cm tall. Leaf blades 2–5 mm wide. Panicles of two to six spicate primary unilateral branches; branches tending to be erect rather than spreading. Spikelets about 3 mm long. In *P. pubiflorum* spikelets more turgid, wider and less regularly arranged on branches.

Less frequent along mid Gulf Coast than *P. pubiflorum*. Fair forage.

Paspalum laeve Michx. var. ***laeve*** **FIELD PASPALUM** Perennial bunchgrasses. Culms to 100 cm tall from firm bases. Sheaths glabrous; ligules membranous; blades 3–10 mm wide. Panicles of three to five (rarely two or six) spicate primary unilateral branches; branches typically 4–10 cm long; pedicels 0.7–2.0 mm long. Spikelets 2.4–3.4 mm long, ovate, glabrous, borne singly and widely spaced; upper florets light brown to straw colored.

var. ***circulare*** (Nash) Fern. **ROUNDSEED PASPALUM** Similar to var. *laeve* except spikelets 2.7–3.2 mm wide, orbicular or suborbicular.

Both varieties found along upper Gulf Coast.

Paspalum langei (Fourn.) Nash **RUSTYSEED PASPALUM** Tufted perennials. Culms to 100 cm tall. Leaves cauline and basal, glabrous. Panicles of two to five spicate primary unilateral branches; branches mostly 4–10 cm long, bearing more or less paired spikelets. Spikelets 2.2–2.6 mm long, elliptic; first glumes present on most spikelets, rusty brown, margins pubescent; lemma of lower florets rusty brown, 3-veined, glabrous; upper florets light brown.

Occasional in sandy woods openings, usually in partial shade along lower and mid Gulf Coast. Good forage; provides limited seed for wildilfe.

Paspalum lividum Trin. **LONGTOM** (Figure 142) Perennials with creeping stolons as much as 1–2 m long. Culms to 70 cm tall, flattened. Leaves cauline; sheaths glabrous, thin, keeled, soon breaking off and exposing yellowish-brown nodes; blades mostly 3–6 mm wide, glabrous to hirsute. Panicles of three to seven spicate primary unilateral branches; branches 1.5–4.0 cm long, 1.5–2.0 mm wide, short, spreading to erect with or without a few scattered long hairs, often becoming dark purple; spikelets imbricated in four rows per branch. Spikelets 2.0–2.5 mm long, glabrous, elliptic or obovate, widely pointed; glumes and lemma of lower florets thin, chartaceous; upper florets finely rugose, straw colored.

Occasional in ditches, swales, coastal flats, along streams, and around marshes of entire Gulf Coast. Good forage. One of the top four species in cattle diets along mid Gulf Coast on mid-successional rangelands. Also provides abundant seeds for birds. Often called "pull-and-be-damned."

Figure 142. *Paspalum lividum*
plant and spikelet (lowermost lemma view) (Gould and
Box 1965).

Paspalum minus Fourn. **MAT PASPALUM** Similar to *P. notatum* but has more slender culms and inflorescences. Culms seldom over 30 cm tall with rhizomatous bases usually forming a dense mat. Lower sheaths and blades often hirsute or hispid. Spikelets 2.0–2.5 mm long and less shiny than in *P. notatum*.

Infrequent in open grasslands or along wooded borders of mid Gulf Coast.

Paspalum monostachyum Vasey **GULFDUNE PASPALUM** (Figure 143) Stout rhizomatous perennials. Culms to 120 cm tall, erect. Leaves basal and cauline, glabrous; blades 2 mm wide, involute. Panicles of one to three spicate primary unilateral branches; branches 10–15 cm long. Spikelets 3.0–3.5 mm long, paired, some with irregularly developed first glumes, glabrous, elliptic; upper lemmas 2.2–2.4 mm long, apex obtuse, light brown or straw colored.

Occasional to frequent on coastal dunes and in sandy sites along coastal woodlands throughout Gulf Coast. Highly desirable forage for cattle; fair wildlife seed value.

Paspalum notatum Flugge **BAHIAGRASS** Densely tufted, rhizomatous perennials. Culms to 75 cm tall, erect. Leaves basal and cauline, glabrous; ligules a dense ring of short hairs; blades 2–6 mm wide, flat, folded, involute, usually firm and tough in texture. Panicles typically of two (occasionally three) spicate primary unilateral branches, branches 4–12 cm long, paired at culm apex, or one slightly below the other. Spikelets 2.8–3.5 mm long, closely imbricate in two rows, glabrous, shiny; upper florets straw colored, about the length of spikelets.

Frequently planted as a pasture grass; occasional on roadsides, along ditches, and other slightly disturbed sites throughout Gulf Coast. Fair forage and hay producer in sandy soils but poor wildlife value.

Paspalum plicatulum Michx. **BROWNSEED PASPALUM** (Figure 144) Perennial bunchgrasses. Culms to 100 cm tall, stiff, erect, glabrous. Leaf sheaths keeled; ligules 3–7 mm long, brown; blades 20–35 cm long, mostly 4–6 mm wide with long pilose hairs above. Panicles with three to eight spicate primary

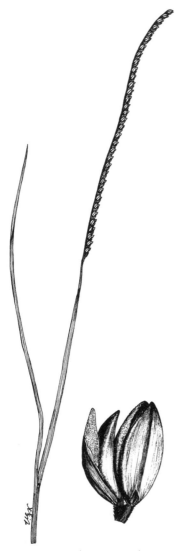

Figure 143. *Paspalum monostachyum* inflorescence and paired spikelets (Gould and Box 1965).

unilateral branches; branches mostly 3–8 cm long. Spikelets 2.5–5.1 mm long; first glumes absent; second glumes dark brown, ovate, apex obtuse; lower lemmas transversely rugose; upper florets dark brown, ovate, shiny, apex obtuse.

Frequent in sandy soils of prairies and open woodlands throughout Gulf Coast. Fair forage; good wildlife seed producer. Often a climax dominant in uplands of coastal prairie. Rio Grande wild turkeys (*Meleagris gallopavo*) have been observed "stripping" mature seed heads.

Paspalum praecox Walt. **EARLY PASPALUM** Rhizomatous perennials. Culms to 150 cm tall. Leaves cauline; sheaths slightly keeled; blades 15–25 cm long, 3–7 mm wide. Panicles with three to six spicate primary unilateral branches, branches 2–7 cm long, flattened, slender with short-pedicelled, paired spikelets. Spikelets 2.2–3.2 mm long, glabrous; lower lemmas 3- to 5-veined; upper florets light brown, minutely papillose.

In moist woodlands and pastures along upper Gulf Coast. Birds and rodents eat seeds.

Paspalum pubiflorum Rupr. *ex* Fourn. var. ***pubiflorum*** **HAIRYSEED PASPALUM** Glaucous perennials. Culms to 100 cm long from decumbent bases. Leaf sheaths pilose; blades wide, glabrous except for a few hairs near base. Spikelets 2.7–3.2 mm

Figure 144. *Paspalum plicatulum* inflorescence and paired spikelets (Gould and Box 1965).

long, elliptic to obovate, pubescent; upper florets light colored. Similar to *P. hartwegianum*, differing by having blunter, more pubescent, and wider leaves (6–15 mm).

Frequent along mid Gulf Coast on clay soils along ditches, oak mottes, swales, and other areas of moist heavy soils; occasional in partial shade throughout coastal region. Fair forage; fair seed producer for birds.

Paspalum setaceum Michx. **THIN PASPALUM** Low, short-lived tufted perennials. Culms to 80 cm tall from knotty bases or short rhizomes. Leaves nearly glabrous to variously pubescent; ligules minute; blades 4–5 mm wide, flat, soft. Spicate racemes or panicles with two to five slender, spicate primary unilateral branches; branches ascending. Spikelets 1.4–2.6 mm long, elliptic to orbicular.

var. ***ciliatifolium*** (Michx.) Vasey **FRINGELEAF PASPALUM** (Figure 145) Distinguised from other varieties by dark green to purplish herbage, wider leaf blades (3–20 mm wide), and spikelets 1.7–2.6 mm long.

var. ***muhlenbergii*** (Nash) D. Banks Distinguished by having pilose leaf blades and conspicuous midvein on lower florets. Herbage light to dark green.

var. ***stramineum*** (Nash) D. Banks Distinguished by yellowish-green foliage and narrow leaf blades (3–15 mm wide). Spikelets 1.6–2.2 mm long, suborbicular, yellow to light green, sometimes spotted; lemma of lower florets rusty brown and pubescent, otherwise similar to second glumes.

Infrequent to common throughout Gulf Coast in a wide range of soils; most frequent in heavily grazed pastures, ditches, and wooded borders. All varieties are fair forage; limited seed production provides only fair wildlife value.

Paspalum unispicatum (Scribn. & Merr.) Nash **ONESPIKE PASPALUM** Rhizomatous perennials. Culms 50–80 cm tall, arising singly or in small clumps. Leaf blades 3–4 mm wide, rather stiff, more or less papillose-hairy. Spicate racemes 7–20 cm long, slender; secondary inflorescences axillary. Spikelets 3.0–3.3 mm long, elliptic to narrowly oblong; first glumes present or absent; upper florets straw colored or light brown.

Infrequent in sandy soils of lower to mid Gulf Coast.

Paspalum urvillei Steud. **VASEYGRASS** (Figure 146) Large, coarse, perennial bunchgrasses. Culms to 2 m tall, numerous, stiffly erect. Leaves basal and cauline; basal sheaths hirsute to sharply hispid, upper sheaths glabrous; ligules membranous; blades 4–15 mm wide, long. Panicles of 8–50 spicate primary unilateral branches; branches 4–13 cm long with spikelets in four rows. Spikelets 2.2–2.7 mm long, conspicuously pubescent.

Infrequent in sandy ditches, swales, and other areas of moist disturbed soils of lower Gulf Coast; frequent along upper Gulf Coast. Poor forage; limited wildlife value except as nesting cover.

Paspalum vaginatum Sw. **SEASHORE PASPALUM** (Figure 147) Low-growing perennials. Culms to 60 cm tall, decumbent. Leaves cauline; sheaths large, straw colored; blades 1–4 mm wide, inrolled. Panicles with paired, spicate primary unilateral branches at culm apex. Spikelets 2.6–4.0 mm long, apex acute, glabrous, in two rows; upper florets straw colored.

Infrequent along Gulf Coast in poorly drained areas with sandy or sandy loam soils, usually in shallow brackish ponds and marshes. Poor to fair forage; good for shoreline stabilization.

Paspalum virgatum L **TALQUEZAL** Large, rhizomatous perennial bunchgrasses. Culms to 2 m tall, unbranched. Leaf blades 30–40 cm long, 9–13 mm wide, flat, margins serrate. Panicles with 10-16 spicate primary unilateral branches; branches 7–15 cm long, spreading, drooping, bearing spikelets in four rows. Spikelets 2.7–3.2 mm long, elliptic to obovate; first glumes absent; second glumes brown, pubescent; upper florets dark brown.

Figure 145. *Paspalum setaceum* var. *ciliatifolium* inflorescence and spikelet (Gould and Box 1965).

Figure 146. *Paspalum urvillei*
plant, (A) spikelet (second glume view), (B) spikelet (lowermost lemma view), and (C) upper floret (palea view) (Gould and Box 1965).

Infrequent along lower and mid Gulf Coast; a grass of moist or marshy open sites.

64. **PENNISETUM** L. C. Rich. • Pennisetum

Culms solid. Leaves basal and cauline; sheaths rounded or keeled; ligules a ciliate membrane; blades flat. Panicles contracted, cylindrical; spicate primary branch a stipe, bearing fascicles of bristles subtending one to five spikelets; bristles frequently in two series. Spikelets dorsally compressed, disarticulation below glumes; florets two, lower sterile, upper fertile; glumes awnless; upper lemma awnless.

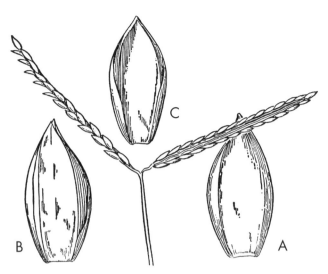

Figure 147. *Paspalum vaginatum*
inflorescence, (A) second glume, (B) spikelet (lower lemma view), and (C) upper floret (palea view)
(Hitchcock 1951).

1. Longer bristles of involucre longer than 3 cm **2**
1. Longer bristles of involucre shorter than 2.5 cm **3**
2(1) Inflorescence 15–30 cm long, purple; lemma of lower florets 1- to 3-(5) -veined .... *P. setaceum*
2. Inflorescence shorter than 10 cm, tawny; lemma of lower florets 7- to 11-veined .... *P. villosum*
3(1). Spikelets sessile within involucre; bristles often united at base to form small disk-shaped cup .... *P. ciliare*
3. Spikelets pedicellate within involucre; bristles free to base, not forming cup **4**
4(3). Apex of peduncle glabrous to slightly puberulent .... *P. orientale*
4. Apex of peduncle hairy, pilose to villous **5**
5(4). Longest bristles to 1.7 cm long; spikelets 5.0–6.6 mm long ....
.... *P. purpureum*
5. Longest bristles to about 1 cm long; spikelets about 4 mm long ....
.... *P. nervosum*

Pennisetum ciliare (L.) Link **BUFFELGRASS** (Figure 148) Tufted perennials. Culms to 100 cm tall, erect to spreading. Leaf sheaths keeled; blades flat and wide. Panicles 5–12 cm long, contracted, densely spikeleted; fascicles of two to four

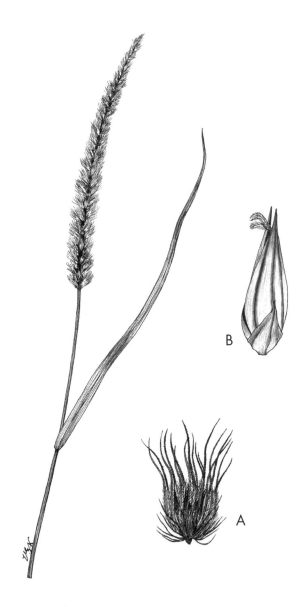

Figure 148. *Pennisetum ciliare*
inflorescence, (A) bur, and (B) spikelet (Gould and Box 1965).

spikelets, purplish, subtended by bristles 4–8 mm long. Spikelets 2.1–5.7 mm long; glumes and lemmas awnless, whitish, lanceolate; upper lemmas 2.0–5.4 mm long.

Frequent in a variety of soils along lower and mid Gulf Coast. Persists in pastures and as a weed of roadsides; a preferred introduced species recommended for pasture seeding following brush control in southern Texas and northern Mexico. Good livestock forage and bird nesting cover.

Pennisetum nervosum (Nees) Trin. **BENTSPIKE PENNISETUM** Tufted perennials from knotty bases. Culms to 3.2 m tall, erect, lower nodes swollen. Leaf sheaths glabrous; ligules 1.5–1.8 mm long, a ciliate membrane; blades 6–10 mm long. Panicles 8–22 cm long, to 2 cm thick, contracted; fascicles of one spikelet, spreading, bristles about 1 cm long, purple. Spikelets 5–6 mm long.

Occurs along roadsides and deep sandy soils of lower Gulf Coast and lower Rio Grande Valley.

Pennisetum orientale L. C. Rich. **LAURISAGRASS** Rhizomatous perennials. Culms 40–150 cm tall, erect, much-branched basally. Leaf sheaths rounded; ligules 0.2–1.4 mm long, membranous; blades to 35 cm long. Panicles 10–25 cm long, contracted; fascicles of one to five spikelets, bristles in two series, inner series longer (to 2 cm), ciliate, stipe scabrous to pubescent. Spikelets 4.4–8.7 mm long.

Occurs as an escaped roadside weed; introduced as a cultivated grass.

Pennisetum purpureum Schumach. **NAPIERGRASS** Caespitose perennials. Culms 2–4 m tall, erect, nodes with a tuft of hairs. Leaf sheaths rounded, ligules 2.0–2.4 mm long, a ciliate membrane; blades to 30–50 cm long. Panicles to 25 cm long, 2.5–3.0 cm wide, contracted, branches spreading; peduncles densely pubescent; fascicles with one spikelet, bristles to 1.7 cm long, golden. Spikelets 5.5–6.5 mm long.

Cultivated for pasture and occasional as a roadside weed along lower to mid Gulf Coast. Highly productive forage species, but becomes unpalatable at maturity.

Pennisetum setaceum (Forssk.) Chiov. **FOUNTAINGRASS** (Figure 149) Densely tufted perennials. Culms to 1.3 mm tall, erect. Leaf sheaths rounded; blades to 35 cm long, to 4 mm wide, glaucous. Panicles 5–30 cm long, cylindrical, central axis angular with pubescent stipes 1–3 mm long; fascicles of one to three spikelets, bristles 14–42 mm long, inner ones plumose. Spikelets 4.4–6.4 mm long.

Occasional as an escaped weed; cultivated.

Pennisetum villosum R. Br. *ex* Fresen. **FEATHERTOP PENNISETUM** (Figure 150) Tufted perennials. Culms 20–75 cm tall, ascending, base may be rhizomatous. Leaves with ligules a ciliate membrane, hairs to 1 mm long; blades to 30 cm long, flat or folded, glabrous. Panicles to 12 cm long, contracted; fascicles of one spikelet, bristles subtended by stipe with long hairs, bristles to about 4 cm long, tawny white, inner bristles plumose. Spikelets 7–9 mm long.

Commonly grown as an ornamental and occasionally persisting out of cultivation throughout Gulf Coast.

65. **PHALARIS** L. • Canarygrass

Culms hollow. Leaves cauline; sheaths open; ligules membranous; blades flat. Panicles contracted, spikelike. Spikelets awnless, with a single fertile floret and one or two scalelike rudimentary florets below, disarticulation above the glumes; glumes longer than florets, subequal and usually winged; upper florets coriaceous, shiny.

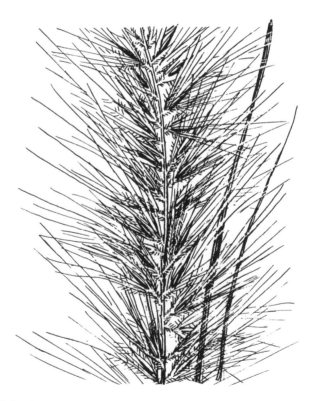

Figure 149. *Pennisetum setaceum*
partial inflorescence (Hitchcock 1951).

Figure 150. *Pennisetum villosum* inflorescence and leaves (Hitchcock 1951).

1.	Reduced florets one, scalelike	*P. minor*
1.	Reduced florets two, scalelike	2
2(1).	Reduced florets broad, more than one-half the length of perfect floret	*P. canariensis*
2.	Reduced florets subulate, less than one-half the length of perfect floret	3
3(2).	Panicles 2–7 cm long; culms to 70 cm tall	*P. caroliniana*
3.	Panicles 6–15 cm long; culms 60–150 cm tall	*P. angusta*

Phalaris angusta Nees *ex* Trin. **TIMOTHY CANARYGRASS** (Figure 151) Glabrous annuals. Culms to 150 cm tall, erect, thick, succulent. Leaves with ligules 3–5 mm long; blades 5–12 mm wide. Panicles 6–15 cm long, 8–10 mm wide. Spikelets with glumes 3.5–4.0 mm long, keels scabrous, apex narrowly winged; reduced florets two, basal, subequal, scalelike; lemma of upper floret thick, shiny, ovate, attenuate, hispid. Caryopses 2.6–3.0 mm long.

Found in ditches, swales, and other moist, open sites along mid and upper Gulf Coast. Good seed producer; often planted in game food plots.

Phalaris canariensis L. **CANARYGRASS** (Figure 152) Tufted, glabrous annuals. Culms to 70 cm tall, erect. Leaves with ligules 2–6 mm long; blades 5–15 cm long, 3–7 mm wide. Panicles 1.5–3.0 (–4.0) cm long, 10–18 mm wide, short, thick. Spikelets with glumes 7–9 mm long, glabrous to sparsely hispid, pale, upper half of keel broadly winged to 1 mm wide; reduced florets 2.5–4.5 mm long, scalelike, subequal; lemma of upper floret 4.5–6.5 mm long, densely appressed-pubescent, narrowly acute or acuminate. Caryopses 3.9–4.2 mm long.

Adventive, generally not persisting outside cultivation; common constituent of birdseed mixes.

Phalaris caroliniana Walt. **CAROLINA CANARYGRASS** (Figure 153) Low succulent annuals. Culms to 70 cm tall, erect. Leaves with blades 6–15 cm long, 3–10 mm wide, flat. Panicles 2–8 cm long, 8–13 mm wide, contracted. Spikelets with glumes 5–6 mm long, keel with greenish wing, wing 0.2–0.5 mm wide; reduced florets narrow, scalelike, somewhat unequal, one-third to one-half the length of

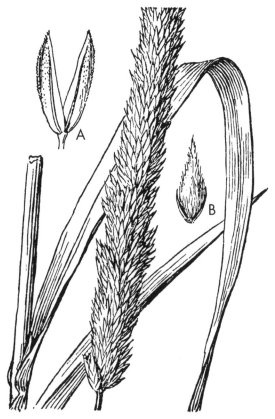

Figure 151. *Phalaris angusta* inflorescence, (A) glumes, and (B) florets (Hitchcock 1951).

Figure 152. *Phalaris canariensis*
plant, (A) spikelet, and (B) two reduced florets (perfect floret above) (Hitchcock 1951).

upper florets; lemma of upper floret 3–4 mm long, shiny, ovate lanceolate, hirsute with whitish hairs. Caryopses 1.7–2.0 mm long, brownish, oblong and minutely rugose.

Found in grasslands and open woodlands on fine-textured soils; especially abundant on roadsides, stream banks, and ditch banks throughout Gulf Coast. Provides fair spring forage for livestock and seed for wildlife.

Figure 153. *Phalaris caroliniana*
plant, (A) spikelet, and (B) three florets (Gould and Box 1965).

Phalaris minor Retz. **LITTLESEED CANARYGRASS** Tufted annuals generally similar to *P. canariensis* but panicles often longer (to 8 cm); glumes narrower with pale green lateral striations; reduced florets about 1 mm long at base of perfect floret; lemma of upper floret mostly 2.5–3.5 mm long.

Adventive along Gulf Coast from chance seedings, but probably not persisting.

66. **PHRAGMITES** Adans.

Plants tall. Culms hollow. Leaves basal and cauline; sheaths open, rounded; ligules a ciliate membrane; blades flat, broad. Panicles open, nodding at maturity, peduncle with a tuft of hairs at base. Spikelets laterally compressed, disarticulation above the glumes; florets several, sterile florets apical; glumes 3-veined, awnless; lemmas 3-veined, awnless, glabrous; rachilla hairy.

Phragmites australis (Cav.) Trin. *ex* Steud. **COMMON REED** (Figure 154) Robust rhizomatous perennials. Culms to 3 m tall, erect, glabrous. Leaves to base of inflorescence; blades 1.5–5.0 cm wide, margins scabrous. Panicles 15–40 cm long, usually drooping, much-branched. Spikelets 10–15 mm long; florets four to eight; rachilla joints villous, hairs 1 cm or longer; glumes, lemmas, and paleas glabrous; first glumes one-half to two-thirds the length of second glumes, 3-veined; second glumes mostly 6–8 mm long, 3- to 5-veined, acute or mucronate; lower lemmas 10–11 mm long, awnless, brown, apex acuminate; paleas to 4 mm long, 2-veined.

Occasional to locally abundant along streams, ditches, and other moist sites, often in shallow water throughout Gulf Coast. Provides fair to good forage and good nesting habitat for mottled ducks; cannot withstand prolonged heavy grazing. Good for shoreline stabilization.

67. **PIPTOCHAETIUM** Presl

Culms hollow. Leaves basal and cauline; sheaths open, rounded; ligules membranous; blades flat to involute. Panicles loosely contracted. Spikelets terete to laterally compressed, disarticulation above the glumes; florets one; glumes equal, membranous, longer than floret; lemmas indurate, with overlapping margins enclosing all but tip of paleas.

Piptochaetium avenaceum (L.) Parodi **BLACKSEED NEEDLEGRASS** (Figure 155) Tufted perennials. Culms to 75 cm tall, slender, stiffly erect. Leaf blades 1 mm wide. Panicles to 20 cm long, open, nodding. Spikelets to 15 mm long; floret one; glumes 10–15 mm long, thin, glabrous with stiff brownish hairs; lemmas 8–10 mm long, dark brown and shining when mature, base hairy; lemma awns 3.5–7.0 cm long, twisted at base.

Found along upper Gulf Coast in shade of sandy woodlands; shade tolerant. Good livestock forage but herbage production low; poor wildlife value.

Figure 154. *Phragmites australis*
plant, (A) spikelet, and (B) floret (Hitchcock 1951).

68. **POA** L. • Bluegrass

Culms hollow. Leaf sheaths mostly open; ligules membranous; blades flat to folded. Panicles open or contracted, rarely a raceme. Spikelets laterally compressed, disarticulation below the glumes, usually with several perfect florets, reduced florets at spikelet apex; glumes keeled; lemmas 5-veined, scabrous on the margins; veins somewhat obscure, glabrous to scabrous to pilose; paleas often ciliolate.

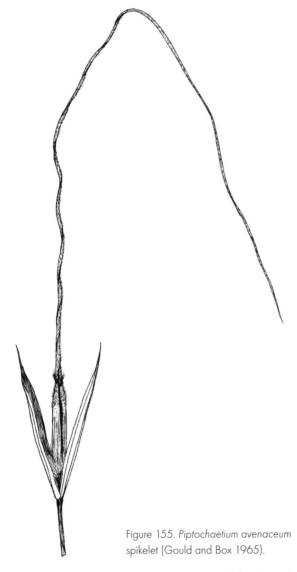

Figure 155. *Piptochaetium avenaceum* spikelet (Gould and Box 1965).

1. Plants annual .... *P. annua*
1. Plants perennial 2
2(1). Plants caespitose, with perfect florets; panicles open, diffuse ....
.... *P. autumnalis*
2. Plants rhizomatous, dioecious; panicles contracted, dense ....
.... *P. arachnifera*

Poa annua L. **ANNUAL BLUEGRASS** (Figure 156) Low, tufted, unbranched annuals. Culms to 30 cm tall, ascending, geniculate. Leaves cauline, glabrous, bright green; ligules 1.5–4.0 mm long, decurrent; blades 2–12 cm long, 1.5–4.0 mm wide, thin, flat. Panicles mostly 3–8 cm long, well-exserted or hidden in basal tuft of leaves, lower branches stiffly spreading and bare of spikelets on lower one-third to one-half. Spikelets with glumes slightly unequal, thin, wide; lower lemmas 3.0–3.5 mm long, hyaline, apex obtuse, 5-veined, veins equally developed, variously pubescent to nearly glabrous, pubescence commonly on midvein and marginal veins.

Found throughout Gulf Coast as a weed in lawns and disturbed sites during late winter to early spring. Palatable but a low forage producer with a relatively short growth period; poor wildlife value.

Poa arachnifera Torr. **TEXAS BLUEGRASS** (Figure 157) Tufted dioecious perennials with slender rhizomes. Culms to 50 cm tall, stiffly erect. Leaves cauline and basal, glabrous; blades 1–5 mm wide, elongate, folded or flat. Panicles 6–16 cm long, contracted, may be lobed. Spikelets with three to six florets; pistillate spikelets densely woolly-pubescent with long, kinky hairs attached at base of lemmas or on rachilla joints immediately below florets; staminate spikelets not conspicuously hairy, but usually with a few long, kinky hairs at base of florets; glumes and lemmas thin, chartaceous, broadly acute or obtuse.

Occurs at wooded borders of prairies along upper Gulf Coast. Good forage.

Poa autumnalis Muhl. *ex* Ell. **AUTUMN BLUEGRASS** (Figure 158) Tufted perennials. Culms to 70 cm tall, slender, weak. Leaves basal and cauline, glabrous; ligules 0.5–1.0 mm long; blades 1.0–4.5 mm wide, lax. Panicles 8–18 cm long with slender, usually paired branches; lower branches spikelet-bearing only near apex. Spikelets 5–7 mm long, florets three to six; first glumes about one-third the length of spikelet; second glumes about one-half; lower lemmas mostly 3.5–4.5 mm long, apex wide and rounded, hyaline, 5-veined, well-defined, midvein and margins hairy below middle but without basal tuft of long, kinky hairs.

Figure 156. *Poa annua*
plant and spikelet (Gould and Box 1965).

Most frequent in pine or mixed-pine hardwood forest along upper Gulf Coast. Fair winter to spring forage.

69. **POLYPOGON** Desf. • Polypogon

Culms hollow. Leaves basal and cauline; sheaths rounded; ligules membranous; blades flat. Panicles contracted, dense. Spikelets laterally compressed, disarticula-

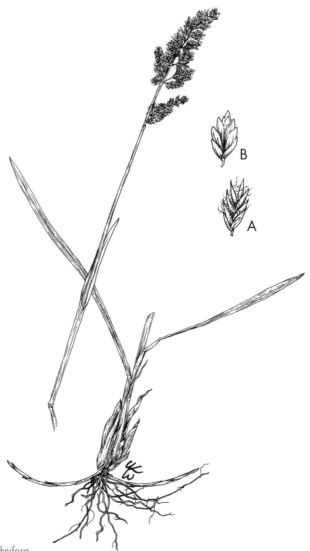

Figure 157. *Poa arachnifera*
plant, (A) pistillate spikelet, and (B) staminate spikelet (Keith Westover).

tion below the glumes; floret one; glumes equal, longer than floret, awned; lemmas membranous, short-awned; rachilla not prolonged beyond floret.

Polypogon monspeliensis (L.) Desf. **RABBITFOOT POLYPOGON** (Figure 159)
Tufted annuals. Culms to 70 cm tall, weak, geniculate, often rooting at lower nodes.

Leaves with blades 3–6 mm wide, flat, glabrous. Panicles to 15 cm long, 1.0–2.5 cm wide, dense, lobed, light green. Spikelets 1.0–1.5 mm long (excluding awns), laterally compressed; glumes scabrous to pubescent with awn 2–10 mm long; lemmas and paleas much shorter than glumes; lemma awns to 1 mm long, delicate.

Found throughout Gulf Coast as a weed along streams, ditches, and swales; occurs in areas of high salinity as well as along bodies of fresh water. Poor livestock and wildlife values.

70. **ROSTRARIA** Trin.

Culms hollow. Leaves mostly basal; sheaths open; ligules membranous; blades flat to involute. Panicles contracted, dense. Spikelets laterally compressed, disarticulation above glumes; florets two to four, reduced floret apical; glumes subequal, shiny, nearly the length of lower floret; lemmas shiny, usually awnless; rachilla extending above the apical floret.

Rostraria cristata (L.) Tzvelev **ANNUAL JUNEGRASS** Tufted annuals. Culms to 40 cm tall, erect. Leaves cauline; blades 2–15 cm long, 1–5

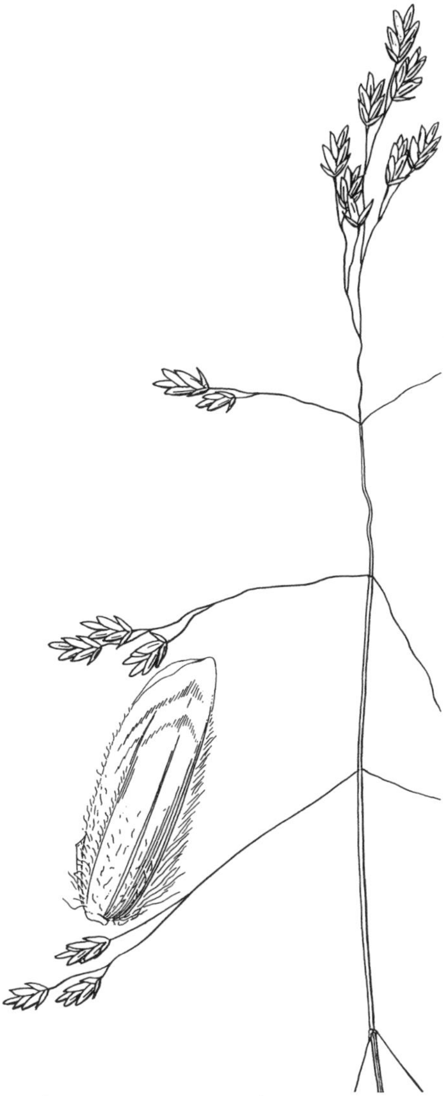

Figure 158. *Poa autumnalis* partial inflorescence and floret (lemma view) (Hitchcock 1951).

mm wide. Panicles 2–7 cm long, dense. Spikelets 4–5 mm long; florets four to six; glumes and lemmas papillose or papillose-hispid on back, margins hyaline and shiny; second glumes and lemmas 2.5–3.0 mm long; lemmas with awn to 2 mm long, apex minutely bifid; paleas narrow, hyaline, awn- tipped.

Adventive along upper Gulf Coast. Poor livestock and wildlife values.

Figure 159. *Polypogon monspeliensis*
plant, (A) glumes, and (B) floret (Hitchcock 1951).

71. **ROTTBOELLIA** L.f.

Culms solid. Leaves cauline; sheaths rounded with sharp papilla-based hairs; ligules a ciliate membrane; blades with white midvein and margin. Spicate racemes terminal and axillary on most culms, with paired spikelets at each node appearing sunken into thick rachis. Sessile spikelets fertile and coriaceous, pedicellate spikelet sterile; sessile spikelet glumes equal, awnless; lemmas membranous.

Rottboellia cochinchinensis (Lour.) W. D.
Clayton **ITCHGRASS** (Figure 160) Robust annuals. Culms to 3 m tall, erect, branching, glabrous; lower nodes developing prop roots. Leaves
with lower sheaths having stiff papilla-based hairs
1–3 mm long, sharp; ligules a ciliate membrane
1.0–1.5 mm long; blades to 60 cm long, 10–23 mm
wide, flat, glabrous above. Spicate racemes to
15 cm long, axillary inflorescences shorter, disarticulation at rachis nodes; spikelets two per node.
Sessile spikelets 4.0–6.5 mm long, awnless; first
glumes flat, apex bifid; second glumes keeled;
upper lemmas hyaline; upper paleas absent; pedicellate spikelets neuter.

Occurs in disturbed sites along upper Gulf
Coast near Port Arthur. Introduced from the Old
World where it is an aggressive weed; ranked 18th
as the worst weed worldwide in the Federal Noxious Weed Act. Common name is derived from the
"itch" caused by contact with stiff, irritating hairs
on leaf sheaths.

72. **SACCHARUM** L. • Plumegrass (adapted from R. D. Webster and R. D. Shaw 1995)

Culms tall, solid. Leaves basal and cauline; sheaths
open; ligules a ciliate membrane; blades flat, wide.
Panicles large, dense, plumose; branches ascending, several per node. Spikelets all alike and perfect, in pairs of one sessile and one pedicellate,
disarticulation at base of sessile spikelet; florets two,
lower sterile, upper perfect; glumes coriaceous,
large, firm, subequal, usually with tuft of long hairs
at base; lemma of lower florets and lemmas of upper florets thin and hyaline; lemma of upper florets with long, straight or loosely twisted awns;
paleas absent. Pedicellate spikelets well developed.
Includes the genus *Erianthus*.

Figure 160. *Rottboellia
cochinchinensis*
inflorescence
(Hitchcock 1951).

1. Lemma awn of upper florets basally spiraled 2

1. Lemma awn of upper florets not basally spiraled 3

2(1). Callus hairs 7 mm or shorter, equal to or shorter than spikelet; inflorescence central axis sparsely hairy .... *S. brevibarbe* var. *contortum*

2. Callus hairs longer than 7 mm, longer than spikelet; inflorescence central axis densely hairy. .... *S. alopecuroideum*

3(1). Callus hairs longer than spikelet; panicles more than 10 cm wide .... *S. giganteum*

3. Callus hairs equal to or shorter than spikelet; panicles less than 8 cm wide .... *S. baldwinii*

Saccharum alopecuroideum (L.) Nutt. **SILVER PLUMEGRASS** Tall, stout perennials. Similar to *S. brevibarbe* var. *contortum* but hairs at base of spikelets 1 cm or longer and more copious. Main panicle axis and branches more or less obscured by silky hairs; lower internode of panicle axis and internode below panicle typically with appressed hair, but usually becoming glabrous with age. Upper lemma awns flattened, loosely twisted, and in loose spirals to well above middle.

Occurs in ditches and swales, and along lake and stream shores of upper Gulf Coast.

Figure 161. *Saccharum baldwinii* inflorescence and leaves (Hitchcock 1951).

Saccharum baldwinii Spreng. **NARROW PLUMEGRASS** (Figure 161) Perennials. Culms to 2 m tall with hard, knotty base; nodes of young culms hispid with long, stiff, deciduous hairs. Leaves basal and cauline; ligules ciliate membranes; blades to 80 cm long, 6–12 mm wide, flat. Panicles 20–40 cm long; branches stiffly erect, hairs not prominent. Spikelets 8–11 mm long, sparsely hairy; glumes about equal, glabrous or scabrous-hispid, brownish; upper lemma awns 14–20 mm long, straight.

Occurs in moist swales and ponds, and along lakeshores and riverbanks of upper Gulf Coast.

Saccharum brevibarbe (Michx.) Pers. var. *contortum* (Ell.) R. Webster
BENTAWN PLUMEGRASS Robust perennials from firm, knotty bases. Culms to 2.5 m tall. Leaves basal and cauline; ligules ciliate membranes, fringed with stiff hairs 1–3 mm long; blades to 80 cm long, mostly 8–18 mm wide, flat. Panicles 20–50 cm long, peduncles glabrous. Spikelets 6–8 mm long, callus with dense tuft of white or tawny spreading hairs about the length of spikelets; glumes about equal, brownish, apex narrow; first glumes often sparsely long-hispid on margins; upper lemma awns 15–22 mm long, slightly flattened at base, loosely twisted and geniculate below middle, terminal half usually straight.

Found along upper Gulf Coast in moist soil of swales, ditches, and stream and lakeshores. Palatable to horses and cattle; decreases with overgrazing. Poor wildlife value, other than providing cover.

Saccharum giganteum (Walt.) Pers. **SUGARCANE PLUMEGRASS** (Figure 162)
Densely tufted perennials in dense clumps from hard, knotty rhizomatous bases. Culms to 3 m tall, erect, nodes densely bearded with hairs 2–6 mm long. Leaves basal and cauline; ligules and collars of leaf densely villous; blades to 90 cm long, to 20 mm wide. Panicles mostly 15–50 cm long, conspicuously hairy, main axis villous. Spikelets 6–8 mm long, brownish; callus hairs copious, brownish, slightly shorter to considerably longer than spikelets; upper lemma awns 12–25 mm long, straight or slightly curved, terete, and untwisted.

Found mostly in wet soils of bogs, swales, or swamps along mid and upper Gulf Coast.

73. SACCIOLEPIS Nash

Culms hollow. Leaves cauline; sheaths open; ligules a ciliate membrane; blades flat. Panicles contracted. Spikelets awnless, dorsally compressed, disarticulation below glumes; florets two, lower sterile, upper fertile; glumes greatly unequal; second glumes saccate at base; upper florets indurate.

Sacciolepis striata (L.) Nash **AMERICAN CUPSCALE** Stoloniferous perennials. Culms 1.5 m or longer, often decumbent or from stoloniferous bases rooting freely at nodes. Leaf blades 8–20 cm long, 6–15 mm wide, thin. Panicles 8–25 cm long, elongated. Spikelets 3.5–4.3 mm long, glabrous, awnless, asymmetrical at base; first glumes acute, greatly reduced and usually one-fourth the length of sec-

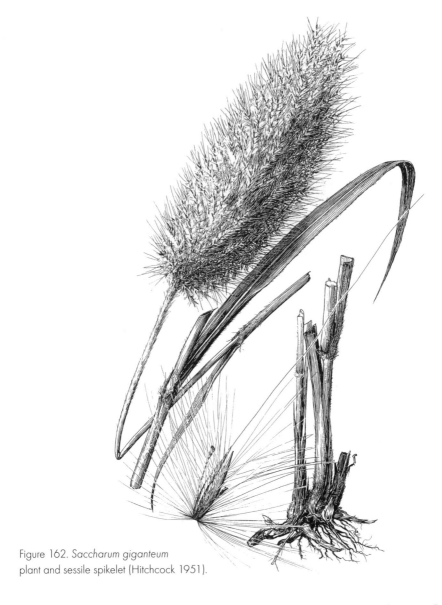

Figure 162. *Saccharum giganteum*
plant and sessile spikelet (Hitchcock 1951).

ond or less; second glumes inflated to saccate at base; 7- to 11-veined; upper florets indurate, much shorter than second glumes, smooth, shiny, apex rounded.

Found along upper Gulf Coast in moist soil of ponds, ditches, and streams.

74. SCHEDONNARDUS Steud.

Culms hollow or solid. Leaves basal; sheaths open; ligules membranous; blades flat, short, spirally twisted, margin white. Panicles of alternate spicate primary branches with widely spaced spikelets. Spikelets laterally compressed, disarticulation above glumes; florets one, glumes unequal; lemmas 3-veined.

Schedonnardus paniculatus (Nutt.) Trel. **TUMBLEGRASS** (Figure 163) Low, tufted perennials. Culms to 70 cm long, wiry, stiffly curving. Leaves glabrous; sheaths keeled; blades to 15 cm long, twisted when dry. Panicles of two to eight spicate primary unilateral branches, much exceeding leafy portion of plant; branches slender, stiffly curved, bearing widely spaced but closely appressed spikelets. Spikelets 3–9 mm long; lemmas 3-veined; paleas the length of lemmas. At maturity inflorescence breaks off at base to become a tumbleweed.

Occasional throughout Gulf Coast, most commonly in clayey soils. Frequent in heavily grazed pastures on clay upland sites, often associated with *Bouteloua rigidiseta*, *Aristida* species, and other "poor quality" forage plants. Poor forage; poor wildlife value.

75. **SCHIZACHYRIUM** Nees • Bluestem

Culms solid. Leaves basal and cauline; sheaths rounded or keeled; ligules membranous; blades flat or folded. Spicate racemes terminal and axillary, numerous per culm. Spikelets paired, dorsally compressed, disarticulation below glumes; sessile spikelet fertile, pedicellate one sterile; sessile spikelet glumes equal; lemmas hyaline; upper lemmas awned.

1.	Lower sheaths and leaf blades villous	*S. scoparium* var. *divergens*
1.	Lower sheaths and leaf blades glabrous to pubescent 2	
2(1).	Plants rhizomatous; sheaths strongly keeled; rachis joints densely villous .... *S. scoparium* var. *littorale*	
2.	Plants tufted, without rhizomes; sheaths only slightly keeled; rachis joints ciliate .... *S. scoparium* var. *scoparium*	

Schizachyrium scoparium (Michx.) Nash **LITTLE BLUESTEM** Tufted perennial bunchgrasses. Culms 50–200 cm tall with or without rhizomes, green or glaucous, branching freely above to produce numerous inflorescences per culm. Leaf sheaths to 10 mm wide, strongly keeled, laterally flattened, glabrous to villous; basal blades 25 cm or longer, 1.5–4.0 (rarely 6.0) mm wide, glabrous or sparsely hispid to villous. Spicate racemes mostly 2.5–5.0 cm long; rachis joints and pedicels ciliate with long, silvery hairs, at least on upper two-thirds. Sessile spikelets 6–8 mm long; first glumes glabrous or scabrous; upper lemmas 8–15 mm long, awns 9–16 mm long. Pedicellate spikelets staminate or neuter, from the length of sessile spikelets to much shorter, awnless or with short, straight awns. Many intergrading forms and varieties.

var. *divergens* (Hack.) Gould **EASTERN LITTLE BLUESTEM** Distinguished by long, shaggy hairs on sheaths and blades. Pedicellate spikelets well developed, often the length of sessile spikelets and with two well developed glumes.

Figure 163. *Schedonnardus paniculatus*
plant, (A) spikelet, and (B) floret (Hitchcock 1951).

Figure 164. *Schizachyrium scoparium* var. *scoparium*
plant, (A) rachis, (B) sessile spikelet, (C) pedicel, and pedicellate spikelet (Hitchcock 1951).

Frequent in open woodlands along upper Gulf Coast; shade tolerant. Good forage and wildlife cover.

var. ***littorale*** (Nash) Gould **SEACOAST BLUESTEM** Variety has well developed rhizomes and more or less densely pubescent rachis joints and pedicels.

Occurs in sandy areas where grazing has been light; usually the dominant forage species throughout Gulf Coast. Once a climax codominant, it has decreased in abundance in the coastal prairie; particularly well adapted to deep sandy sites. Good forage; good wildlife cover.

var. *scoparium* (C. E. Hubb.) Gould **LITTLE BLUESTEM** (Figure 164) Non-rhizomatous variety with glabrous to sparsely hispid leaves. Spicate raceme rachis and pedicels hairy, but not densely villous. Pedicellate spikelets narrower and shorter than sessile spikelets.

Codominant of coastal prairies and wooded openings throughout Gulf Coast. Good forage for cattle; poor wildlife forage, but provides good cover.

76. SECALE L. • Rye
Culms hollow. Leaves cauline; sheaths rounded; ligules membranous; blades flat. Spikes bilateral with one spikelet per node. Spikelets laterally compressed, disarticulation above glumes; florets two, rachilla extended above second floret; glumes equal; lemmas with an asymmetrical keel extending into an awn.

Secale cereale L. **RYE** (Figure 165) Tufted annuals. Culms to 120 cm tall, erect. Spikes 5–12 cm long, about 1 cm wide, dense, bilateral. Spikelets 6–16 mm long, florets two, borne singly, closely imbricate; rachilla flattened, densely hairy on margins, continued above upper florets as short stipe; glumes narrow, subequal, acuminate; lemmas wide, 5-veined, usually asymmetrical, tapering to a stout awn; awns straight, scabrous.

Frequent on roadsides. The common rye cereal planted for grain and forage. Good forage; good wildlife food and cover.

77. SETARIA Beauv. • Bristlegrass
Culms solid. Leaves basal, cauline, or both; ligules a ciliate membrane or a ring of hairs; blades usually flat. Panicles contracted, cylindrical, usually spikelike; spikelets, at least in part, subtended by one to several bristles representing reduced branchlets; bristles antrorsely or retrorsely barbed, disarticulation above bristles, leaving discoid or cup-shaped callus. Spikelets similar to those of *Panicum*, except upper lemmas occasionally rugose.

1.	Plants annual	2
1.	Plants perennial	6
2(1).	Bristles retrorsely scabrous	*S. adhaerans*
2.	Bristles antrorsely scabrous	3
3(2).	Bristles 4–12 below each spikelet	*S. pumila*

3.	Bristles 1–3 below each spikelet	4
4(3).	Spikelets 1.8–2.5 mm long	5
4.	Spikelets 2.8–3.1 mm long	*S. italica*
5(4).	Upper florets smooth	*S. magna*
5.	Upper florets rugose	*S. corrugata*

Figure 165. *Secale cereale*
plant, (A) spikelet, and (B) floret (palea view) (Hitchcock 1951).

6(1).	Bristles present only below terminal spikelets of inflorescences or branches 7
6.	Bristles present below all or nearly all spikelets................................. 9
7(6).	Spikelets 2.4–3.0 mm long; first glumes 1.2–1.5 mm long ... *S. ramiseta*
7.	Spikelets 2.9–3.6 mm long; first glumes 1.8–2.2 mm long.................... 8
8(7).	Leaf blades 1.5–3.0 mm wide .... *S. reverchonii*
8.	Leaf blades 5–7 mm wide .... *S. firmula*
9(6).	Bristles 4–12 below each spikelet .... *S. parviflora*
9.	Bristles one to three below each spikelet 10
10(9).	Inflorescences 2–5 cm long; leaf blades 2–3 mm wide........... *S. texana*
10.	Inflorescences 6–22 cm long; leaf blades 5 mm or wider 11
11(10).	Culm nodes pubescent; leaf blades 10–20 mm wide .... *S. scheelei*
11.	Culm nodes glabrous; leaf blades 5–15 mm wide 12
12(11).	Palea of lower florets nearly the length of palea of perfect florets........ .... *S. macrostachya*
12.	Palea of lower florets one-half to three-fourths the length of palea of perfect florets .... *S. leucopila*

Setaria adhaerans (Forssk.) Chiov. (Figure 166) Weak, trailing annuals. Culms 20–70 cm tall, geniculate, nodes glabrous. Leaf sheaths glabrous; ligules 1–2 mm long, a ring of hairs; blades 5–14 mm wide, flat, hispid on both surfaces, hairs papilla-based. Panicles 2–8 cm long, dense, tightly contracted; bristles one below each spikelet, retrorsely scabrous, longer than spikelets. Spikelets 1.5–2.0 mm long, oblong; glumes unequal; upper florets finely transversely rugose.

Common adventive weed in disturbed sites all along Gulf Coast.

Setaria corrugata (Ell.) Schult. Coarse annuals. Culms to 100 cm tall, decumbent or geniculate, rooting at lower nodes. Leaf sheaths hispid; blades 15–30 cm long, 4–7 mm wide, thin. Panicles 3–15 cm long, densely contracted, cylindrical, central axis scabrous and hispid; bristles 7–15 mm long, one to three below each spikelet, antrorsely scabrous. Spikelets 1.8–2.5 mm long; glumes unequal; lowermost lemma about equal to upper floret; upper florets coarsely, transversely rugose.

Infrequent on sandy, usually disturbed soils along upper Gulf Coast.

Setaria firmula (A. S. Hitchc. & Chase) Pilger (Figure 167) Tufted perennials. Culms to 40 cm tall, stiffly erect from a firm base. Leaves cauline; ligules 1.5–2.0 mm long, a ring of hairs. Panicles 6–15 cm long, contracted, bristles developed only below spikelets terminating the short, appressed branchlets or inflorescence apex. Spikelets mostly 3.0–3.2 mm long; glumes unequal; upper florets rugose.

Frequent on deep sandy soil, usually in heavily grazed areas of open prairie along lower Gulf Coast. Often associated with *Urochloa ciliatissima*. Good forage; good seed producer.

Setaria italica (L). Beauv. **FOXTAIL MIL-LET** (Figure 168) Annuals with large, dense, lobed panicles to 30 cm long and 3 cm wide. Spikelet color and awn length variable.

Cultivated annual of diverse habits with many commercial strains; often planted as part of plot mixes for game birds. Found infrequently in mid Gulf Coast.

Setaria leucopila (Scribn. & Merr.) K. Schum. **PLAINS BRISTLEGRASS** (Figure 169) Tufted perennials. Culms to 100 cm tall, stiffly erect, green or glaucous. Leaf sheaths villous; ligules 1–2 mm long, fringed with hairs; blades 2–5 mm wide. Panicles 6–15 cm long, cylindrical, tightly contracted; bristles 4–15 mm long, one below each spikelet. Spikelets 2.0–2.7 mm long; lower floret paleas one-half to three-fourths the length of lemma; upper florets finely rugose.

Locally abundant in prairie associations on clay and clay loam sites in early successional stages of revegetation following disturbance along lower and mid Gulf Coast. Similar in morphology to *S. macrostachya* and *S. texana*. Good forage; good seed producer.

Setaria macrostachya Kunth in H.B.K. **PLAINS BRISTLEGRASS** Stout perennial bunchgrasses. Culms to 120 cm tall, thick. Panicles 10–25 cm long, 1–2 cm wide, contracted; bristles 10-20 mm long, usually one below each spikelet. Spikelets shorter than 2 mm; upper florets coarsely rugose.

Infrequent to common along lower and mid Gulf Coast. Similar to *S. leucopila*, but taller, with shorter, strongly inflated spikelets; leaf blades usually wider. Fair forage for livestock and wildlife; large seed provides good food for wildlife.

Figure 166. *Setaria adhaerans* spikelet and bristle (Gould and Box 1965).

Figure 167. *Setaria firmula*
plant, spikelet, and bristle (Gould & Box, 1965).

Setaria magna Griseb. **GIANT BRISTLEGRASS** Coarse annuals. Culms to 4 m tall, 1–2 cm thick at base. Leaves cauline; ligules 2–3 cm long, a ciliate membrane; blades 20–40 cm long, 1–3 cm wide, scabrous, especially upper surface. Panicles 14–45 cm long, contracted, dense, main axis scabrous to densely villous; bristles 1–2 cm long, yellowish, usually one or two below each spikelet. Spikelets 2.0–2.5 mm long, lower florets well developed, staminate or occasionally perfect; upper florets smooth and shiny.

Infrequent along coastal marshes, canals, and ditches of upper Gulf Coast. Large seeds provide good food for wildlife.

Setaria parviflora (Sw.) Kerguelen **KNOTROOT BRISTLEGRASS** (Figure 170) Weak, tufted perennials. Culms to 60 cm tall, stiffly erect from firm, knotty base, often with short rhizomes. Leaves usually glabrous; sheaths keeled; blades 4–7 mm wide, flat. Panicles 3–8 cm long, cylindrical, spikelike; bristles 4–12 below each spikelet, antrorsely scabrous. Spikelets 2.0–2.8 mm long; both glumes shorter than lower lemmas; first glumes slightly less than one-half the length of lower lemmas; second glumes slightly more than one-half the length; upper florets transversely rugose, acute.

Locally abundant throughout Gulf Coast in loamy and clay soils, especially in areas of poor drainage. Fair forage; good seed producer for wildlife.

Setaria pumila (Poir.) Roem. & Schult. **YELLOW BRISTLEGRASS** (Figure 171) Tufted annuals. Culms to 120 cm tall, geniculate below, branching at basal nodes; glabrous. Leaf sheaths keeled; ligules a ciliate membrane, short; blades 4–10 mm wide. Panicles 3–15 cm long, cylindrical, densely contracted; bristles 4–12 below each spikelet. Spikelets mostly 3.0–3.5 mm long; upper lemmas conspicuously rugose.

Found along mid to upper Gulf Coast on roadsides and in waste places. Good seed producer for wildlife.

Setaria ramiseta (Scribn.) Pilger (Figure 172) Tufted rhizomatous perennials. Culms to 60 cm tall, erect, contracted. Leaf sheaths sparsely hirsute; ligules to 2 mm long, a ciliate membrane; blades 2–4 mm wide, flat. Panicles to 15 cm long; bristles only below terminal spikelet of branches or inflorescence apex. Spikelets 2.4–2.8 mm long, upper florets rugose.

Occasional on sandy soils throughout lower and mid Gulf Coast. Closely related to *S. reverchonii* but

Figure 168. *Setaria italica* inflorescence and upper floret (Hitchcock 1951).

Figure 169. *Setaria leucopila*
plant and spikelet (Gould and Box 1965).

with shorter, consistently flat blades, short bristles, and smaller spikelets. Fair forage and wildlife seed producer.

Setaria reverchonii (Vasey) Pilger **REVERCHON BRISTLEGRASS** (Figure 173) Tufted perennials. Culms 30–70 cm long, stiffly erect. Leaves basal and cauline; basal leaves hirsute or villous. Panicles 6–20 cm long, contracted, slender; bristle subtending terminal spikelets of branches and inflorescence apex, longer than associated spikelets. Spikelets 2.6–4.0 mm long; first glumes about one-half the length of second glumes; upper florets rugose.

Occasional on clay and clay loam sites, usually on or near caliche outcrops throughout Gulf Coast. Fair forage and wildlife seed producer.

Setaria scheelei (Steud.) A. S. Hitchc. **SOUTHWESTERN BRISTLEGRASS** (Figure 174) Tall, coarse perennials. Culms to 125 cm tall, erect to spreading; nodes puberulent. Leaves basal and cauline; ligules to 2 mm long, ciliate membrane; blades mostly 15–30 cm

Figure 170. *Setaria parviflora* inflorescence and spikelet (Gould and Box 1965).

long, 5–18 mm wide, thin, flat, dark green, scabrous to finely pubescent. Panicles 15–35 cm long, typically tapering from 5 cm above base to apex, but not infrequently columnar; branches short, lower branches 1–4 cm long, spreading or contracted; bristles 15–35 mm long, usually one below each spikelet. Spikelets 2.1–2.6 mm long, ovate or ovate-oblong; upper florets conspicuously rugose.

Grasses of the Texas Gulf Prairies and Marshes

Figure 171. *Setaria pumila*
plant, (A) spikelet (first glume view), (B) spikelet (second glume view), and (C) upper floret (palea view) (Hitchcock 1951).

Frequent along lower to mid Gulf Coast, mostly in sandy loam soils and usually in shade of trees or shrubs. Good forage; large seed provides good food for wildlife.

Setaria texana W.H.P. Emery **TEXAS BRISTLEGRASS** Tufted perennials. Culms 15–70 (-90) cm tall, strictly erect or decumbent, wiry, freely branched at and above base; nodes glabrous. Leaf sheaths ciliate on margins; ligules a ciliate membrane with hairs to 1 mm long; blades thin, 5–15 (-20) cm long, 2–4 (-5) mm wide, mostly flat. Panicles 2–6 cm long, 5 mm wide, contracted, spikelike, tapering above. Panicle axis puberulent; bristles 3–10 mm long, usually one below spikelets. Spikelets 1.8–2.1 mm long; first glumes less than one-half the length of spikelets; second glumes about two-thirds the length of mature lemmas of lower florets; palea of lower florets rudimentary to slightly more than one-half the length of lemmas; upper florets finely rugose in transverse lines.

Found along lower and mid Gulf Coast. Closely related to *S. leucopila, S. texana* plants are distinguished from depauperate *S. leucopila* with difficulty. *Setaria texana* grows in partial shade and is particularly well adapted to growth in the sandy soils of oak and mesquite mottes in southern Texas. Fair livestock and wildlife values.

Figure 172. *Setaria ramiseta* plant and spikelet (Gould and Box 1965).

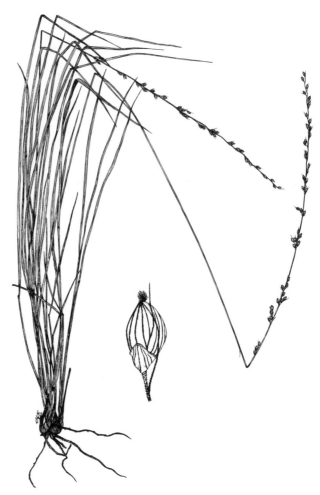

Figure 173. *Setaria reverchonii*
plant, spikelet, and bristle (Gould and Box 1965).

78. **SORGHASTRUM** Nash • Indiangrass

Culms solid, unbranched. Leaves basal and cauline; ligules membranous; blades flat. Panicles open, branches racemose with paired spikelets, sessile spikelets perfect, pedicellate ones represented only by the pedicel. Spikelets dorsally compressed, disarticulation below glumes; florets two, lower reduced, upper perfect; glumes subequal, flat, indurate; lemmas membranous; upper lemma with geniculate awn.

1. Awn once-geniculate, 1.0–1.6 cm long; rhizomes present; inflorescence generally tan to yellowish at maturity .... *S. nutans*

1. Awn twice-geniculate, 2.5–4.0 cm long; rhizomes absent; inflorescence generally dark to chestnut-brown at maturity .... *S. elliottii*

Sorghastrum elliottii (Mohr.) Nash **SLENDER INDIANGRASS** (Figure 175) Tufted perennials. Culms to 1.8 m tall, slender. Leaves with ligules 2–4 mm long, membranous, truncate or variously lobed, thickened laterally to form stiff sheath auricles; blades mostly 3–8 mm wide, long, attenuate. Panicles 15–25 cm long, narrow, loose. Spikelets mostly 5.5–7.0 mm long, dark brown; pedicels slender,

Figure 174. *Setaria scheelei* showing two inflorescence forms (Gould and Box 1965).

flexuous, often curved; upper lemmas 23–35 mm long; lemma awns dark brown, twisted and usually twice-geniculate. Pedicels with brownish hairs, pedicellate spikelets absent.

Usually found in sandy soil in or along woodland margins of upper Gulf Coast. Good forage and wildlife cover.

Sorghastrum nutans (L.) Nash **YELLOW INDIANGRASS** (Figure 176) Rhizomatous perennials. Culms to 2 m tall, stiffly erect; nodes hispid. Leaf sheaths with erect auricles; ligules 2–5 mm long. Panicles 15–30 cm long, contracted, yellowish; branches, branchlets, pedicels, and spikelets hirsute. Sessile spikelets 6-8 mm long; lemma awns 1.0-1.5 cm long, once-geniculate. Pedicellate spikelets absent; pedicels hairy.

Found only on well managed ranges or in protected areas throughout Gulf Coast; once an important constituent of coastal prairie climax vegetation. Good livestock forage; good wildlife cover.

79. **SORGHUM** Moench • Sorghum

Culms solid or hollow. Leaves basal and cauline; sheaths open; ligules membranous or ciliate membranes; blades flat. Panicles open or contracted, branches numerous and racemose. Spikelets generally in pairs, one sessile and fertile, one pedicellate and sterile; except at branch apex where spikelets occur in threes, with two pedicellate and sterile; glumes indurate, subequal; lemmas membranous; upper lemmas with geniculate twisted awn, awn early deciduous.

1.   Plants perennial, rhizomatous .... *S. halapense*
1.   Plants annual, without rhizomes .... *S. bicolor*

Sorghum bicolor (L.) Moench **GRAIN SORGHUM** Large annuals. Culms to 3 m tall. Leaves basal and cauline; blades 1–5 cm or wider, long, thin. Panicles 10–25 cm long, highly variable, compact. Spikelets 4–6 mm long, awnless; glumes pubescent, usually with a shiny spot on back.

The common grain and forage sorghum; many varieties or races such as sudangrass, milo, broomcorn, and kafir. Good forage and grain plant.

Sorghum halepense (L.) Pers. **JOHNSONGRASS** (Figure 177) Tall, coarse perennials with stout, creeping rhizomes. Culms to 2 m tall, stout. Leaf blades 8–20 mm wide, glabrous with conspicuous white midvein. Panicles 15–40 cm long,

Figure 175. *Sorghastrum elliottii* inflorescence (Hitchcock 1951).

open, pyramidal. Spikelets in pairs, one sessile and perfect, one pediceled and staminate or neuter, at branch apices spikelets in threes. Upper lemmas of sessile spikelets awned or awnless; lemma awns delicate, geniculate, deciduous.

Found throughout Gulf Coast as a weed in crops and along roadsides. Widely used for livestock forage; causes prussic acid poisoning when grazed under stress conditions. Declines rapidly under moderate, continuous grazing; persists under non-grazed conditions. Good wildlife food and cover.

Figure 176. *Sorghastrum nutans*
plant and sessile spikelet with empty pedicel (Gould and Box 1965).

80. **SPARTINA** Schreb. • Cordgrass

Culms solid or partially hollow. Leaves usually basal and cauline; sheaths rounded; ligules a ring of hairs; blades flat or involute. Panicles of two to numerous spicate primary unilateral branches, spikelets pectinately arranged. Spikelets laterally compressed, disarticulation below glumes; floret one, glumes unequal, the second short-awned, keeled, 1- to 3-veined; lemmas 3-veined, keeled, awned or awnless; paleas with two closely placed veins.

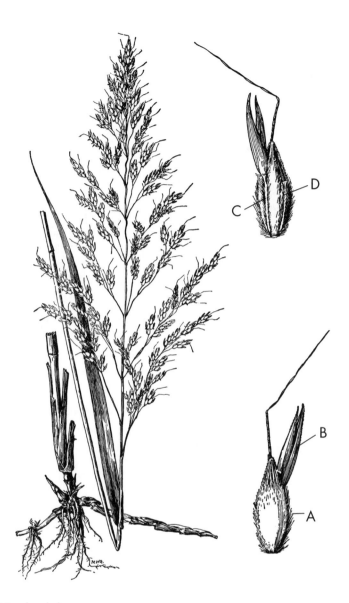

Figure 177. *Sorghum halepense*
plant, (A) sessile spikelet, (B) pedicellate spikelet, (C) pedicel, and (D) branchlet (Hitchcock 1951).

1. Plants without rhizomes; culms in large clumps 2
1. Plants rhizomatous; culms single or in clumps 3
2(1). Panicle branches 9–15, spreading to erect .... *S. bakeri*
2. Panicle branches 16–35, tightly appressed .... *S. spartinae*
3(1.) Panicle branches appressed, ten or more; second glumes glabrous ....
.... *S. alterniflora* var. *glabra*
3. Panicle branches spreading, few to many; second glumes strongly scabrous 4
4(3). Leaf blades 1–4 mm wide; culms under 1.5 m tall; panicle branches two to seven .... *S. patens*
4. Leaf blades 10–23 mm wide; culms 2.0–3.5 m tall; panicle branches 12–25 .... *S. cynosuroides*

Spartina alterniflora Loisel. var. *glabra* (Bigel.) Fern. **SMOOTH CORDGRASS** (Figure 178) Robust, rhizomatous perennials. Culms to 2.5 m tall, solitary or tufted. Leaves cauline; lower sheaths wide; blades 25–40 cm long, 2–4 mm wide, tapered to a long point, margins serrate. Panicles 15–35 cm long; several spicate primary unilateral branches, appressed with spikelets on one side. Spikelets 8–14 mm long; glumes glabrous, keeled, awnless or apiculate; lemmas 3-veined, awnless, slightly shorter than paleas.

Occasional to locally abundant in tidal flats, bayou margins, swales, and bays throughout Gulf Coast. Fresh herbage has disagreeable odor. Good livestock forage; good fish habitat; valuable wildlife food, particularly for geese (*Branta, Anser,* and *Chen* species).

Spartina bakeri Merr. Densely tufted perennials. Culms to 2 m tall, erect, from hard, knotty bases. Leaves basal and cauline; ligules a fringe of short hairs; blades mostly 3–7 mm wide. Panicles of 15 spicate primary unilateral branches; branches 5–9 cm long, erect to spreading, widely spaced. Spikelets 9–12 mm long; glumes acute, acuminate or abruptly short-awned, keel scabrous; first glumes usually slightly less than one-half the length of second glumes; lemmas rounded at apex, slightly shorter than paleas.

Occasional along upper Gulf Coast in marshes and bayous. Fair forage in winter and spring if burned in the fall; tough and unpalatable in summer.

Spartina cynosuroides (L.) Roth **BIG CORDGRASS** Robust, rhizomatous perennials. Culms to 3.5 m tall. Blades 1.0–2.5 cm wide. Panicles with 12–25 spicate primary unilateral branches; branches 4–9 cm long, loosely contracted or spreading. Spikelets 10–14 mm long; glumes awnless, keel sharply scabrous; first glumes usually less than one-half the length of second glumes; lemmas and paleas blunt at apex; lemma midvein scabrous above.

Gould (1975) indicated species was known only from the Port Arthur-Orange area at the mouth of the Sabine River, growing mainly in shallow water along bayous and tideland flats. Fair forage for cattle, ducks, and geese after marshes are burned in fall.

Spartina patens (Ait.) Muhl. **MARSHHAY CORDGRASS** (Figure 179) Tufted or rhizomatous perennials. Culms to 1.5 m tall, erect. Leaves with narrow blades. Panicles 3–15 cm long, bearing 2–15 spicate primary unilateral branches; branches 2–7 cm long. Spikelets 7–17 mm long; glumes unequal, first glumes one-half the length of second glumes; lemmas and paleas blunt; paleas slightly longer than lemmas.

Frequent throughout Gulf Coast; rhizomatous form widespread and common on beaches, sandy flats, and low dune margins of tidal flats on lower Gulf Coast; tufted form on muddy bayous and marshlands of upper coastal region. Good forage; good wildlife cover, especially for geese and muskrats (*Ondatra zibethicus*).

Spartina spartinae (Trin.) Merr. *ex* A. S. Hitchc. **GULF CORDGRASS** (Figure 180)

Figure 178. *Spartina alterniflora* var. *glabra* partial inflorescence and spikelet (Hitchcock 1951).

Tufted perennials in dense clumps. Culms to 130 cm tall, erect to ascending. Leaves tough; blades 5 mm wide or less, long, firm, involute. Panicles 15–25 cm long with 15–30 spicate primary unilateral branches; branches short, tightly ascending. Spikelets mostly 6–8 mm long; first glumes narrow, one-half the length of second glumes; second glumes blunt, often short-awned. Lemmas blunt, awnless.

Figure 179. *Spartina patens*
inflorescence and spikelet (Hitchcock 1951).

Frequent to locally abundant in moist saline sites throughout Gulf Coast, mostly on clayey soils. Dominates, sometimes to the exclusion of other species; thousands of hectares of gulf cordgrass occur in inundated areas inland. Good winter cattle and geese forage when burned and properly grazed; good wildlife nesting and cover, especially for wetland margin species. Good bird nesting habitat.

81. **SPHENOPHOLIS** Scribn. • Wedgescale
Culms hollow. Leaves cauline; sheaths open;
ligules membranous; blades flat. Panicles usually dense and contracted. Spikelets usually
with (one) two or three florets, awnless, laterally compressed, disarticulation below glumes;
glumes dissimilar in size and shape; lemmas
membranous, yellowish-white.

1. Second glume apex rounded; panicle contracted; second glume width one-third to one-
half the length .... *S. obtusata* var. *obtusata*
1. Second glume apex rounded; panicle
loose; second glume width less than one-third
the length .... *S. obtusata* var. *major*

Sphenopholis obtusata (Michx.) Scribn. var.
obtusata **PRAIRIE WEDGESCALE** (Figure
181) Tufted annuals. Culms to 70 cm tall,
erect. Leaves with ligules 1–3 mm long; blades
4–10 cm long, 2–8 mm wide, flat. Panicles
5–20 cm long, dense, contracted. Spikelets
1.5–5.0 mm long; florets two or three, awnless, glabrous to scabrous; first glumes 1–4
mm long, acute; second glumes conspicuously obovate, one-third to one-half as wide
as long.

var. *major* (Torr.) Erdman Variety similar
to *S. obtusata* but with more acute glumes, second glumes less than one-third as wide as long,
and a more open panicle.

Infrequent along mid and upper Gulf Coast
in moist prairies, stream banks, and swales.
Grows in partial shade in moist, sandy or sandy loam. Poor forage value.

Figure 180. *Spartina spartinae*
inflorescence and spikelet (Gould
and Box 1965).

82. **SPOROBOLUS** R. Br. • Dropseed
Culms solid or pithy. Leaves basal and/or cauline; sheaths round or keeled; ligules
a ring of hairs or a short ciliate membrane; blades flat, folded or involute. Panicles

open or contracted, spikelets pedicellate. Spikelets laterally compressed, disarticulation above glumes, awnless; floret one; glumes usually unequal, 1-veined, first glume usually shorter than lemma; lemmas 1-veined; paleas 2-veined, usually splitting at maturity and appearing as an extra lemma. Spikelets similar in general aspect to those of *Muhlenbergia* but lemmas 1-veined, thin, awnless.

1. Plants with extensive rhizomes .... *S. virginicus*
1. Plants without rhizomes 2
2(1). Pedicels 5–8 mm long .... *S. silveanus*
2. Pedicels 4 mm or shorter 3

Figure 181. *Sphenopholis obtusata* var. *obtusata* plant and spikelet (Gould and Box 1965).

Grasses of the Texas Gulf Prairies and Marshes

3(2).	Spikelets 1.0–2.5 mm long **4**
3.	Spikelets 3–7 mm long **7**
4(3).	Glumes about equal, one-half to two-thirds the length of floret .... *S. indicus*
4.	Glumes unequal, first glume short, second glume about the length of floret **5**
5(4).	Lower sheaths strongly keeled, compressed .... *S. buckleyi*
5.	Lower sheaths rounded **6**
6(5).	Culms 10–40 cm tall; lower panicle branches distinctly whorled; inflorescences 3–15 cm long; spikelets about 1 mm long .... *S. coromandelianus*
6.	Culms 40 cm tall or taller; lower panicle branches not distinctly whorled; inflorescences 10–40 cm long; spikelets about 1.5–2.5 mm long .... *S. cryptandrus*
7(4).	Lemmas pubescent .... *S. compositus* var. *clandestinus*
7.	Lemmas glabrous **8**
8(7).	Lower panicle branches whorled **9**
8.	Lower panicle branches not whorled **10**
9(8).	Inflorescences 0.6–1.6 cm wide, cylindrical; branches with spikelets to near base, appressed .... *S. purpurascens*
9.	Inflorescences 3–6 cm wide, pyramidal; branches without spikelets near base, spreading .... *S. junceus*
10(8).	Panicles 17–35 cm wide, open .... *S. airoides*
10.	Panicles less than 2 cm wide, contracted **11**
11(10).	Primary panicle branches 12–35, dense; leaf blades 2 mm or wider; culm bases 2–5 mm wide .... *S. compositus* var. *compositus*
11.	Primary panicle branches 8–18, dense; leaf blades less than 2 mm wide; culm bases less than 2 mm wide .... *S. compositus* var. *drummondii*

Sporobolus airoides (Torr.) Torr. **ALKALI SACATON** (Figure 182) Coarse perennials. Culms to 170 cm tall, in dense clumps. Leaf blades 3–6 mm wide, usually involute with long, silvery hairs at base. Panicles 20–45 cm long, ovate; branches to 15 cm long, stiffly erect to spreading, one per node. Spikelets 2.8–3.2 mm long, pedicels 1.5 mm long; glumes yellowish-white, lanceolate; first glumes one-fourth the length of second glumes; lemmas and paleas whitish, glabrous.

Occasional to frequent on sand and calcareous shale soils and vegetated flats on Padre Island and coastal bays of lower and mid Gulf Coast. Synonymous with *S. tharpii* A. S. Hitchc.

Sporobolus buckleyi Vasey **BUCKLEY DROPSEED** Densely tufted perennials. Culms to 110 cm tall, slender, erect, strongly compressed, unbranched. Leaf sheaths laterally keeled; collars purple-tinged, pubescent; blades 4–12 mm wide, glabrous, lowermost short, upper elongate. Panicles 15–40 cm long, open. Spikelets 1.3–2.0 mm long, purplish; glumes lanceolate, unequal; first glumes 0.6–1.0 mm long; lemmas and paleas nearly equal length; paleas wider than lemmas, often splitting as grains mature. Grains about 1 mm long, flattened laterally.

Found along lower Gulf Coast in loamy soil of shaded habitats.

Figure 182. *Sporobolus airoides*
plant, (A) glumes, (B) floret, and caryopsis (Hitchcock 1951).

Sporobolus compositus (Poir.) Merr. var. *compositus* **TALL DROPSEED** (Figure 183A, B, D, E) Tufted perennials. Culms to 120 cm tall, 2–5 cm wide at base, erect; cleistogamous spikelets in axillary panicles, partially or entirely enclosed within sheath. Leaf blades elongate, flat or folded, glabrous. Panicles 5–30 cm long, contracted, often entirely enclosed in inflated, subtending sheath. Spikelets 4–6 mm long; glumes keeled with bright green midvein; second glumes about twice the length of first glumes; lemma apex rounded, longer than glumes; paleas well developed, conspicuous. Grains 1.6–2.0 mm long.

Found along upper Gulf Coast in open piney woods. Poor forage.

var. *clandestinus* (Biehler) Wipff & S. D. Jones (Figure 183C) Stout perennials. Culms to 100 cm tall, erect, nodes glabrous or glaucous below. Leaves basal and cauline; blades flat. Panicles 5–10 cm long, narrow with erect to appressed branches, partially enclosed in terminal sheath. Spikelets 5–7 mm long, flattened laterally, awnless; glumes unequal, keeled, scabrous; lemmas 4–5 mm long, mottled with purple, appressed pubescence; paleas longer than lemmas, appressed pubescence. Grains 2–3 mm long, reddish-orange. Similar to var. *asper* and var. *drummondii* but differs in having pubescent lemmas.

Occasional throughout Gulf Coast, mostly in open, sandy loam sites.

var. *drummondii* (Trin.) Kartesz & Gandhi **MEADOW DROPSEED** Perennials. Culms slender, stiffly erect, in moderate clumps. Panicles contracted, small, usually developed on axillary branches at upper nodes and terminally. Similar to var. *asper* except with thinner culms (1–2 mm), narrower terminal sheaths (0.8–2.0 mm wide when folded), and shorter primary panicle branches.

Frequent throughout Gulf Coast in open prairies, wooded borders, and along road rights-of-way. Apparently a mid-successional species in recovering prairies; found on heavy clay soils along mid Gulf Coast. Poor forage; fair bird nesting cover; good rodent cover.

Sporobolus coromandelianus (Retz.) Kunth **WHORLED DROPSEED** (Figure 184) Low, tufted perennials. Culms to 55 cm tall, ascending. Leaves mostly in basal tufts; collars yellow, glabrous; ligules about 0.5 mm long, membranous; blades thin, flat, glabrous or with a few long hairs near base. Panicles 4–7 cm long, open, pyramidal with short, spreading branches, at least some in definite whorls. Spikelets 1.6–2.0 mm long, awnless, pedicels glabrous; glumes unequal; lemmas and paleas glabrous.

Occasional to frequent on coastal sands and fine-textured soils, usually at margins of saline sites. Poor forage.

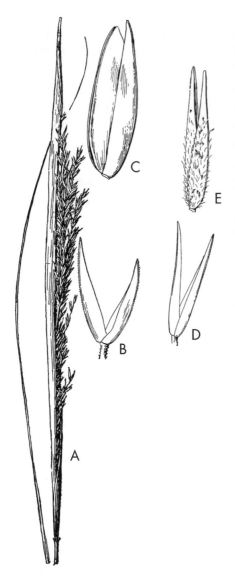

Sporobolus cryptandrus (Torr.) Gray **SAND DROPSEED** (Figure 185) Tufted perennials. Culms 40–100 cm tall, mostly erect. Leaf sheaths with tufts of long, white hairs (2–4 mm long) on either side of collar, upper margins ciliate-pubescent; blades 8–25 cm long, 2–5 mm wide. Panicles 15–30 cm long, partially enclosed by sheaths; branches with spikelets nearly to base or naked on lower 5–10 mm; secondary branches and branchlets appressed. Spikelets 1.5–2.4 mm long, short-pediceled; light brown or plumbeous, or purple-tinged; glumes thin, membranous, acute; first glumes about one-half the length of second glumes; second glumes equaling or slightly shorter than lemmas; lemmas the length of spikelets; paleas well developed, slightly shorter than lemmas; grain about 1 mm long, reddish-orange, oblong, flattened laterally.

Present on disturbed sites throughout Gulf Coast, especially on sandy or sandy loam sites. Occasional but never abundant on well managed native pastures. Fair forage; increases under grazing.

Figure 183. *Sporobolus compositus* var. *compositus*
(A) inflorescence, (B) glumes, (C) floret (var. *clandestinus*), (D) glumes, and (E) floret (Hitchcock 1951).

Sporobolus indicus (L.) R. Br. **SMUTGRASS** (Figure 186) Strongly tufted perennials. Culms to 100 cm tall, erect. Leaves tough, basal and cauline; blades 10–30 cm long, 1–5 mm wide, commonly involute, tapering to a long apex, flexuous, some filiform. Panicles 10–30 cm long, narrowly contracted; lower branches erect, dense. Spikelets 1.4–2.0 mm long; glumes subequal, translucent;

first glumes less than one-half the length of lemmas; second glumes acute, one-half to two-thirds the length of lemmas; lemmas and paleas of same texture as glumes and lemmas. Grains obovate, flattened laterally, reddish-brown; apex somewhat truncate.

Rare to occasional in sandy loam soils, usually in yards or other disturbed places throughout Gulf Coast. Poor forage.

Sporobolus junceus (Beauv.) Kunth
PINEYWOODS DROPSEED Tufted perennials. Culms to 100 cm tall, un-branched. Leaves basal, long; sheaths margins glabrous or sparsely hispid-ciliate with long, white hairs at throat; blades 1–2 mm wide, lower blades wider mostly 13–30 cm long, upper blades short. Panicles 10–25 cm long, narrow but open, gradually tapering at apex; branches usually simple, in rather widely spaced verticils, lower branches 2.0–3.5 cm long without spikelets on lower one-half. Spikelets 3.0–3.8 mm long, appressed along branches, brownish or bronze-purple; glumes unequal, glabrous, narrowly acute or acuminate; first glumes 1.2–3.0 mm long; second glumes 3.0–3.8 mm long; lemmas and paleas glabrous, slightly shorter than second glumes. Grains about 1.5 mm long, plump, brownish, minutely rugose, asymmetrically oblong.

Figure 184. *Sporobolus coromandelianus* inflorescence and spikelet (Gould and Box 1965).

Frequent in pine barrens and Coastal Plains of upper Gulf Coast. Fair forage; increases under grazing. Seeds eaten by birds and rodents.

Figure 185. *Sporobolus cryptandrus* plant, (A) glumes, and (B) floret (Hitchcock 1951).

Sporobolus purpurascens (Sw.) Hamilt. **PURPLE DROPSEED** Generally similar to *S. junceus* except for inflorescence shape. Tufted perennials. Culms 25–90 cm tall, erect, unbranched above base. Leaves basal; blades 8–15 cm long, 2–5 mm wide, tapering. Panicles 10–25 cm long, contracted, interrupted below; branches 0.8–1.5 cm long, the lower occasionally to 2–3 cm long in well-defined verticils, appressed or narrowly spreading, dense. Spikelets purple or bronze-tinged, similar to *S. junceus*; first glumes 1.6–2.5 mm long, acute; second glumes 3.0–4.5 mm long, acute; lemmas and paleas equal to second glumes; paleas frequently splitting as the grains mature. Grains 2.0–2.2 mm long, about 1 mm wide, reddish-brown.

Occasional in sandy soils, mostly on coastal prairie or oak mottes of lower and mid Gulf Coast. Fair forage; seeds eaten by birds and rodents.

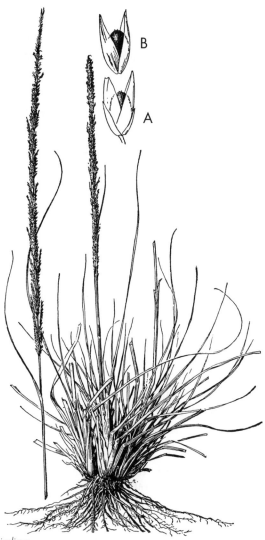

Figure 186. *Sporobolus indicus*
plant, (A) spikelet, (B) floret, and caryopsis (Hitchcock 1951).

Grasses of the Texas Gulf Prairies and Marshes

Sporobolus silveanus Swallen **SILVEUS DROPSEED** Densely tufted perennials. Culms to 120 cm tall, slender, erect. Leaves basal; lower sheaths firm, shiny, becoming flat and chartaceous with age; blades 15–20 cm long, 1–2 mm wide, loosely folded. Panicles 20–50 cm long, somewhat open. Spikelets 5–6 mm long, purple; glumes acuminate, subequal; first glumes 3.0–4.5 mm long, 1-veined; second glumes 4–6 mm long, about the length of lemmas and paleas; lemmas 5–6 mm long, subacute. Grains 2.0–2.5 mm long, about 0.8 mm wide, oblong.

Infrequent in pine and hardwood forests of upper Gulf Coast.

Sporobolus virginicus (L.) Kunth **SEASHORE DROPSEED** (Figure 187) Low, coarse rhizomatous perennials, arising singly or in small clusters. Culms to 65 cm tall, smooth and shining; nodes several to many. Leaves cauline; blades mostly 3–10 cm long, 1.5 mm wide, conspicuously distichous, firm, usually tightly involute upon drying. Panicles 2–8 cm long, contracted to spicate, dense. Spikelets 1.8–3.2 mm long; glumes subequal; second glumes 1.8–3.2 mm long, equaling or often slightly longer than lemmas; paleas same size and texture as lemmas.

Occurs throughout Gulf Coast on sandy beaches, tidal flats, and inland salt marshes. Good forage for livestock and geese following controlled burns in the fall.

83. STENOTAPHRUM Trin.

Culms solid, much-branched. Leaves basal and cauline; sheaths keeled; ligules a ciliate membrane; blades folded. Panicles of spicate racemes with one to three spikelets per node, spikelets sunken into branches or rachis. Spikelets awnless, dorsally compressed, disarticulation below the glumes; florets two, lower sterile, upper fertile.

Stenotaphrum secundatum (Walt.) O. Ktze. **ST. AUGUSTINEGRASS** (Figure 188) Low, mat-forming, stoloniferous perennials. Culms 10–30 cm tall, rooting at lower nodes. Leaves glabrous; ligules a ciliate membrane; blades mostly 3–15 cm long but longer on sterile shoots, 4–10 mm wide, thick, flat to folded, apex obtuse or rounded. Panicles or spicate racemes 5–10 cm long; branches short, stout, closely placed, appressed; branches bearing one to three sessile or subsessile spikelets; spikelets partially embedded in one side of wide, thick, flattened branch or rachis. Spikelets 4–5 mm long, florets two, lower staminate or neuter, upper perfect; first glumes short but well developed, irregularly rounded; second glumes

Figure 187. *Sporobolus virginicus*
plant and spikelet (Gould and Box 1965).

and lower lemmas about equal, glabrous, awnless; upper lemmas chartaceous, ovate, awnless, margins thin and flat.

Commonly used as lawngrass in southern and southeastern Texas; otherwise found only as an escapee near maintained lawns. Seldom produces seed; propagated by sprigs and sod clumps. Poor livestock and wildlife values.

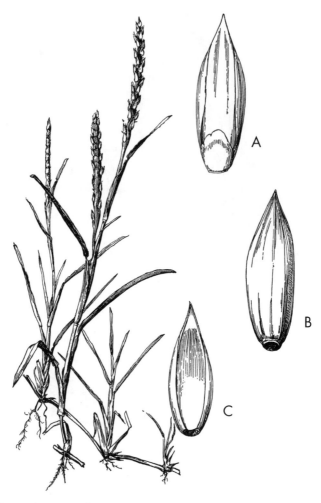

Figure 188. *Stenotaphrum secundatum*
plant, (A) spikelet (first glume view), (B) spikelet (second glume view), and (C) upper floret (palea view) (Hitchcock 1951).

84. TRACHYPOGON Nees

Culms solid. Leaves basal and cauline; sheaths keeled; ligules membranous, blades flat or involute. Spicate racemes terminal with paired spikelets at each node; short-pedicelled spikelet staminate; long-pedicelled spikelets fertile. Long-pedicelled spikelets dorsally compressed, disarticulation below glumes; florets two; upper lemmas with densely pubescent awn.

Trachypogon secundus (Presl) Scribn. **CRINKLEAWN** (Figure 189) Tufted, perennial bunchgrasses. Culms to 120 cm tall; nodes densely bearded, becoming glabrate. Leaf blades 20–30 cm long, 1–6 mm wide, often involute. Spicate racemes 10–18 cm long; spikelets paired, one subsessile and awnless, one with a slightly longer pedicel and long-awned. Subsessile spikelets 6–8 mm long, staminate; first glumes strigose-pubescent. Longer-pediceled spikelets perfect, equal in length and appearance to subsessile spikelets; upper lemmas with stout awn 4–6 cm long; lemma awns loosely twisted and contorted, densely plumose below with hairs mostly 2–6 mm long.

Found along lower and mid Gulf Coast, including barrier islands, on open pastures in loose, sandy soils; more frequent south and west. "Crinkleawn" refers to the long, twisted, densely hairy awns. Good livestock forage and wildlife cover; decreases under livestock grazing.

85. TRAGUS Haller • Burgrass

Culms solid. Leaves basal and cauline; sheaths rounded; ligules a ring of hairs; blades flat or folded. Panicles spikelike with burs of two to five spikelets per central axis node. Spikelets with disarticulation below the "bur" spikelet cluster; floret one; second glumes with three rows of hooked spines.

Tragus racemosus (L.) All. **STALKED BURGRASS** Low annuals. Culms to 30 cm tall, geniculate to spreading. Leaves with ligules a dense ring of short hairs; blades short, 2–5 mm wide, flat, margins usually coarsely hispid. Panicles 2–8 cm long, spikelike; spikelets two to five in short-pedicellate burlike clusters. Spikelets with two florets; first glumes reduced or absent; second glumes with five rows of hooked spines; lemmas 3-veined, veins extending into awns.

Infrequent along lower and mid Gulf Coast in sandy woodland sites.

86. TRICHLORIS Fourn. *ex* Benth.

Culms hollow, flattened at base. Leaves basal and cauline; sheaths keeled or terete, open; ligules a ciliate membrane; blades flat. Panicles of digitate or subdigitate spicate primary unilateral branches. Spikelets dorsally compressed, disarticulation above glumes; florets three or four with two fertile and basal, and one or two reduced at apex; glumes unequal; lemmas 3-veined and 3-awned. Grain narrowly elliptic with pericarp free.

Trichloris pluriflora Fourn. **MULTIFLOWERED FALSE RHODESGRASS** (Figure 190) Tufted or stoloniferous perennials. Culms to 150 cm tall, erect.

Figure 189. *Trachypogon secundus*
plant and spikelet (Hitchcock 1951).

Leaves cauline; blades 5-10 mm wide. Panicles of 10–20 spicate primary unilateral branches; branches to 20 cm long, mostly in one or two irregular verticels at culm apex, ascending, bases pilose. Spikelets 5–6 mm long; florets four; glumes subequal, whitish; second glumes extending into awn about 2 mm long; lower lemmas 3-awned, middle awn 6–7 mm long, lateral awns of lemmas 3.5–4.5 long; paleas slightly longer than lemmas.

Occasional on many sites along lower and mid Gulf Coast. Good forage and seed producer; decreases under heavy livestock grazing.

Figure 190. *Trichloris pluriflora*
inflorescence and spikelet (Gould and Box 1965).

87. **TRICHONEURA** • Anderss.

Culms solid. Leaves basal and cauline; sheaths rounded; ligule a ciliate membrane; blades flat. Panicles contracted. Spikelets laterally compressed, disarticulation above glumes; florets several, sterile one apical; glumes unequal, the length of first floret, awned; lemmas 3-veined.

Trichoneura elegans Swallen **SILVEUSGRASS** (Figure 191) Robust annuals. Culms to 70 cm long; erect or partially decumbent with many nodes. Leaves with scabrous sheaths; blades 3–7 mm wide, flat, scabrous. Panicles 5–24 cm long, contracted, branches with spikelets short-pedicellate. Spikelets with five to eight florets; glumes long, 1-veined, acuminate; lemmas 3-veined, awnless or mucronate, margins conspicuously ciliate on lower one-half.

Infrequent in deep sands inland and on Padre Island along lower and mid Gulf Coast.

88. **TRIDENS** Schult. & Schult. • Tridens (adapted from Gould and Box 1965)

Culms solid. Leaves basal and cauline; sheaths open; ligules a ciliate membrane or a ring of hairs; blades flat. Panicles open or contracted. Spikelets laterally compressed, disarticulation above glumes, florets several, reduced florets at apex; glumes unequal to subequal; lemmas 3-veined, the veins with short hairs basally, awnless, or the midvein extended as a short mucro; paleas slightly shorter than lemmas.

1.	Panicles open, branches spreading	2
1.	Panicles contracted, branches appressed	5
2(1).	Pedicels of lateral spikelets 1 mm or shorter	*T. ambiguus*
2.	Pedicels of lateral spikelets, at least some, longer than 1 mm	3
3(2).	Spikelets 4–6 mm long, lemmas 1.8–3.0 mm long	*T. eragrostoides*
3.	Spikelets 6 mm or longer, lemmas 3.1–5.0 mm long	4
4(3).	Panicles 6–15 cm long, lower branches to 8 cm long	*T. texanus*
4.	Panicles 15–40 cm long, lower branches 10–20 cm long	*T. flavus* var. *flavus*
5(1).	Glumes equal to or longer than all florets	*T. strictus*
5.	Glumes shorter, or only slightly longer, than first florets	6
6(5).	Lemma veins glabrous	*T. albescens*
6.	Lemma veins hairy at base	7
7(6).	Lemma midvein pubescent on lower half, mucronate	*T. congestus*
7.	Lemma midvein pubescent to well above middle, not awned or mucronate	*T. muticus* var. *muticus*

Tridens albescens (Vasey) Woot. & Standl. **WHITE TRIDENS** (Figure 192) Rhizomatous perennials from hard, knotty bases. Culms to 90 cm tall, erect to ascending. Leaf sheaths glabrous; ligules a ciliate membrane; blades 1–4 mm wide, glaucous. Panicles 8–25 cm long, 0.6–1.5 cm wide with short, appressed branches, contracted, dense. Spikelets 4–10 mm long, florets 4–11, pedicels glabrous; glumes unequal, whitish; lemmas about 3 mm long, whitish to purple-tinged, rounded, lateral veins glabrous; paleas awnless, the length of lemmas.

Figure 191. *Trichoneura elegans*
inflorescence and spikelet (Gould and Box 1965).

Occasional to frequent on fine-textured soils, usually growing in moist or poorly drained areas throughout Gulf Coast. Fair forage value, contributing significantly to forage in native pasture mixtures; large seeds eaten by birds and rodents.

Figure 192. *Tridens albescens*
plant, (A) spikelet, and (B) floret (Gould and Box 1965).

Tridens ambiguus (Ell.) Schult. **PINEBARREN TRIDENS** Tufted perennials from firm, knotty bases. Culms to 125 cm tall, glabrous, stiffly erect. Leaves with blades 2–5 mm wide, firm, apex often infolded, glabrous. Panicles 8–20 cm long, narrow. Spikelets 4–6 mm long, florets four to six; glumes glabrous, acute; lemmas 3–4 mm long, veins ciliate basally, apex slightly notched, midvein and often lateral veins excurrent as minute mucros; paleas about the length of lemmas; palea veins ciliolate, enlarged, and bowed out at base.

Infrequent along upper Gulf Coast in piney woods and road rights-of-way bordering wooded areas.

Tridens congestus (L. H. Dewey) Nash **PINK TRIDENS** (Figure 193) Tufted or rhizomatous perennials. Culms to 75 cm tall. Leaves glabrous; ligules shorter than 0.5 mm, a ciliate membrane; blades long, bright green beneath, glaucous above. Panicles 5–8 (–10) cm long, 1.2–2.5 cm wide, contracted, congested. Spikelets 5–10 mm long, light colored, rosy or light violet-tinged; lemma veins with short hair near base.

Adapted to tight, poorly drained soils both on upland clay sites and saline marshy grasslands bordering Gulf Coast. Generally, closely associated and similar to *T. albescens*, but can be distinguished by usually shorter panicles and more pubescent lemmas pink-tinged, rather than purple or rosy-purple, as in *T. albescens*. Grazing value similar to *T. albescens*.

Tridens eragrostoides (Vasey & Scribn.) Nash **LOVEGRASS TRIDENS** (Figure 194) Tufted, perennial bunchgrasses. Culms to 100 cm tall, stiffly erect, glabrous, nodes glabrous or sparsely bearded. Leaves with ligules 1.2–3.0 mm long and thinmembranous, lacerate, glabrous; blades mostly 1.5–5.0 mm wide, elongate, scabrous to sparsely pilose, narrowing at base of attenuate apex. Panicles 10–30 cm long, open; branches usually lax, drooping without spikelets at base, pedicels 1.5 mm or longer. Spikelets 3–7 mm long, florets 5–12; glumes awnless, often purple colored, glabrous, acute or acuminate, 1-veined; lemmas 2.0–3.2 mm long, puberulent on veins to well above middle; apex rounded or notched, midvein usually excurrent as a mucro; paleas shorter than lemmas, not enlarged and bowed out at base, veins glabrous or scabrous. Caryopses 1.0–1.3 mm long.

Occasional in lower and mid Gulf Coast on clays and clay loams, usually along fencerows or protected by shrubs. Good forage.

Tridens flavus (L.) A. S. Hitchc. var. *flavus* **PURPLETOP** (Figure 195) Perennial bunchgrasses. Culms to 1.8 m tall, slender. Leaves with lower sheaths keeled; collars pubescent; blades to 10 mm wide, flat, apex attenuate. Panicles 10–30 cm long, large, open; branches drooping, mostly glabrous. Spikelets 5–9 mm long, florets four to eight; glumes and lemmas often mucronate.

Common but infrequent along mid and upper Gulf Coast. Grows mainly on sandy soils in woodland sites. Good livestock forage; seeds eaten by birds and rodents.

Tridens muticus (Torr.) Nash var. *muticus* **SLIM TRIDENS** (Figure 196) Tufted perennials. Culms to 50 cm tall, erect; nodes bearded. Leaves glabrous to scabrous; blades 1–2 mm wide, narrow. Panicles 8–25 cm long, contracted. Spikelets 8–13 mm long; glumes unequal, thin; lemma midveins ciliate-pubescent on lower one-half.   Infrequent along lower and mid Gulf Coast. Fair forage; seeds eaten by birds and rodents.

Tridens strictus (Nutt.) Nash **LONGSPIKE TRIDENS** Stout, tufted perennials. Culms to 1.5 cm tall, erect, glabrous. Leaf blades long, 3-8 mm wide, apex long-attenuate, involute. Panicles 10–36 cm long, narrow, contracted; axis, branches, and pedicels glabrous or nearly so; branches to 6 cm long, strictly erect to appressed, pedicels short. Spikelets 4–7 mm long, florets 5–11; glumes 4–7 mm long, subequal, conspicuously longer than other spikelets; lemmas 2–3 mm long, veins ciliate or pubescent at base, apex notched and mucronate, lateral veins often excurrent as mucro; paleas wide, awnless.

Occasional in prairie along mid and upper Gulf Coast.

Tridens texanus (S. Wats.) Nash **TEXAS TRIDENS** Perennial bunchgrasses. Culms to 75 cm tall, slender, erect. Leaf blades thin, flat. Panicles to 16 cm long, open or contracted. Spikelets 6–13 mm long, large, florets six or seven; glumes 1-veined, nearly equal; lemma veins pubescent below middle; lemmas and paleas thin, tinged with pink or purple.

Occasional on sandy loam or clay loam soils, usually under protection of shrubs along lower and mid Gulf Coast.

89. TRIPLASIS · Beauv.

Culms solid. Leaves cauline; sheaths rounded, lower sheaths enclosing cleistogamous inflorescences; ligules a ring of hairs; blades flat or involute. Panicles exserted or included in upper sheath, branches spreading. Spikelets laterally compressed, disarticulation above glumes; florets two to four, sterile floret above; glumes unequal; lemmas 3-veined, veins ciliate, awned from between lobes.

Figure 193. *Tridens congestus* inflorescence and spikelet (Gould and Box 1965).

Triplasis purpurea (Walt.) Chapm. **PURPLE SANDGRASS** (Figure 197) Tufted annuals. Culms to 100 cm tall, decumbent to erect to spreading; nodes numerous, pubescent, purple-tinged. Axillary inflorescences with cleistogamous spikelets in axils of enlarged sheaths; spikelets with one floret. Terminal panicles 3–11 cm long, pyramidal, relatively small. Spikelets 6–10 mm long, florets two to four;

Figure 194. *Tridens eragrostoides*
inflorescence and spikelet (Gould and Box 1965).

glumes tapering, apex notched, awnless; lemmas 3-4 mm long, veins densely short-
pubescent, apex obtuse and notched, awned or mucronate; paleas narrow, veins
silky-villous. Caryopses 1.5–2.0 mm long, yellow-brown, firm.

Occasional in sandy wooded openings, deep sands, and dunes throughout Gulf
Coast.

90. **TRIPSACUM** L.

Plant monoecious. Culms solid. Leaves basal and cauline; sheaths rounded; ligules a ciliate membrane; blades flat and wide. Panicles or spicate racemes; branches racemose; staminate spikelets above beadlike pistillate spikelets.

Figure 195. *Tridens flavus* var. *flavus*
plant (Gould 1978), (A) spikelet, and (B) floret (palea view) (Hitchcock 1951).

Figure 196. *Tridens muticus* var. *muticus*
plant, (A) glumes, and (B) florets (Gould and Box 1965).

Tripsacum dactyloides (L.) L. **EASTERN GAMAGRASS** (Figure 198) Rhizomatous perennials. Culms to 3 m tall in large clumps. Leaves glabrous; sheaths shiny;
ligules a ciliate membrane; blades 30–75 cm long, 10–25 mm wide. Panicles of
racemose branches or spicate racemes; branches 12–25 cm long; spicate racemes
or racemose branches with staminate spikelets above and pistillate spikelets below. Staminate spikelets 6–10 mm long, awnless, florets two. Pistillate spikelet
glumes 6–8 mm long, membranous, flat, several-veined, subsessile, usually solitary, hard and bony, indurate; lemmas of lower and upper florets of pistillate spike-

lets thin and hyaline, often reduced. Staminate portion of inflorescence deciduous as a whole, pistillate portion breaking up at nodes into hard, shiny, beadlike units.

Most frequent along banks of brackish streams and ditches close to Gulf Coast. Once a common and productive constituent of inland prairies, it is good livestock forage and used as a pasture grass or hay on fertile bottomland and prairies; provides good wildlife cover and seed.

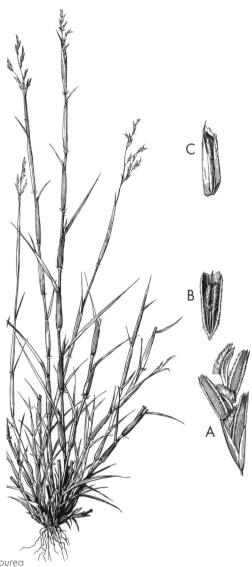

Figure 197. *Triplasis purpurea*
plant, (A) spikelet, (B) floret, and (C) cleistogamous spikelets of lower sheaths (Hitchcock 1951).

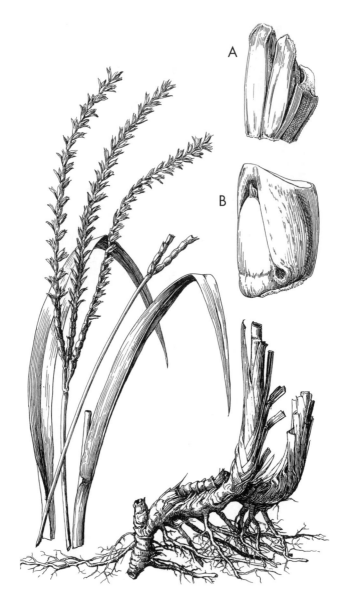

Figure 198. *Tripsacum dactyloides*
plant, (A) staminate spikelets and branch section, and (B) pistillate spikelets and branch section
(Hitchcock 1951).

91. **TRISETUM** Pers. • Trisetum
Culms hollow. Leaves basal and
cauline; sheaths open; ligules membranous; blades flat. Panicles open
or contracted. Spikelets laterally
compressed, disarticulation above
glumes; florets two to four, perfect;
glumes subequal to unequal, longer
than florets, rachilla prolonged
above upper floret; lemmas usually
awned from just below the bifid
apex.

Trisetum interruptum Buckl.
PRAIRIE TRISETUM (Figure 199)
Tufted annuals. Culms to 40 cm tall,
geniculate, nodes purple. Panicles to
15 cm long, narrow, contracted.
Spikelets about 5 mm long, florets
two or three; glumes subequal, awnless, shorter than spikelets; lemmas
3.5–5.0 mm long, apex toothed with
twisted awn 5–8 mm long.

Infrequent on sandy soil along
mid and upper Gulf Coast.

92. **TRITICUM** L.
Culms hollow. Leaves cauline;
sheaths rounded, auricles well developed; ligules membranous;
blades flat. Spikes bilateral with one
spikelet per node. Spikelets laterally
compressed, disarticulation above
the glumes, florets two to five, ster-
ile floret apical or absent; glumes nearly equal; lemmas asymmetrically keeled,
awned or awnless.

Figure 199. *Trisetum interruptum*
inflorescence and spikelet (Gould and Box
1965).

Triticum aestivum L. **WHEAT** (Figure 200) Tufted annuals. Culms to 100 cm tall, erect. Leaves with fingerlike auricles; blades to 2 cm wide. Spike to 12 cm long, spikelets single at nodes. Spikelets 10–15 mm long, florets two to five; glumes broad, keeled to one side, awned or awnless; lemmas long-awned to awnless; paleas well developed.

Occasional as an escapee, mainly along road and railroad rights-of-way throughout Gulf Coast. The common wheat planted for grain or forage. Good forage and grain for livestock and wildlife.

93. UNIOLA L.

Culms solid. Leaves mainly basal; sheaths open; ligules a ciliate membrane; blades flat to involute. Panicles drooping. Spikelets awnless, laterally compressed, disarticulation below glumes; florets 10–30, lowermost one to four florets sterile, several fertile florets, and apical florets sterile; glumes unequal; lemmas 9-veined.

Uniola paniculata L. **SEA-OATS** (Figure 201) Stout, rhizomatous perennials. Culms to 1.5 m tall, occurring singly or in clumps. Leaf sheaths about two-thirds the length of internodes, glabrous; ligules a dense ring of hairs; blades to 80 cm long, 5–10 mm wide, flat. Panicles to 50 cm long, contracted. Spikelets 2.0–3.5 cm long, to 2 cm wide, florets 12–20, laterally compressed, smooth, shiny, disarticulation below glumes; glumes subequal, acute, awnless; lemmas wide, acute, keeled, awnless; paleas about the length of lemmas, margins winged, serrate.

Common on dunes and sandy flats all along Gulf Coast and barrier islands. An important dune builder and binder; used successfully in artificial plantings on Padre Island. Poor forage; provides good wildlife cover; rodents utilize seeds.

94. UROCHLOA Beauv. • Signalgrass

Culms solid, branched. Leaves basal and cauline; sheaths rounded and keeled; ligules a ring of hairs or a ciliate membrane; blades flat, sometimes margin crisp. Panicles open contracted or of several spicate primary unilateral branches; branches with spikelets oriented with first glumes abaxial and adaxial to the primary branch axis. Spikelets dorsally compressed, disarticulation below the glumes; florets two, lower one sterile, upper one fertile; glumes awless, unequal; second glumes and lowermost lemmas similar in size and texture; upper florets indurate, finely rugose to rugose, margins clasping palea.

Figure 200. *Triticum aestivum*
plant, (A) spikelet, (B) floret (palea view), (C) awned inflorescence, and (D) nearly awnless inflorescence (Hitchcock 1951).

1. Panicles of spicate primary unilateral branches (occasionally primary branches have short secondary branches) 2
1. Panicles open or contracted but not having spicate primary unilateral branches 6

Figure 201. *Uniola paniculata*
inflorescence and floret (Hitchcock 1951).

2(1). Spikelets less than 2.5 mm long; plants annual .... *U. reptans*

   2. Spikelets 2.6 mm or longer; plants annual or perennial 3

3(2). Leaf blade margins crisp; plants annual .... *U. panicoides*

   3. Leaf blade margins flat not crisp; plants annual or perennial 4

4(3). Spikelets less than 3 mm long; plants perennial .... *U. mutica*

   4. Spikelets greater than 3.5 mm long; plants annual or perennial 5

5(4). Lowermost lemma apex reticulate veined; plants annual .. *U. platyphylla*

5. Lowermost lemma apex not reticulate veined; plants perennial ....
.... *U. mosambicensis*

6(1). Apex of second glumes and lowermost lemmas reticulate veined ....
.... *U. fasciculata*

6. Apex of second glumes and lowermost lemmas not reticulate veined ... 7

7(6). Spikelets 4.5 mm or longer, glabrous to conspicuously hairy; plants annual; leaf blades more than 10 mm wide .... *U. texana*

7. Spikelets less than 4.5 mm long, sparsely pubescent; plants perennial; leaf blades less than 6 mm wide .... *U. ciliatissima*

Urochloa ciliatissima (S. Buckl.) R. D. Webster **FRINGED SIGNALGRASS** Tufted perennials. Culms to 40 cm tall, erect with spreading stolons; internodes short; nodes swollen. Leaf blades mostly 3–5 mm wide. Inflorescence a panicle. Spikelets to 4 mm long; florets 2; second glume and lower lemma margins hispid, hairs about 1 mm long.

Frequent on sandy and sandy loam soils. Sometimes referred to as "sandhill grass," it functions as a soil binder in sandy areas subject to wind erosion. Provides fair forage during periods of vigorous growth. Large seeds provide food for birds. Usually associated with *Setaria firmula*.

Urochloa fasciculata (O. Swartz) R. D. Webster **BROWNTOP SIGNALGRASS** (Figure 202) Tufted annuals. Culms to 120 cm long, sometimes decumbent. Leaves basal and cauline; ligules ciliate membranes; blades flat. Panicles 5–15 cm long with few racemose branches. Spikelets 2–3 mm long, yellowish-brown; second glumes and lower lemmas with reticulate cross veins; upper lemmas rugose.

Locally frequent in dry lake beds and disturbed areas on clay sites. Poor forage.

Urochloa mosambicensis (Hack.) Dandy Tufted or stoloniferous perennials. Culms to 150 cm tall with papilla-based hairs, rooting at lower nodes. Leaves cauline with papilla-based hairs; sheaths pubescent; ligules 1–2 mm long; blades 3–7 mm wide, flat. Panicles 5–12 cm long with 3–10 spicate primary unilateral branches; branches terminating in a spikelet; pedicels with 1–3 conspicuous hairs, hairs about 1.5–3.0 mm long. Spikelets with first glumes oriented away from primary branch.

Found along mid Coast in Jim Wells County.

Figure 202. *Urochloa fasciculata*
plant, (A) spikelet (first glume view), and (B) upper floret (palea view) (Gould and Box 1965).

Urochloa mutica (P. Forrsk.) T. Q. Nguyen **PARAGRASS** Coarse perennials.
Culms to 4–5 m long, thick, decumbent, trailing. Leaves basal and cauline; sheath
nodes and collars densely pubescent; blades 10–30 cm long, 0.5–1.5 cm wide.
Panicles 12–20 cm long with 8–18 spicate primary unilateral branches; branches
widely spaced, spreading, basal portion villous. Spikelets more or less paired on
flattened branches. Spikelets 2.8–3.4 mm long, glabrous; first glumes acute;
second glume and lemma of lower florets about equal; upper florets finely rugose.

Introduced along Gulf Coast as a forage grass and now rather frequent along waterways, resacas, and in coastal marshes along lower Coast. Good forage for livestock and good seed producer for birds.

Urochloa panicoides P. Beauv. **LIVERSEED GRASS** Vigorous annuals. Culms to 80 cm long, ascending to prostrate, rooting at lower nodes, glabrous to pubescent. Leaf sheath margins pubescent to ciliate; ligules 1.0–1.5 mm long; blades to 20 cm long, 5–18 mm wide with papillose hairs, margins crisp, flat. Panicles of 2–10 spicate primary unilateral branches; branches to 6 cm long, spreading. Spikelets 3–5 mm long; first glumes 1.3–1.6 mm long, oriented away from primary branch, 3–5-veined, one-fourth the length of second glumes; upper florets transversely rugose, apex rounded.

Adventive in lawns, roadsides, and other disturbed areas along lower Coast.

Urochloa platyphylla (Munro *ex* Wright) R. D. Webster **BROADLEAF SIGNALGRASS** (Figure 203) Spreading annuals. Culms to 50 cm tall, stoloniferous, weak, rooting at lower nodes. Leaves relatively thick, glabrous; blades 6–18 mm wide. Panicles of 2–6 spicate primary unilateral branches, branches widely spaced. Spikelets 4.0–4.5 mm long, glabrous, ovate; first glumes short, blunt; second glumes and lowermost lemmas subequal; lower lemmas reticulate cross-veined; upper florets finely rugose.

Found on disturbed soils in moist open sites of mid and lower Coast. Poor forage.

Urochloa reptans (L.) **SPRAWLING SIGNALGRASS** Low, weedy, mat-forming annuals. Culms decumbent, stoloniferous, rooting at nodes; upright culms to 30 cm long, becoming erect, branching extensively. Leaves cauline; sheaths keeled, glabrous, margins hirsute; ligules to 1.5 mm long; blades 2–6 cm long, to 1 cm wide, margins crisp. Panicles of 4–14 spicate primary unilateral branches; branches spreading; pedicels bearing few long silvery, bristlelike hairs. Spikelets 1.8–2.1 mm long; first glumes about 0.4 mm long; second glumes and lower lemmas slightly apiculate; upper florets transversely rugose.

Occasional on disturbed soils throughout Coast; most frequent on heavy clay soils; a common weed of flower beds, gardens and fields.

Urochloa texana (S. Buckl.) R. D. Webster **TEXAS SIGNALGRASS** (Figure 204) Coarse annuals. Culms to 110 cm tall, decumbent, branching above base, pubescent. Leaves cauline; ligules are rings of hairs to 4 mm long; blades 1–2 cm wide,

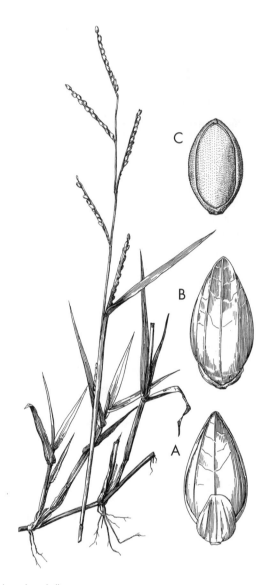

Figure 203. *Urochloa platyphylla*
plant, (A) spikelet (first glume view), (B) spikelet (second glume view), and (C) upper floret (palea view) (Hitchcock 1951).

pubescent. Panicles 10–20 cm long, contracted. Spikelets 5.0–5.7 mm long, ovate-lanceolate; glumes and lemmas awnless; upper florets about 2 mm long; paleas rugose.

Seasonally abundant on disturbed soils. Often grows as a weed of cultivated fields, generally in sand and sandy loam soils. Fair grazing value for livestock and a good producer of seeds for wildlife. Deer have been observed to relish the early growth.

Figure 204. *Urochloa texana*
inflorescence and spikelet (Gould and Box 1965).

95. VASEYOCHLOA A. S. Hitchc.

Culms solid. Leaves basal and cauline; sheaths rounded; ligules a ring of hairs; blades flat to involute. Panicles open or contracted. Spikelets not conspicuously compressed, disarticulation above glumes; florets five to ten, sterile florets apical; glumes unequal; lemmas 7- to 9-veined; paleas keeled on margins.

Vaseyochloa multinervosa (Vasey) A. S. Hitchc. **TEXASGRASS** (Figure 205) Tufted perennials. Culms to 100 cm tall, erect, slender. Panicles 6–20 cm long, drooping. Spikelets 10–20 mm long, florets 6–11; glumes obtuse, shorter than lemmas; lower lemmas 5–7 mm long, 7- to 11-veined, prominent, awnless, slightly hairy on back, apex rounded; paleas splitting at maturity. Caryopses with horn-like style bases, dark brown or black at maturity.

Locally abundant on sandy sites inland and near coastline along lower and mid Gulf Coast. Fair to good forage; good wildlife cover.

96. VULPIA Gmel. • Sixweeksgrass

Plants annual. Culms hollow. Leaves basal and cauline; sheaths rounded; ligules membranous; blades flat or involute. Panicles occasionally reduced to racemes. Spikelets laterally compressed, disarticulation above glumes; florets two to several, sterile florets apical; glumes unequal; lemmas with apical awns or awnless.

1. Lemmas glabrous to scabrous .... *V. octoflora* var. *octoflora*
1. Lemmas sparsely to densely pubescent .... *V. octoflora* var. *hirtella*

Vulpia octoflora (Walt.) Rydb. var. *octoflora* **COMMON SIXWEEKSGRASS** (Figure 206) Tufted annuals. Culms to 60 cm tall, erect to ascending. Leaf blades 1–2 mm wide, involute. Panicles or racemes 4–15 cm long, contracted. Spikelets with florets 6–11; glumes narrowly pointed, glabrous or scabrous; lemma awn-tipped to awned, awns 0-6 mm long.

Occurs on most sites along Gulf Coast; most frequent around ant beds and other disturbed areas. Poor livestock and wildlife values.

var. *hirtella* (Piper) Henr. **HAIR SIXSWEEKSGRASS** Similar to var. *octoflora* but with strongly scabrous to densely pubescent lemmas.

97. WILLKOMMIA Hack.

Culms solid. Leaves mostly basal; sheaths rounded; ligules a ciliate membrane; blades folded, involute or flat. Panicle of two to several spicate primary unilateral

Figure 205. *Vaseyochloa multinervosa*
plant, (A) spikelet, (B) lemma, (C) mature floret showing split palea, and (D) caryopsis (Hitchcock 1951).

Figure 206. *Vulpia octoflora* var. *octoflora*
plant and spikelet (Hitchcock 1951).

branches; branches appressed. Spikelets awnless, laterally compressed; floret one; glumes unequal; lemmas 3-veined.

Willkommia texana A. S. Hitchc. **TEXAS WILLKOMMIA** (Figure 207) Tufted perennials in small clumps. Culms to 40 cm tall from a firm base. Leaves with ligules a ciliate membrane; blades 4–10 cm long, 1–3 mm wide. Panicles of several appressed spicate primary unilateral branches. Spikelets about 4 mm long,

Figure 207. *Willkommia texana* var. *texana*
plant, (A) spikelet (first glume view), (B) spikelet (second glume view), (C) lemma, and (D) floret (palea view) (Hitchcock 1951).

awnless, floret one, sessile on short branches of main culm axis; first glumes short; second glumes and lemmas about equal in length.

Occasional in hard, tight soil bordering cattle trails, swales, and small lakes along mid and upper Gulf Coast. Poor forage.

98. ZEA L.

Plants monoecious. Culms solid or spongy, thick, tall. Leaves cauline; sheaths rounded; ligules membranous; blades flat, wide. Staminate panicles apical, branches racemose with paired spikelets. Pistillate inflorescences axillary (corn cob), concealed by several spatheate sheaths; spikelets numerous in many rows.

Zea mays L. **CORN** (Figure 208) Monoecious annuals. Culms to 3 m tall, succulent. Leaf blades 6 cm or wider, elongate, flat. Spikelets unisexual; staminate spikelets with two florets at plant apex. Pistillate inflorescences enclosed in numerous axillary sheaths of culm with spikelets paired in rows on thickened woody base (cob).

Common cultivated corn; seldom found outside planted fields. High food value for humans; important forage and grain for livestock and wildlife.

99. ZIZANIOPSIS Doell

Plants monoecious. Culms hollow. Leaves basal and cauline; sheaths rounded; ligules membranous; blades flat and wide, with coarsely serrate margins. Panicles open, large; branches ascending, staminate spikelets below and pistillate ones above. Pistillate spikelets short-awned, disarticulation below glumes; floret one; glumes absent; lemmas 7-veined; paleas 3-veined. Staminate spikelets awnless; glumes absent; lemmas 7-veined; paleas 3-veined.

Zizaniopsis miliacea (Michx.) Doell & Aschers. **MARSHMILLET** (Figure 209) Coarse, rhizomatous perennials. Culms 3 m or taller. Leaf blades long, 8–22 mm wide, succulent. Panicles large, spreading, bearing staminate and pistillate spikelets. Staminate spikelets positioned below pistillate spikelets on inflorescence branches; lemmas of pistillate spikelets 7-veined, bearing slender awns at apex; paleas of pistillate spikelets 3-veined; staminate spikelets with six stamens, awnless. Caryopses about 3 mm long, globose.

Present in shallow water along freshwater lakes, marshes, and rivers of mid and upper Gulf Coast. Often present as dense stands in brackish coastal marshes. Readily grazed by cattle, but of limited forage value because of limited access. Good wildlife food and cover, especially as seed for waterfowl; good for shoreline stabilization and for use in reconstructed wetlands.

Figure 208. *Zea mays*
(A) branches of staminate inflorescence, (B) staminate spikelet, (C) pistillate inflorescence, (D) pistillate spikelet after flowering, and (E) pair of pistillate spikelets with attached rachis (Hitchcock 1951).

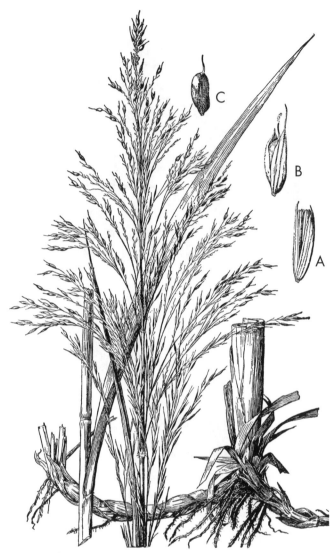

Figure 209. *Zizaniopsis miliacea*
plant, (A) staminate spikelet, (B) pistillate spikelet, and (C) caryopsis (Hitchcock 1951).

— Glossary

A- Prefix meaning without.

Abaxial Located on the side away from the axis.

Achene One-seeded, dry indehiscent fruit with a relatively thin wall; the seed coat is not fused to the ovary wall.

Acuminate Gradually tapering to a sharp point; point is drawn out.

Acute Sharply pointed, but less tapering than acuminate; angle 90° or less.

Adaxial Located on the side nearest the axis.

Adhere To stick to.

Adherent Sticking or clinging.

Adnate Fusion of unlike parts (e.g., fusion of palea to the caryopsis in *Bromus*).

Adventitious roots Roots developing from basal culms, nodes, or some structure other than the seed.

Adventive Term used to denote an exotic species established by chance or accidental seeding.

Aggregate Cluster, or the forming of a group with objects in close proximity.

Alternate Located singly at each node; an arrangement of parts (e.g., leaves) at different heights along an axis.

Annual Completing life cycle from seed to maturity to death within one year or one season.

Anther Pollen bearing portion of the stamen.

Antrorse Directed upward or forward toward the apex; the opposite of retrorse.

Apex Uppermost tip of a structure.

Apices Plural of apex.

Apical Located at the tip.

Apiculate Ending in a short, flexible point.

Appendage Secondary or projecting part.

Appressed Lying against an organ in the direction of the apex.

Aristate Provided with a short awn or bristle from the apex, edge, or back of an organ.

Aromatic Having an odor, fragrant or otherwise; bearing volatile essential oils.

Articulate Jointed; a node for natural separation of parts.

Ascending Sloping or rising obliquely upward.

Asexual Without sex; sexless; not involving gametes.

Asymmetrical Not having planes dividing the structure into mirror-image halves.

Attenuate Gradually narrowing to a pointed apex or base; sharper than acute.

Auricle Fingerlike appendage or flange of tissue at the junction of the blade and sheath in some grasses; holds the split sheath to the culm.

Autumnal Growth form for late summer and fall (e.g., *Dichanthelium*).

Awn Extension of the vein (nerve) of spikelet bracts beyond the leaflike tissue.

Axil Upper angle between an organ (e.g., branch) and its axis.

Axillary Occurring in an axil.

Axis (axes) Central stem(s) of an inflorescence, particularly of a panicle.

Barbed Retrorse projections or hairs.

Basal Referring to the base or location there; the lower portion of a structure.

Bearded Bearing long, stiff hairs (e.g., at culm nodes of *Dichanthium*).

Bi- Two.

Bifid Apex with one cleft, or having two teeth.

Bilateral Two-sided; structures on two sides of an organ.

Bisexual Having both sexes (e.g., flower or floret); a hermaphrodite.

Blade Part of the leaf above the sheath.

Bloom Waxy covering on surfaces (e.g., fruits and leaves); usually results in a bluish color.

Bract Modified leaf, often scalelike (e.g., glumes, lemmas, paleas).

Branch Lateral stem or part of the panicle inflorescence.

Bristle Stiff, slender hair or appendage similar to a hog's bristle; in *Setaria*, *Pennisetum,* and a few other grasses; a highly reduced branch without a spikelet at the apex.

Bud Undeveloped stem, branch, leaf, or flower.

Bulb Subterranean bud with fleshy scales (e.g., those of an onion).

Bur Rough or prickly covering surrounding the fruits or spikelets in some genera (e.g, *Cenchrus*).

Caespitose (cespitose) Tufted; several stems in a close tuft.

Callus Indurate downward extension of the mature lemma in *Stipa, Aristida,* and other genera; hard, pointed base of spikelet (e.g., *Heteropogon*).

Capillary Very slender or hairlike.

Capitate In a globular cluster or head.

Capitellate Possessing a minute swelling at the apex.

Cartilaginous Firm and tough, but flexible; like cartilage.

Caryopsis One-seeded, dry indehiscent fruit or grain of grasses with a lateral embryo; the seed coat is adnate to the pericarp.

Cauline Belonging to the stem (e.g., stem leaves).

Central axis Main axis of the inflorescence.

Central groove Longitudinal depression in the sides of pedicels in *Bothriochloa*.

Cespitose See caespitose.

Ciliate Fringed with hairs on the margin.

Ciliolate Minutely ciliate.

Clasping To hold parts together; holding.

Cleistogamous Applied to flowers or florets fertilized without opening; must be self-fertile.

Cluster Several similar things (e.g., bracts or spikelets) grouped together.

Coleoptile Protective sheath for the young shoot in the embryo.

Collar Area on the outer (abaxial) side of a leaf at the junction of the sheath and blade.

Column Lower, undivided part of the awns in certain *Aristida* species.

Compact Short and dense.

Compressed Flattened strongly (most often laterally); keeled.

Concave Dished inward; an existing hollow.

Connate Fusion of like parts (e.g., sheath margins forming a tube).

Continuous Rachis or other organ that does not disarticulate.

Contracted Narrow or dense inflorescences, the branches being appressed or short.

Convex Rounded on the surface.

Cordate Heart-shaped base and pointed apex of a structure (e.g., a leaf blade).

Coriaceous Having a leathery texture.

Corm Short, bulblike stem.

Crisp Undulating in a horizontal plane.

Crown Persistent base of a perennial.

Culm Jointed grass stem composed of nodes, internodes, leaves, and axillary buds.

Cylindrical Shaped like a tube, round in cross section with parallel margins.

Deciduous Not persisting, falling away in less than one year.

Decumbent Curved upward from a horizontal or inclined base (e.g., stems).

Deflexed Turned abruptly downward.

Deltoid Triangular in outline; shaped like the Greek letter delta.

Dense Refers to inflorescences having crowded spikelets.

Depauperate Stunted.

Dermal Pertaining to the epidermis.

Diffuse Open and much-branched; spread widely.

Digitate Parts (three or more) arising from the summit of a structure (e.g., branches of the *Chloris* inflorescence).

Dilated Expanded, enlarged, or widened.

Dioecious Unisexual, the staminate and pistillate flowers being on separate plants.

Disarticulate (disarticulation) Naturally separating at the nodes (joints) at maturity.

Discoid Resembling a disk or platter.

Distichous Obviously in two ranks, and like the rungs of a ladder in appearance.

Divergent Extending away from an axis by degrees.

Dorsal Referring to the back of an organ, away from the axis; abaxial surface.

Elliptic Arching margins of leaf that is pointed at both ends, about two times longer than wide.

Elongate Narrow, with the length several times greater than the width or thickness.

Emarginate Having a slightly notched apex.

Embedded Appearing or growing as part of another structure.

Endosperm Nutritive tissue near the embryo of the seed; develops from a fusion of polar nuclei and sperm nucleus.

Entire Having a continuous margin without teeth or lobes.

Equal Same length or width.

Erect Upright in relation to the ground; perpendicular to the ground.

Erose Irregularly toothed on the margins or at the apex; appearing to be chewed off.

Exserted Protruding (e.g., the inflorescence from the sheath).

Fascicle Small bundle or cluster.

Fertile Capable of producing a fruit or caryopsis.

Fibrous Resembling a mass of fiber; threadlike, but may appear branched.

Filiform Threadlike; long and narrow.

First glume Lowermost glume; odd-veined, an empty bract.

Flabellate Broadly, wedge- or fan-shaped.

Flexuous Bent gradually in one direction and then another.

Floral axis Structure connecting the palea and flower to the rachilla.

Floret Lemma, floral axis, and palea with the included flower (pistil, stamen, and lodicules) or caryopsis (floret with all parts).

Flowering Blooming or being in flower; covered with flowers.

Fruit Ripened ovary.

Fusiform Spindle-shaped; widest near the middle and tapering in toward both ends.

Geniculate Bent sharply, like a bent knee.

Gibbous Swollen on one side; see the second glume of *Sacciolepis*.

Glabrate Almost glabrous.

Glabrescent To become glabrous (without hairs) as a particular plant structure ages or matures.

Glabrous Without hairs of any type.

Glandular Bearing glands.

Glaucous Waxy bloom or white covering of a surface; in plants, usually a blue-green color.

Globose Round or spherical.

Glumes Pair of bracts at the base of the spikelet; odd-veined, empty bracts that may be awned or awnless.

Habit General appearance or aspect of a plant; growth form.

Herbaceous Having the character of an herb (not woody);
grasses, grasslike plants, and forbs are herbs.

Hirsute Covered with coarse, straight, and rather stiff hairs, usually perpendicular to the surface.

Hispid Rough with erect, bristly hairs.

Hyaline Thin and translucent or transparent.

Imbricate Overlapping (e.g., shingles on a roof).

Imperfect Having unisexual flowers (i.e., either stamen or pistil [carpels], but not both).

Inconspicuous Hard to see; not striking to the eye.

Indehiscent Not opening at maturity, staying closed (e.g., anther or fruit).

Indicator categories:

> **Upland** Not included in the *National List of Plant Species that Occur in Wetlands: Texas* (Reed 1988).
>
> **Facultative upland** Usually occurs in upland or non-wetlands (probability 67–99%), but occasionally found in wetlands (probability 1–33%).
>
> **Facultative** Equal likelihood of occurring in wetlands or non-wetlands (probability 34–66%).
>
> **Facultative wetland** Usually occurs in wetlands (probability 67–99%), but occasionally found in non-wetlands.
>
> **Obligate wetland** Under natural conditions, occurs in wetlands (probability >99%).

Indurate Hard.

Infertile Incapable of sexual reproduction.

Inflated Puffed up; bladdery.

Inflorescence Flowering part of a plant, above the uppermost leaf or portion thereof.

Inrolled Having the margin rolled toward the midvein; involute.

Intercalary Meristematic tissue occurring in an area other than at the apical meristem; tissue at the base of the internode in young culms.

Internode Portion of a culm between two successive nodes.

Involucre Cluster of bristles or sterile branchlets below the spikelets (e.g., *Cenchrus* and *Pennisetum*).

Involute Rolled inward from the edges so that the upper surface is within.

Joint Node of a grass culm, spikelet, inflorescence, or any other node.

Keel Sharp fold at the back of a compressed sheath, glume, lemma, palea, or caryopsis.

Lacerate Appearing torn on the margin; irregularly cleft.

Lanate Woolly covering of short, dense hairs.

Lanceolate Shape or outline resembling the head of a spear; pointed at both ends and widest below the middle.

Lateral Refers to the sides.

Leaf Lateral organ of a grass culm, typically consisting of a sheath, blade, ligule, and auricles.

Lemma Odd-veined bract of a spikelet occurring above the glumes; the abaxial bract of the floret, either awned or awnless.

Ligule Adaxial appendage, membrane, ciliate membrane, or ring of hairs on the inside of a leaf at the junction of sheath and blade.

Linear Long and narrow with parallel margins.

Lobed Projecting portion of an organ in which the divisions are less than half the distance to the base or midrib; usually rounded at apex.

Lodicules Two or three membranous parts at the base of the grass flower; thought to be reduced perianth.

Longevity Life span of an organism; in plants, annual, biennial, or perennial.

Margins Edges (e.g., the leaf edge or margins).

Mat-forming Low growth form resembling a pad.

Membranous Thin, soft, pliable.

Meristem Undifferentiated cell capable of developing into a number of organs and/or tissues; a growing point.

Mesic Characterized by an intermediate moisture supply (e.g., a type of habitat or soil).

Midrib Central vein of a leaf or leaflet.

Midvein Central vein or vascular bundle of a leaf, lemma, glume, or similar structure.

Minute Very small.

Monocotyledons Plants having one cotyledon or seed leaf.

Monoecious Having staminate and pistillate flowers on the same plant but each sex on different flowers.

Motte Small grove or clump of trees.

Mucro Minute awn or excurrent midvein of an organ (e.g., on a lemma).

Mucronate Tipped with a short point or tip like an awn; usually the short extension of a vein beyond the leafy tissue.

Muticous Blunt, or without a definite point.

Neuter Without sexual structures; not having stamens or pistils.

Node Joint of a culm, inflorescence, or spikelet.

Ob- Prefix meaning inversely.

Obconic Solid figure with the shape of a cone; widest at the apex and pointed at the base.

Oblique Having unequal sides; slanting.

Oblong Object with round ends and parallel margins, three times longer than wide.

Obovate Egg-shaped, with widest part above the middle.

Obovoid Solid that is obovate in outline.

Obpyriform Pear-shaped, with the wide end toward the apex.

Obtuse Pointed with an angle greater than 90°; broad, pointed apex or base.

One-sided Secund; arranged only on one side.

Open Loose, spreading (e.g., inflorescences with few spikelets and long branches).

Opposite Structures paired at the nodes and placed one on each side of the node; stamen inserted directly in front of the petal; leaves are also opposite.

Orbicular Approaching a circular outline.

Oval Broadly elliptical, but with rounded ends; similar to oblong, but not as long.

Ovate Egg-shaped, with the widest part below the middle.

Ovulate Bearing ovules.

Ovule Structure within the ovary that will become the seed after fertilization.

Paired Occurring in twos (e.g., two spikelets per node).

Palea Abaxial bract of a floret; two-veined, arising from the floral axis.

Panicle Inflorescence type in which the central axis branches and rebranches.

Papilla Minute nipple-shaped projection.

Papillose Having minute nipple-shaped projections on the surface.

Pectinate Arrangement of parts resembling the teeth of a comb (e.g., the spikelets on *Bouteloua hirsuta*).

Pedicel Stalk of a single spikelet or flower, except for spikelets on a spike inflorescence.

Pedicellate Having a pedicel or stalk.

Peduncle Stalk or stem of an inflorescence.

Pendulous Drooping; hanging downward; suspended.

Perennial Growing more than two years; completing several reproductive cycles.

Perfect Flowers having both stamen and pistils (carpels).

Pericarp Ripened ovary wall after becoming a fruit.

Persistent Remaining attached, either after other parts have been shed or for a considerable period.

Petiole Stalk of a leaf blade.

Pilose Covered with long, soft hairs that are typically straight.

Pinnate Having two rows of lateral divisions along the main axis.

Pistil Seed producing structure of a flower with ovary, style, and stigma.

Pistillate Applied to spikelets bearing female parts only and to an inflorescence or a plant with female flowers.

Pithy Spongy (e.g., culm of *Saccharum*).

Pitted (pit) Marked with small depressions or pits.

Plano-convex Flat on one side and convex on the other.

Playa Dried-up lake basin.

Plumbeous Lead colored.

Plumose Feathery in appearance, having fine hairs on each side.

Primary branch Any branch arising from the main axis; all branches coming from the central axis of a grass inflorescence.

Primary unilateral branch Any branch originating from the central or main axis of a panicle inflorescence with spikelets along one side, or what appears to be one side.

Prophyll First leaf of a lateral branch; a sheath with two veins.

Prostrate Lying flat on the ground.

Puberulent Minutely pubescent.

Pubescent Covered with short, soft hairs.

Pulvini Swelling at the base of a leaf or branch of the inflorescence.

Punctate Covered with glandular dots, pits, or depressions.

Pungent Having a sharp point and/or an acrid taste.

Pyramidal Triangular in outline; shaped like a pyramid.

Raceme Inflorescence type in which all the spikelets are pedicellate on the rachis.

Racemose Having branches similar to racemes, with some combination of sessile and short pedicellate spikelets.

Rachilla Axis of the spikelet; structure to which glumes, lemma, and floral axis are attached.

Rachis Axis of a spike, spicate raceme, or raceme inflorescence.

Range condition Current productivity of rangeland relative to that land's natural productivity.

Reduced Smaller in size, frequently lacking parts; in flowers, the sexual parts may be absent.

Reduced floret Staminate or neuter floret; if highly reduced (e.g., to awnlike structures), sometimes called a rudimentary floret.

Reflexed Bent downward or backward from the apex.

Resaca Old riverbed (e.g., an oxbow).

Resinous Characterized by a viscous substance or resin.

Reticulate In the form of a network (e.g., some types of netted venation).

Retrorse Pointing downward toward the base (e.g., barbs on *Cenchrus* [sandbur]).

Revolute Turned under along the margins toward the abaxial surface.

Rhizome Horizontal, underground stem with modified leaves at the nodes.

Rhizomatous Having rhizomes; horizontal underground stems with nodes and internodes.

Rosette Cluster of spreading or radiating basal leaves (e.g., in *Dichanthelium*).

Rounded Having an arched apex, rather than a pointed and angled apex.

Rudiment Imperfectly developed organ or part, specifically used in reference to florets; the rudiment of a spikelet is formed by the structures of a reduced sterile floret.

Rudimentary Not fully developed, and nonfunctional.

Rugose Wrinkled or folded; having horizontal folds in the surface.

Saccate Swollen or saclike in shape; see the second glume of *Sacciolepis.*

Scabrous Rough to the touch, caused by short, stiff, angled hairs on the surface.

Scarious Thin, dry, and membranous; not green (e.g., the margins of a *Poa* lemma).

Second glume Uppermost of the two glumes; an odd-veined, empty bract of the spikelet.

Secondary Not primary, subordinate; the branches arising from the primary branches.

Series Number or group of similar objects arranged in a row.

Serrate Saw-toothed, with the teeth angled toward the apex; having sharp teeth.

Sessile Without a pedicel or stalk.

Setaceous Slender and bristlelike.

Setae Rigid bristle; sharp, pointed bristle.

Sheath Lower part of a leaf enclosing the culm; typically open or split and overlapping at the margins.

Sinuate Having a wavy margin.

Solitary Single; one.

Spathe Modified leaf sheath subtending, and often enclosing, some of the inflorescence.

Spatheate Having a spathe.

Spherical Shaped like a globe or a ball.

Spicate Spikelike; resembling a spike inflorescence but having both sessile and pedicellate spikelets or flowers.

Spicate raceme Raceme with both sessile and pedicellate spikelets on a rachis.

Spike Unbranched inflorescence in which the spikelets are sessile on the rachis (main axis).

Spikelet Basic unit of a grass inflorescence, typically consisting of two glumes (except in some species where one or both glumes are lacking), one or more florets, and a rachilla.

Spines Sharp, pointed, stiff bodies arising from the epidermis; in grasses, spines are usually flattened and modified inflorescence branches.

Spiral Arrangement of objects along the outline of a coiled spring.

Spreading Branches diverging widely from the main axis.

Squarrose To spread rigidly at a right angle; usually, the shape of bracts.

Stamen Male organ of a flower, consisting of the pollen bearing anther on a slender filament; the collective term for stamen is androecium.

Staminate Containing the stamen but not the pistil.

Sterile Without pistils; not capable of producing a seed; a sterile floret may be staminate or neuter.

Stipe Small stalk to a fascicle of spikelets; see the stalk of *Pennisetum.*

Stolon Horizontal, aboveground stem with modified leaves, nodes, internodes, and axillary buds.

Stoloniferous Bearing horizontal aboveground stems that root at the nodes.

Striate Marked with longitudinal grooves or lines; appearing striped.

Sub- Prefix used to denote a lesser degree, an inferior rank, or a lower position.

Subequal Nearly equal in length.

Subtend To be below and close to; refers to position.

Subterranean Belowground or below the soil.

Subulate Awl-shaped.

Succulent Fleshy, soft, or juicy.

Terete Cylindrical and slender (e.g., the normal culm of a grass plant).

Terminal Borne at or belonging to the extremity or summit; distal.

Tessellate Having a surface marked with square to rectangular depressions.

Tiller Erect, lateral shoot.

Tomentose Vesture of dense, short, and soft, matted hairs.

Transverse Crossing the width of an object.

Triad Group of three, as applied to spikelets of *Chrysopogon* or *Hordeum; Hordeum* consisting of a sessile spikelet and two pedicellate spikelets; in *Chrysopogon*, the triad represents a reduced racemose branch.

Triangular Three-sided.

Truncate Apex or base of a structure that is flat or ends abruptly, appearing to be cut off.

Tuberculate Bearing small projections or warty protuberances.

Tufted Caespitose; bunched.

Turgid Swollen, appearing to be filled from within.

Undulate Gently wavy margins.

Unilateral One-sided or turned to one side (e.g., the spikelet arrangement on the branches of *Bouteloua*).

Unisexual Spikelets or flowers containing either stamens or pistils, but not both.

Vein Vascular bundles, veins, or ribs of the blades, glumes, lemmas, and paleas.

Velvety Vesture of dense, medium-length hairs.

Vernal Growth form for spring and early summer.

Verrucose Covered with warty protuberances.

Verticil Whorl of parts arising from a common point or from around an axis.

Verticillate In whorls or verticils.

Vestigial Not fully developed; rudimentary.

Vestiture Surface coverings (e.g., hairs, wax, or scales).

Villous Having long, soft, unmatted hairs; shaggy.

Viscid Sticky; glutinous.

Whorl(ed) Cluster of three to several branches around the inflorescence axis.

Winged Bearing a projection or border near the margins resembling a wing.

Xeric Dry soil or habitat.

— References

Allred, K. W. 1982. Describing the Grass Inflorescence. *J. Range Manage.* 35:672–75.

———. 1984. Morphological Variation and Classification of the North American *Aristida purpurea* Complex (Gramineae). *Brittonia* 36:382–95.

———. 1993. *A Field Guide to the Grasses of New Mexico.* Las Cruces: Agr. Exp. Sta., New Mexico State University.

Allred, K. W., and F. W. Gould. 1983. Systematics of the *Bothriochloa saccharoides* Complex (Poaceae: Andropogoneae). *Syst. Bot.* 8:168–84.

Coffey, C. R., and J. Valdes-R. 1986. *Monerma cylindrica* (Poaceae: Monermeae), New to Texas. *Sida* 11:352–53.

Correll, D. S., and M. C. Johnston. 1970. Manual of the Vascular Plants of Texas. Texas Research Foundation, Renner.

Cronquist, A., A. H. Holmgren, J. R. Reveal, and P. K. Holmgren. 1977. *Intermountain Flora,* Vol. 6. New York: Columbia University Press.

Gould, F. W. 1951. *Grasses of the Southwestern United States.* Tucson: University of Arizona Press.

———. 1975. *The Grasses of Texas.* College Station: Texas A&M University Press.

———. 1978. *Common Texas Grasses: An Illustrated Guide.* College Station: Texas A&M University Press.

Gould, F. W., and T. W. Box. 1965. *Grasses of the Texas Coastal Bend.* College Station: Texas A&M University.

Gould, F. W., and C. A. Clark. 1978. *Dichanthelium* (Poaceae) in the United States and Canada. *Ann. Mo. Bot. Gard.* 65:1088–1132.

Gould, F. W., and R. B. Shaw. 1983. *Grass Systematics,* 2nd ed. College Station: Texas A&M University Press.

Hatch, S. L., and J. Pluhar. 1993. *Texas Range Plants.* College Station: Texas A&M University Press.

Hatch, S. L., K. N. Gandhi, and L. E. Brown. 1990. *A Checklist of the Vascular Plants of Texas.* MP-1655. College Station: Texas Agr. Exp. Sta.

Hatch, S. L., C. W. Morden, and B. M. Woie. 1984. *The Grasses of the National Range Research Station, Kiboko (Kenya).* MP-1573. College Station: Texas Agr. Exp. Sta.

Hignight, K. W., J. K. Wipff, and S. L. Hatch. 1988. *Grasses (Poaceae) of the Texas Cross Timbers and Prairies.* MP-1657. College Station: Texas Agr. Exp. Sta.

Hitchcock, A. S. 1951. *Manual of the Grasses of the United States,* 2nd ed. A. Chase, revision author. Misc. Publ. 200. Washington, D.C.: United States Dep. Agr.

Jones, F. B. 1982. *Flora of the Texas Coastal Bend,* 3rd ed. Corpus Christi: Mission Press.

Kartesz, J. T., and R. Kartesz. 1980. A Synonymized Checklist of the Vascular Flora of the United States, Canada, and Greenland in *The Biota of North America,* Vol. II. Chapel Hill: University of North Carolina Press.

Leithead, H. L., L. L. Yarlett, and T. N. Shiflet. 1976. *100 Native Forage Grasses in 11 Southern States.* Agriculture Handbook No. 389. Washington, D.C.: Soil Conservation Service. United States Dep. Agr.

Lonard, R. I. 1993. *Guide to the Grasses of the Lower Rio Grande Valley, Texas.* Edinburg: The University of Texas-Pan American Press.

McKenzie, P. M., L. E. Urbatsch, and C. Aulbach-Smith. 1987. *Eustachys caribea* (Poaceae), a Species New to the United States and a Key to *Eustachys* in the United States. *Sida* 12:227–32.

McMahon, C. A., R. G. Frye, and K. L. Brown. 1984. *The Vegetation Types of Texas—Including Cropland.* Bull. 7000-120. Austin: Texas Parks and Wildlife Dep.

Powell, A. M. 1994. *Grasses of the Trans-Pecos and Adjacent Areas.* Austin: University of Texas Press.

Reed, P. B., Jr. 1988. *National List of Plant Species that Occur in Wetlands: Texas.* Washington, D.C.: United States Fish and Wildlife Service.

Shaw, R. B., and R. D. Webster. 1987. The genus *Eriochloa* (Poaceae: Paniceae) in North and Central America. *Sida* 12:165–207.

Smeins, F. E., D. D. Diamond, and C. W. Hanselka. 1982. Coastal Prairie. Chapter 13 in *Ecosystems of the World 8A—Natural Grasslands.* R. T. Coupland, editor. New York: Elsevier Press. pp. 269–90.

Snow, N., and G. Davidse. 1993. *Leptochloa mucronata* (Michx.) Kunth is the correct name for *Leptochloa filiformis* (Poaceae). *Taxon* 42:413–17.

Stubbendieck, J., S. L. Hatch, and C. H. Butterfield. 1992. *North American Range Plants.* 4th ed. Lincoln: University of Nebraska Press.

Webster, R. D. 1992. Character Significance and Generic Similarities in the Paniceae (Poaceae: Panicoideae). *Sida* 15:185–213.

Webster, R. D., and R. B. Shaw. 1995. Taxonomy of the Native North American Species of *Saccharum* (Poaceae: Andropogoneae). *Sida* 16:551–80.

Wipff, J. K., and S. L. Hatch. 1992. *Eustachys caribea* (Poaceae: Chlorideae) in Texas. *Sida* 15:160.

Wipff, J. K., and B. S. Rector. 1993. *Rottboellia cochinchinensis* (Poaceae: Andropogoneae) New to Texas. *Sida* 15:419–24.

Wipff, J. K., R. I. Lonard, S. D. Jones, and S. L. Hatch. 1993. The Genus *Urochloa* (Poaceae: Paniceae) in Texas, including Unreported Species for the State. *Sida* 15:405–13.

— Index